REMEMBERING
ORWELL

Conceived and compiled by
STEPHEN WADHAMS

Introduction by George Woodcock

Based on interviews recorded for the Canadian Broadcasting Corporation's radio program, "George Orwell: A Radio Biography."

PENGUIN BOOKS

Penguin Books Canada Ltd., 2801 John Street, Markham, Ontario, Canada
  L3R 1B4
Penguin Books Ltd., Harmondsworth, Middlesex, England
Penguin Books, 40 West 23rd Street, New York, New York, 10010, U.S.A.
Penguin Books Australia Ltd., Ringwood, Victoria, Australia
Penguin Books (N.Z.) Ltd., 182-190 Wairau Road, Auckland 10, New
Zealand

Published in 1984

Manufactured in Canada by Webcom Limited
Typesetting by Jay Tee Graphics Limited
Design by Brant Cowie

CANADIAN CATALOGUING IN PUBLICATION DATA

Main entry under title:
Remembering Orwell

Based on interviews recorded for the CBC program
"George Orwell: a radio biography", broadcast
Jan. 1984.
ISBN 0-14-007458-9

1. Orwell, George, 1903-1950.   2. Authors, English -
20th century - Biography.   I. Wadhams, Stephen.

PR6029.R8Z8 1984   828'.91209   C84-098718-8

To Jack and Joan

Contents

CHAPTER FIVE
1984

Preface

It is with some discomfort that I note I am an exact contemporary — thirty-nine years old in 1984 — of Winston Smith, the hero of George Orwell's *Nineteen Eighty-Four*, and I am writing this on 4 April, the very day on which Smith began his rebellion against Big Brother by starting a diary. Luckily, the resemblance appears to end there.

Winston Smith's job at the Ministry of Truth was to rewrite history. This book is intended to preserve it in its rawest and perhaps most powerful form. I was in an airport bookshop in April 1982 when I picked up a copy of Professor Bernard Crick's *George Orwell: A Life*. Crick was the first person to gain full access to Orwell's papers, and his book was a meticulously researched, massively detailed biography. I have been a radio journalist most of my working life, and flipping through the pages on my short flight from Toronto to Ottawa I began to hear in my mind a rich and fascinating radio program: a series of broadcasts which would transport the listener to all the places Orwell had been — Eton, Burma, Paris, Wigan, Catalonia, and the Scottish Hebrides. Fortunately my senior managers at the Canadian Broadcasting Corporation could hear it too, and they backed my proposal from the beginning.

In the spring of 1983 I was released to work full-time on a five-hour radio biography of Orwell,* and in June, armed with a sheaf of addresses and telephone numbers culled from Professor Crick's files and supplemented by some sleuthing of my own, I set to work recording the interviews which form the basis of this book. In nine weeks I put three thousand miles on a hired car, criss-crossing England and Scotland and making a side trip to Spain in a hectic but fascinating whirl of hard work. A few people on my list declined to be interviewed, but by August I had met virtually everyone with interesting first-hand recollections of George Orwell, or Eric Blair as he is still known to many. These surviving relatives, friends, and acquaintances turned out to be an astonishingly mixed group socially. I was welcomed into homes ranging from a huge and, I was assured, haunted Scottish border house to small brick row houses in Wigan and Barnsley. I threaded my way along narrow country lanes to find cottages hidden behind high walls and hedges. Even if I arrived late, frustrated and exhausted, my apologies were invariably waved away and I was presented with a calming cup of tea. Orwell's England, decent and humane, was alive and well in the summer of 1983.

The result of my work is a collection of memories — nothing more, nothing less. All the people I spoke to saw only fractions of the "total" Orwell; their memories of their encounters with him are coloured by their own personalities and political perspectives. Sometimes two people's recollections of the same incident are contradictory. These are the familiar limitations of oral history. This book does not attempt to be another biography of Orwell; it is, rather, a composite portrait of the man and of the people he chose to know.

---

* "George Orwell: A Radio Biography" was first broadcast on the Stereo Network of the Canadian Broadcasting Corporation on 1 January, 1984, and simultaneously on 240 public radio stations in the United States.

The spur to collect these accounts came just in time. In the summer of 1983 it was still possible for me to meet more than seventy people who had known Orwell — people who ranged in age from sixty to ninety-five — and to collect reminiscences spanning his entire life. Now, less than a year later, I am sorry to say that at least four of the people I met have died: Christopher Eastwood, Sir John Grotrian, Lydia Jackson, and Joan Mullock.

Interviews are always exploratory, often repetitive, and generally rather jumbled conversations. In preparing them for this book, I have, to varying degrees, reorganized the material into a more comprehensible form, and in every case I have removed my prompting questions. Because this editing involves only the rearrangement of verbatim quotations, the verbal mannerisms and hence the "flavour" of each interview have been preserved.

STEPHEN WADHAMS
Toronto
4 April, 1984

Introduction

When I met George Orwell, early in World War II, he was neither popular nor famous, though he stood on the verge of becoming both. By this time half his career already lay behind him, but the important years, though there would be few of them, lay ahead.

He had published four novels, which were modest critical successes and a great deal less than best-sellers: *Burmese Days, A Clergyman's Daughter, Keep the Aspidistra Flying,* and, the best of his early fiction, *Coming Up for Air.* He was best known for the books that were half autobiography and half reportage, books that called attention to wrongs that should be righted: *Down and Out in Paris and London, The Road to Wigan Pier,* and *Homage to Catalonia.*

The reportages showed most openly Orwell's special characteristic as a writer: that he invented very little, preferring to write from experience. Indeed, he often experienced in order to write. He put on ragged disguises to mingle among the tramps and beggars of England so that he could gather the material on living in poverty that he would use in *Down and Out in Paris and London.* He went on a special expedition, financed by his publisher Victor Gollancz, into the northern industrial towns, to collect the facts and impressions that formed the basis for *The*

Road to Wigan Pier. When he went to Spain in 1936-37 and actually took part in the civil war, the idea of writing about it was always in his mind; he kept elaborate diaries on the fighting he witnessed, and as soon as he got back to England he sat down to write *Homage to Catalonia.* The principal characters of *A Clergyman's Daughter* and *Keep the Aspidistra Flying* worked respectively in a secondhand bookshop and in a sleazy private school; Orwell had done both, so that even his fiction came pretty directly from experience.

Another important feature of those early Orwell books was that he never just described an experience; he always drew some political conclusion from it. *The Road to Wigan Pier* began as an account of what Orwell actually saw in the industrial towns, where he lived among the workers just as he had once wandered the roads in the company of tramps, but it ended as a highly polemical discussion of the aims and methods of socialism — a discussion most socialists found opinionated and presumptuous. And *Homage to Catalonia*, after its descriptions of fighting against the Francoists in Aragon and then against the communists in Barcelona who were trying to gain control behind the Loyalist lines, built up to a passionate denunciation of the distortion of historical truth by liberal journalists in England who accepted the manufactured Stalinist version of events.

In all this, Orwell fitted rather well into the 1930s, when his literary career began. Reportage was fashionable then, fiction tended to be didactic, and writers were inclined to be politically committed. Orwell's commitment differed from that of most writers at that time; he became a revolutionary socialist, as many of us did, but he also became a lifelong anti-communist as a result of his experiences in Spain, whereas most of the well-known younger writers of the time, like Auden and Spender and Day Lewis, were attached to the communist cause. In fact, his divergence from the current trend probably did less to harm Orwell's popularity and critical acceptance than he imagined. One of the finest of all his early essays, "Shooting an Elephant," appeared in John Lehmann's Marxist-leaning *New Writing*.

Orwell had virtually no popular following before the 1940s. His books were published in small editions, and he wrote for left-wing magazines with small circulations. His admirers were mostly fellow writers, who appreciated his clear vernacular prose and his honest reportage and were often amused by his aggressively argumentative manner and his crotchety opinions. He was regarded then as an eccentric rather than an original writer, and nobody — least of all Orwell himself, who lived with a chronic sense of failure — would have taken a bet on his becoming a famous writer and a perennial best-seller. He seemed destined for the role of a struggling second-rater, and even the life he planned for himself — living and writing in a country cottage with a little store attached to it by which he could earn at least the rent — seemed to confirm this destiny.

But the war changed that destiny. It was then that I encountered him in person, though I had been reading his books and his articles and wondering what kind of a man he was ever since *Down and Out in Paris and London* appeared in 1933. It was 1942, and Orwell was working at the BBC in London. When the war began he abruptly changed from a left-wing war resister into a socialist patriot supporting Britain's entry into the war, but because of his ailing lungs he was unacceptable for the army. Finally he found the war work he longed for, as a radio producer beaming literary programs to India. At the same time he started on the period of prolific and often splendid journalism that served as the prelude to his last and great books, *Animal Farm* and *Nineteen Eighty-Four*.

Among other assignments, he began to write regular "London Letters" for the New York *Partisan Review* — opinionated and readable if not always accurate assessments of what was going on in wartime England. In one of these "Letters" he publicly attacked a literary magazine I was then editing, *Now*, for its pacifist inclinations. In the next issue of the *Review* I replied with an attack on Orwell's inconsistencies. He answered with an equal show of anger.

So I was surprised when my friend the Indian novelist Mulk Raj Anand came to me one evening in a Soho pub and told me Orwell would like me to take part in one of the panels of writers he was arranging for broadcast to India. I was curious. I accepted. When I got to the BBC I found that the panel consisted of two writers I knew, Herbert Read and William Empson, and two I did not, the World War I poet Edmund Blunden and Orwell himself. Orwell was by far the tallest man there, lean and gangling, with enormous feet (he wore size twelves) and deep lines down his long and hollow-eyed face that made one think immediately of the Knight of the Sorrowful Countenance, Don Quixote. We talked of poetry into the microphone and then went off to a pub near the BBC, where Orwell remarked sardonically that if two hundred Indian students heard us we would be doing well. He noticed my hands were ingrained with dirt from the market garden I was then cultivating, and he seemed to approve. Nevertheless we soon afterward got involved in an acrimonious correspondence about the BBC, from which, despite his defence of his position, it seemed clear that he was disillusioned with the bureaucracy and the emphasis on propaganda, as distinct from facts, that was inevitable in a wartime broadcasting organization.

The next time I saw Orwell he had left the BBC, after expressing his disillusionment to Rayner Heppenstall with the comment "I'm just an orange that's been trodden on by a very dirty boot." It was an odd meeting. I got on a London double-decker bus in Hampstead, and when I climbed to the top deck I saw a crest of dark brown hair that I remembered. Orwell turned around and waved me to the seat beside him; he had recognized me crossing the street toward the bus. Almost immediately he looked at me earnestly. "You know, Woodcock," he said, "it's all very well to quarrel on paper, but that shouldn't make any difference to one's personal relationships."

I would go to see him at *Tribune*, the left-wing socialist magazine run by Aneurin Bevan of which he became literary editor, and would find him trying to fit his long legs behind a tiny desk whose drawers were filled with unprintable manuscripts he had accepted because the writers were young or poor. He once said nobody could be an effective editor who had once had to live by reviewing books.

Orwell and I shared the habit of working at night and meeting other writers during the day, and we would often lunch together at restaurants around Fleet Street. Orwell would eat with patriotic and masochistic delight the dreadful wartime dishes that were offered and would regale us with prophesies of the future so pessimistic that even Herbert Read, the most taciturn of Yorkshiremen, once remarked to me as we walked away from one such lunch, "My God, Orwell *is* a gloomy bird!"

Orwell's first wife, Eileen, died early in 1945. After that he would come often on his own to our flat in Highgate, or my wife and I would go to his place in Islington if we did not decide to meet in Soho and end the evening on the red plush banquettes of the Café Royal, which was virtually unchanged since the days when Oscar Wilde patronized it. In our house it was a climb to the fourth floor, and when Orwell got to the top he would be wheezing from his aching lungs, and when he started to speak it would be in a levelled-off Eton voice, for the timbre had been permanently affected by a throat wound received in the Spanish civil war.

Eventually the conversation might narrow down into a monologue on some subject that was on Orwell's mind. This was the time he was writing the column called "As I Please" in *Tribune*, and I found that he had the habit of rehearsing his pieces, as it were, by talking them over. This was why he could write an article on the typewriter and present it to the editor — who was often himself — with hardly any corrections. One evening we would be led into a discussion on the merits of the peat fire that was filling Orwell's sitting room with acrid smoke. Another evening it would be the virtues of various kinds of tea and the right way to brew and to drink it. (Twelve spoonfuls in a large teapot, if I remember rightly.) And sure enough, two or three weeks or a month later there would be columns on peat and tea appearing somewhere or other over Orwell's signature. A little later on the discussion became less homely, and at various dinners and high teas and lunches and quick drinks in saloon bars, I heard expounded almost every idea expressed in *Nineteen Eighty-Four,* though I had no inkling of the plot until the book appeared; the actual shape of a novel Orwell kept very secretively to himself until the book was actually published.

I also noticed, as others did, that Orwell was oddly secretive about his other friendships; he tended to compartmentalize them. He knew great numbers of people — as became evident when so many were found to speak about him for the CBC program, "George Orwell: A Radio Biography," broadcast on New Year's Day 1984 — but he gave each one of them the feeling that he or she was a special friend. I think this was one of his great virtues. Friendship was very important to him, and some of his closest friendships, like those with me and Stephen Spender and Julian Symons, were those that had been tested by original disagreement. When he and I first became friends he was having difficulty in getting *Animal Farm* published and asked if a small anarchist press with which I was associated might consider it. The other editor with whom I discussed it dismissed the idea without reading the book, because Orwell had been attacking anarchists. Yet later, when I introduced her to him, they became friends and she took the best photographs of Orwell. All the problems over *Animal Farm* were forgotten.

One evening Orwell came to dinner with a little green book in his hand, which he quietly laid on the table. It was an inscribed copy of *Animal Farm,* which had finally found its way into print, and from that moment Orwell's fame began. (Months later the book would be accepted by the American Book-of-the-Month Club, and prosperity would be added to fame.) That day Orwell invited me to a slap-up lunch at a Greek restaurant in Percy Street, and there we discussed his plans. He had already made up his mind to go to Jura, partly to get away from the editors who were daily pestering him for articles, and partly to take his adopted son Richard out of reach of the war he felt was coming soon. He intended to set up a trust fund for Richard out of the money from *Animal Farm*; already he had decided that he himself was a poor actuarial risk. We talked of the book he was just beginning, which became *Nineteen Eighty-Four*, and he was sceptical about the idea that it would repeat the success of *Animal Farm*. "I'll be lucky if I make five hundred quid out of it," he said of what became one of the century's great best-sellers.

Then he went off to Jura, and after that, I saw him only on a couple of visits to London, one of which was during the terrible winter of 1946-47, when he was in bed much of the time with what he called bronchitis; it was the beginning of the tuberculosis of which he eventually died in 1950. I never saw him after *Nineteen Eighty-Four* was published in June 1949, for in the spring of that year my wife and I came to Canada. "I believe there's incredible fishing if you care about that," George said to me just before we left. He did care about fishing. But I knew that it was something else about North America that preyed on his mind: his last two books, the ones that earned him the fame he had never enjoyed before, had been swept into the propaganda of the cold war in such a way that he had come to be regarded as a socialist-hating conservative rather than a socialist who wished to save his beliefs from the aberrations of the Russian communists.

Orwell is still largely misunderstood in North America, where the modern neoconservatives happily claim him as their own, and this I think is because he belongs so firmly in the English tradition of literary radicalism. The fact that he shared the insights of contemporary continental European writers, mainly ex-communists like Arthur Koestler, Franz Borkenau, and Ignazio Silone, who had seen through the Soviet myth, does not detract from the fact that he expressed his insights in a peculiarly English way, adopting Swift's *Gulliver's Travels* as his distant model for *Animal Farm*.

Herbert Read once said that "Defoe was the first writer to raise journalism to a literary art; Orwell perhaps the last." And, limiting though the definition may seem, it does place Orwell clearly in the line of dissenting didacticism to which he belongs, a line that continued in the radical tradition from Defoe to Cobbett and Dickens, to Gissing — that sad failure in whom Orwell saw so much of himself — and to H.G. Wells.

Orwell grew beyond the facile, shiny, Utopian side of Wells, and this may explain why, when the master and the disciple met, they quarrelled, and Wells memorably denounced Orwell as "that Trotskyite with big feet." But the Wells of the negative Utopias, like *The Sleeper Awakes* and *The Island of Dr Moreau,* is strongly present in Orwell's vision, and so also is the Wells of the lower-middle-class genre novels, *Kipps* and *Mr Polly* and *Tono Bungay*.

Dickens was probably Orwell's favourite among the Victorian novelists, and though Orwell sought for a prose far less decorated than that of Dickens, there is no doubt that the emotional if not the aesthetic affinities were considerable. Orwell wrote a long and particularly fine essay on Dickens, and I have always felt that the pen portrait of the novelist at the end of that piece characterized Orwell as well as his subject: "He is laughing, with a touch of anger to his laughter. It is the face of a man who is always fighting against something, but who fights in the open and is not frightened, a type hated with equal hatred by all the smelly little orthodoxies which are now contending for our souls."

Orwell treated Dickens as a nineteenth-century liberal with all the generous urges and angers of his kind, and though the times made him describe himself as a socialist, it was in Dickens's company that he really belonged. There was nothing of the modern-day conservative about Orwell, but a great deal of the Tory in William Cobbett's sense: the man of social conscience who sees the ancient values of community and decency foundering and who seeks in some radical way to reassert them. And here one sees another line of English writing to which Orwell certainly belongs, that of the great moralistic essayists, whose concern for justice accorded with their search for the clearest prose in which to write of it. Hazlitt as well as Cobbett stands among Orwell's ancestors — Hazlitt who claimed, "I never wrote a line that licked the dust."

It has often been said that Orwell was more important as a man than as a writer. I do not think this is true, or that one can make facile distinctions of that kind in the case of any writer, but the fact remains that he possessed a strange and compelling character and projected more than most writers the image of a deeply moral man. Sixteen years after Orwell's death our common friend Herbert Read wrote to me, "His personality, which remains so vivid after all these years, often rises like some ghost to admonish me." Read was clearly not alone; the many interviews collected in this volume show, in memories that have remained surprisingly clear over the years, how strongly Orwell's nature impressed itself upon those who knew him.

GEORGE WOODCOCK
Vancouver
4 April, 1984

Chronology

1903   Eric Arthur Blair (George Orwell) is born on 25 June at Motihari in Bengal. His father, Richard Walmesley Blair, is a sub-deputy opium agent in the Indian Civil Service. His mother, Ida Mabel Blair (née Limouzin), is the daughter of a teak merchant in Moulmein, Burma. They have one older child, Marjorie Frances, born on 21 April 1898.

1904   Mrs Blair returns to England with Eric and Marjorie, and settles in Henley-on-Thames.

1908   On 6 April Mrs Blair gives birth to a second daughter, Avril Nora.

1911   In September Eric is sent to St Cyprian's, a private boarding school in Sussex.

1912   Richard Blair retires from the Opium Department. The Blairs move to Shiplake, not far from Henley.

1914   On 2 October a local newspaper publishes Eric Blair's first printed work, a patriotic poem called "Awake! Young Men of England."

1915   The Blairs move back to Henley-on-Thames.

1916   Eric Blair leaves St Cyprian's at Christmas.

1917   Eric spends the Lent term at Wellington College. In May he enters Eton as a King's Scholar.

1921   Eric Blair leaves Eton. The Blair family moves to the Suffolk seaside resort of Southwold.

1922   In October Eric leaves England to take up a post with the Burma Police, arriving in Mandalay in November.

1927   In August Eric returns to England on leave and while there decides to resign from the Burma Police. He then goes "tramping" in the East End of London.

1928 In the spring, Eric Blair goes to Paris. On 6 October his first professional article is published in *Le Monde*. His first published article in England, "A Farthing Newspaper," appears on 28 December in *G.K.'s Weekly*.

1929 In February Eric is seriously ill with pneumonia and spends several weeks in the Hôpital Cochin. After working as a dishwasher and kitchen porter in the autumn, he returns to England.

1930 Eric begins writing regularly for the literary journal *Adelphi*. In October he completes a draft of *Down and Out in Paris and London*.

1931 Eric begins writing *Burmese Days*.

1932 In April Eric begins teaching in a private school in Hayes, West London.

1933 Victor Gollancz publishes *Down and Out in Paris and London* on 9 January, choosing "George Orwell" from a list of pseudonyms suggested by Eric Blair.

Before Christmas Eric is very ill again with pneumonia and decides to give up teaching.

1934 Orwell begins writing *A Clergyman's Daughter* while convalescing at his parents' home in Southwold.

In October *Burmese Days* is published in New York, and Orwell takes a part-time job in a bookshop in Hampstead, London.

1935 Early in the year Orwell begins work on *Keep the Aspidistra Flying*.

On 11 March Victor Gollancz publishes *A Clergyman's Daughter* and the same month Orwell meets the woman who will become his wife, Eileen O'Shaughnessy.

On 24 June Victor Gollancz publishes *Burmese Days*.

1936   From January to March Orwell researches living and working conditions of the poor in Wigan, Liverpool, Manchester, and Barnsley.

On 20 April Victor Gollancz publishes *Keep the Aspidistra Flying*. Orwell moves to a small cottage in Wallington, Hertfordshire where he marries Eileen O'Shaughnessy on 9 June.

By December he has finished writing *The Road to Wigan Pier* and left for Spain, enlisting in the militia of the POUM (Workers' Party of Marxist Unification).

1937   In January Orwell goes to the front line at Alcubierre and joins a contingent sent to Spain by the Independent Labour Party. In February Eileen arrives in Barcelona and starts work in the ILP office there, visiting Orwell at the front for two days in the middle of March.

On 8 March *The Road to Wigan Pier* is published by Victor Gollancz.

On 20 May Orwell is shot in the throat by a sniper's bullet. He decides to leave Spain to seek proper medical treatment, and escapes to France with Eileen on 23 June. Returning to Wallington, he begins writing *Homage to Catalonia*. Victor Gollancz refuses to publish it, fearing it would "harm the fight against fascism." In September Fredric Warburg agrees to publish the book.

1938   In March Orwell suffers a tubercular lesion in one lung and enters a sanatorium in Kent. He and Eileen spend the winter in Morocco, where he writes *Coming Up for Air*.

1939   At the end of March Orwell and Eileen return to Wallington.

On 12 June Victor Gollancz publishes *Coming Up for Air*. On 28 June Orwell's father, Richard Blair, dies of cancer at the age of eighty-two.

On the outbreak of war in September, Orwell is rejected by the army as medically unfit. Eileen begins work in the Censorship Department.

1940 On 11 March Orwell's new book of essays, *Inside the Whale*, is published by Victor Gollancz.

On 10 May Orwell joins the Home Guard and is made a sergeant.

In August he begins writing a short book calling for an English revolution. It is titled *The Lion and The Unicorn*.

1941 In February *The Lion and The Unicorn* is published.

On 18 August Orwell joins the BBC as a producer in the Indian service.

1942 Orwell works at the BBC and writes articles for *Horizon, Partisan Review, Tribune, The New Statesman and Nation,* and the *Observer*. Eileen moves from the Censorship Department to the Ministry of Food.

1943 Orwell's mother Ida Blair, aged sixty-seven, dies of a heart attack on 19 March.

In November Orwell resigns from the BBC, begins writing *Animal Farm,* and joins the socialist journal *Tribune* as Literary Editor. He also begins writing a free-ranging weekly column "As I Please" for *Tribune* in December.

1944 In February Orwell finishes *Animal Farm* and begins a frustrating search for a publisher.

In June Eileen gives up her job in order to adopt a three-week-old baby boy whom the Orwells name Richard Horatio Blair.

After living in a series of flats in London the Orwells move to 27b Canonbury Square, Islington, at the beginning of October. In the same month Fredric Warburg agrees to publish *Animal Farm*.

1945 In February Orwell gives up his job at *Tribune* and travels to France to report for the *Observer*. In March, while in Cologne, he receives news that Eileen has died under anaesthetic during an operation for the removal of her uterus.

Animal Farm is published by Secker and Warburg on 17 August. Orwell hires a young housekeeper to look after himself and Richard. In September he stays for nearly two weeks in a crofter's cottage on the Hebridean island of Jura, where he decides to rent a house.

1946 On 3 May Orwell's older sister Marjorie dies of kidney disease at the age of forty-eight. Later in May Orwell moves to a large farmhouse at the remote north end of Jura. His sister Avril comes to live with him.

On 26 August *Animal Farm* is published in New York by Harcourt Brace. Half a million copies are sold by the Book of the Month Club.

Orwell begins working on *Nineteen Eighty-Four*. He spends the winter in London.

1947 In April Orwell returns to Jura. During the summer he works on *Nineteen Eighty-Four,* finishing the first draft in September and then taking to his bed, exhausted. Just before Christmas he enters a hospital near Glasgow where tuberculosis is diagnosed.

1948 In July Orwell returns to Jura. He completes the second draft of *Nineteen Eighty-Four*, types a final copy, and sends it to his publisher on 4 December. He is by now seriously ill.

1949 In January Orwell enters a sanatorium in southern England, where he corrects the proofs of *Nineteen Eighty-Four* in March. The book is published in London on 8 June and in New York on 13 June. In July it is the American Book of the Month Club selection.

On 3 September Orwell moves to University College Hospital, London.

On 13 October he marries Sonia Brownell, editorial assistant at *Horizon,* in a special hospital ceremony.

1950 Orwell dies of pulmonary tuberculosis on 21 January. He is forty-six. On 26 January he is buried in the churchyard of All Saints, Sutton Courtenay.

CHAPTER ONE

To Burma and Back

*I was born into what you might describe as
the lower-upper-middle class.*
GEORGE ORWELL
THE ROAD TO WIGAN PIER

George Orwell pinpointed his social roots with some care, and indeed it is possible to view the story of his life as an attempt to escape from the English class system at a time when it was more rigid and confining than it is today. The heroes of Orwell's fiction invariably try to break loose from "the system" — and invariably fail.

What is curious about Orwell's social climbing is that he wanted to climb down rather than up the ladder, "to go native in his own country," to understand and write about the underdog from solid personal experience.

This opening chapter examines the background of the man who was born Eric Arthur Blair, the mould his society and family prepared for him, and his willingness to fill that mould. His parents certainly wanted him to conform. They made considerable financial sacrifices to send him to "good" schools where he would meet the right people. But from the beginning he appears to have tried to break out of the mould. The general consensus among his childhood friends and schoolmates is that the young Eric Blair was always strangely on the outside, observing but rarely joining in — and then usually to challenge and find fault. The picture given is that of an abrasive, free-thinking individual, but intelligent fault-finding is a far cry from open revolt: the young Blair was not a radical.

In fact, he did not swerve from the path ordained for him by his background until, after finishing his education at Eton, he spent five years in the colonial police force in Burma. The inequities and oppression he saw there had a lasting effect on him. In his writing he describes these years as traumatic. The "dirty end of Empire" left him with an "enormous weight of guilt," which he felt he could expunge only by understanding and identifying with the oppressed classes of his own country.

The Old Etonian who chooses, as Orwell did, to go tramping or to walk bent double through the cramped underground tunnels of a Lancashire coal mine in search of social injustice runs the risk of being called a pretender. Indeed, Orwell was accused by some of making his name as a writer on the backs of the working men he wrote about.

The fact remains that he wanted very badly to be accepted by the working-class people he met, but he faced ingrained resistance from two sides: the men themselves, who often called him "Sir," and his own sense of self — his lower-upper-middle-class self.

Whatever the sources of Orwell's identification with the oppressed people of his time, he continued to write about them all his life. It has been suggested that everything he saw and heard was simply fodder for his typewriter. The persistent baiting and arguing of his youth may have been his way of honing points before committing them to paper. And Burma may well have been, as George Woodcock suspects, George Orwell's first research trip.

Baby Eric

George Orwell was born Eric Arthur Blair on 25 June, 1903 in the small Indian town of Motihari on the Ganges River. His father, Richard Walmesley Blair, worked as a sub-deputy opium agent in the Imperial Service. His mother, Ida Mabel (née Limouzin), was born in England to a French father and an English mother but grew up in

Moulmein, Burma, where her father was a teak merchant. In 1904 Ida Blair returned to England to settle and prepare for her husband's retirement in the town of Henley-on-Thames, bringing with her her daughter Marjorie, then aged seven, and Eric, who was not yet two years old.

JANE MORGAN, one of only four surviving relatives, is the daughter of Orwell's sister Marjorie. Among the Blair family treasures in her possession is her grandmother Ida Blair's diary for 1905.

> Grandma was quite a gal, judging from her diary. She went to the theatre and saw Sarah Bernhardt, went swimming, developed photographs — all sorts of things that you wouldn't expect an Edwardian woman to be doing. But of course there are also little diary entries like 'Very busy as I had no maid.' Oh, here you are, you see — Grandma went to Wimbledon, Saturday the 8th of July: 'Went to Wimbledon to see the tennis finals. I saw Miss Sutton win the ladies' and Mr Doherty the gentlemen's singles . . . glorious day.' And the previous Wednesday she spent 'all day on the river.' That would be the regatta at Henley. She had quite a nice time, really. And old man Blair was still slaving away in the Opium Department!

Ida Blair's diary for 1905 provides evidence that baby Eric suffered from a weak chest.

> Yes, you see, there are accounts here. This is February 1905: 'Baby not at all well, so I sent for the doctor who said he had bronchitis.' And then the next day: 'Baby about the same. We changed him into somebody else's room this afternoon. . .' Wednesday: 'Baby is better. . . Baby improving every day now, calling things beastly.' I mean, if he had bronchitis when he was small it might have started a lifelong weakness, mightn't it? Bronchitis is pretty serious. Baby was ill again here — oh, look! 'Got a wire saying that baby was ill. I got the wire at 8:30 while bathing, and I was in the train at 9:10.'

What's this? Baby must have been ill again, in November. . . 'Baby came downstairs today. . . Baby worse, so sent for the doctor.' That's three times in a year, isn't it?

St Cyprian's

In the autumn of 1907 Eric's father came home on leave. On 6 April 1908 Ida Blair gave birth to a second daughter, Avril. Eric became the middle child of three, with one sister five years older and the other five years younger. Because of the wide age range he later wrote that he was a lonely child "who soon developed disagreeable mannerisms which made me unpopular throughout my schooldays" ("Why I Write").

In 1908 Eric was sent to a small Anglican convent school in Henley. Then, in September 1911, at the age of eight, he left home to attend St Cyprian's, a private boarding school in Sussex. In a famous essay called "Such, Such Were the Joys," George Orwell portrays his life at St Cyprian's in gruesome terms, presenting a picture of a boy powerless to fend off the bullying of the other boys and the persecution of the staff. But his letters home are lively and do not appear to have been censored to present the school in a favourable light. Jane Morgan possesses these early letters from Eric Blair to his mother.

'June 2nd, 1912. St Cyprian's. My Darling Mother, I hope you are all right. Thank you for your letter. I think I would like a gun mettle (*sic*) watch for my birthday. Thank you for the card you sent me. Will you send my coat and my bathing dress. If you send one of my old pairs, don't send those beastly things which come all over my body. I'm first in Latin, eighth in English and French, and second in Arithmetic. With lots of love from Eric Blair.'

And here's another one. This is December the 8th. It doesn't say which year, but the writing is more mature, isn't it? It says, 'My Darling Mother, I hope you are quite well. We have had a magic lantern lecture and a fancy dress dance on Friday. I went to the dance as a footman with a red velvet coat and a white silk flowered waistcoat, and red silk trousers, and black stockings and a lace frill and a wig. One of the boys went as a pirate, and three as revolutionaries. One went as a sunflower, one as Puss in Boots and another as a frog and one as the White Rabbit in *Alice in Wonderland,* and a lot of other things. . . On Wednesday we had a lovely lecture all about the moon. It was awfully interesting. And Mr Siller showed us what an eclipse of the moon was, with a football with sugar on the top.'

This one is the 18th of February 1912: 'The boys went to see an *aeroplane* on Thursday, but I and a lot of the other chaps played footer. And we won easily, nine–three . . . If there are any tadpoles in the rain tub, please don't let any leeches in, because I certainly don't want to come home and find that all the tadpoles are eaten up by the beasts of leeches. I'm fifth in French and English. First in Latin, and second in Arith. With lots of love from E.A. Blair.'

'On Thursday, we played ordinary football. I was in the third game, and was goalkeeper in the second half, and they only got past the half-way line twice while I was in goal, but both of those times nearly a goal. And I had to be jolly quick to pick them up and kick them, because most of the chaps on the other side were in awful rats, and they were running at me like angry dogs. . . From your loving son, Eric Blair.'

SIR JOHN GROTIAN was a fellow student with Eric Blair at St Cyprian's. He was a year younger than Blair, but his brother, the late Brent Grotrian, was an exact contemporary. What makes Sir John's memory of the school, its proprietors, Mr and Mrs Wilkes, and Eric Blair especially valuable is that even now he has not read anything George Orwell wrote. His recollections of the boarding school are his own, and quite independent of Orwell's.

I never read anything of his, I'm afraid, chiefly because I wasn't attracted by him. There wasn't any loophole where I could get in and make friends. He wasn't forthcoming — unlike the other Anglo-Indian boys at the school, who were very easy to make friends with and very attractive people. I thought he was deadly dull.

He was round faced, with straight hair, not in the least the bearded, long-faced number he turned out to be. I don't think he was any good at sports. Neither he nor my brother were footballers or cricketers. Blair and my brother both got bullied. I can remember very well the whole school booing and chasing them and getting them up against the wall of the gymnasium, with a view to bashing at them, but what they'd done I really don't know. I didn't go to the aid of my brother as I ought to have done, because I was too cowardly. I just hid myself.

I can't think what anyone would have had against Blair. He was quite harmless. Maybe he had reprimanded some of the smaller boys because they were making a noise when he was trying to work. I think he was a born bookworm and would have liked to have been left in peace to pursue his own line of studies.

St Cyprian's was a fairly typical English prep school. Its function was to prepare boys for entry into English public schools, particularly the most prestigious ones — Eton, Harrow, and Wellington. This meant a lot of hard work in the classrooms and a daily routine designed to toughen up the boys and develop "character."

I don't know what woke us up, but we all got up about half past seven and scrambled into our dressing gowns and rushed downstairs, probably barefoot, into the swimming bath. We had to dive in one end and swim to the other and get dry on the towels that hung all round the bath and which were sopping wet. Then upstairs and into proper clothes, then downstairs again to the asphalt, where we had to do ten minutes or a quarter of an hour of physical training. Then, if you please, *chapel.* All this on an empty stomach. Chapel for about ten minutes, a hymn or two and a prayer or two, then into the school dining room for breakfast.

Breakfast would be about half past eight. We had very thick slices of bread and margarine with a scrape of jam. And when I say thick, I mean half an inch thick. We had porridge every day, from two-handled pewter bowls. They were called 'porringers.' They were strong and didn't break when the servants were washing them up. There were servants in those days, which was wonderful. And it was the custom when you left the school to have either a mug or a porringer engraved with your name and date.

Every morning Mrs Wilkes used to eat a grapefruit for breakfast, in front of the boys, who didn't get a grapefruit, of course. In those days it was a newly invented thing; they had just started importing them into England. Mrs Wilkes had a round face, and she was enormously fat, especially after she had had her fifth child, which she had while I was there. She had a job getting slim again. Mr Wilkes had a slight stoop and a pince-nez, or at any rate rimless glasses, and I don't think he was really very interested in the school at all. I think Mrs Wilkes was the driving force. Mr Wilkes's nickname was 'Sambo,' whereas Mrs Wilkes's nickname was 'Flip.'

According to Sir John Grotrian, Mr Wilkes would sit at one end of the breakfast table, Mrs Wilkes at the other, and almost before the boys had finished their breakfast, Mrs Wilkes would start teaching them scripture.

You were supposed to learn a given half dozen verses of the Bible which you could say by heart, a different lot every morning. And on Sundays you were set some kind of a question which involved reading at least a chapter on the Bible, and it was then that you got cross-examined and asked questions about it, immediately after breakfast. You stood up and answered your question if you'd done your homework. People who couldn't answer the question got their hair pulled. And that's why Eric Blair had his hair so greasy, so that Mrs Wilkes couldn't pull it so hard. I saw Blair 'blubber' once, as we called it, but I expect he was reduced to tears more often by Mrs Wilkes. He was a nervous type, really.

In his essay about St Cyprian's, Orwell caricatures Mrs Wilkes as a "flirtatious queen, surrounded by courtier lovers, laughing and joking and scattering largesses." Grotrian remembers that the boys tried to "suck up" to her, to win her favour. The reward might be a shopping tour of Eastbourne.

Every day at breakfast time she would detail about four boys to accompany her into the town, and there one could look at shop windows and so forth, and then walk back. I remember asking her on one of these occasions, 'Do you remember, Ma'am, when boys come back to see you, when they're twenty years older? Do you remember them? They must have changed very much!' 'No,' she said, 'none of you ever change at all. You're exactly the same twenty years on.' I begin to see the point now; people are.

Soon after Eric Blair arrived at St Cyprian's, he suffered a prolonged bout of bed-wetting, and for this sin he was caned by Mr Wilkes. But the first two years at the school were probably no more difficult for him to endure than they were for any other small boy uprooted from hearth and home and planted in the tough, regimented society of an English prep school. His early letters home offer glimpses of a boy coming to terms fairly cheerfully with his new environment.

But the atmosphere at St Cyprian's changed for the worse for Eric Blair in his third year at the school, when it was decided he was "scholarship material" and would be "crammed" for special scholarship examinations. (He did win a scholarship — two, in fact: one to Wellington and another to Eton.) At this time Mr Wilkes informed Eric of a great and awful secret: he had been taken on at half fees and was now expected to repay the favour by working hard and winning the scholarship, which would not only assure Blair a good future but also enhance the glory — and financial security — of the school.

The scholarship boys were, Sir John Grotrian remembers, "a chosen few," while the rest of the boys were groomed for the less exacting common entrance examinations. The teaching all the boys received was not, apparently, a wide-ranging, freewheeling education: its main purpose was to enable them to pass their entrance examinations.

It struck me that we were just members of a herd, and all got the same treatment. It may not have been so, of course. There may have been specialized gentleness or harshness for whatever boys were deemed to need it, but it didn't come my way. The teaching was mainly just learning facts. History, for example, was just a list of names and dates — the dates of battles and the names of kings and queens coming to the throne. It was more the history of personalities, but that's the way it was taught in those days. Mrs Wilkes taught all the history in the school because she rather specialized in history, with a view to getting somebody at St Cyprian's to win the Harrow history prize.

Like Eric Blair, John Grotrian was beaten during his time at the school.

I can't remember what for, but I think only about twice. The things one got beaten for seemed so inappropriate, particularly when you were beaten for not being good at games. It wasn't going to make anyone any better at games by beating them, was it? The main beating offences were cheating, I think, and failing to play football hard enough. At night both the matron and the assistant masters used to put on soft slippers and creep out and listen if anyone in the dormitories was talking. If they were caught, it was reported to Mr Wilkes, but I don't think that was a beatable offence. I think you'd only get a reprimand.

JOHN WILKES is the eldest son of Mr and Mrs Wilkes, the proprietors of St Cyprian's. He attended the school for a while in a class one year ahead of Eric Blair's. Wilkes dismisses most of Orwell's attacks on St Cyprian's, particularly Orwell's allegation that he was picked on by Mrs Wilkes, as "nonsense."

My mother certainly never regarded him as an enemy or anything like that. I know she had a great respect for him and was very much hurt when he said the things about the school he did. My mother was rather inclined to have favourites. I don't think Eric Blair was either a favourite or not. I'm not at all sure that he wasn't one of her favourites. But I don't think my mother showed any boy undue impartiality. I think she showed that she was very fond of them. And my father very seldom beat a boy. He didn't like it, even though it was common practice in those days. No, he very seldom did it. He hated doing it. He would only beat a boy for some really bad offence. I knew Eric Blair was a pretty bright boy and likely to get a scholarship, but he didn't have any notable characteristics. He was, to my mind, just one of the chaps.

John Wilkes's memory of life at St Cyprian's is as benign as Orwell's is harsh.

My mother used to teach the top history set and my father the top classical set, she in her sitting room and he in his study. She played the piano very well, and on Sunday evenings the senior boys and her own children would come into the drawing room, and we would sing a hymn or two to her playing. They also had a chapel where the local vicar used to come and take a service every Sunday — a delightful man. On Monday mornings, I remember, only French was allowed to be talked aloud at breakfast. You got considerable silences, actually, among otherwise chatterbox boys, but still, they had to try and say something to one another. It was one way of coaxing them into learning French.

I suppose every prep school wants to get scholarships, but the boys weren't crammed at all. I think they were well taught. I think my father chose very good staff, absolutely splendid. Most of them went on to be headmasters of schools themselves, actually. And of course during the war it was very hard to run a school. Food was a fearful problem. We really were hungry. Some people have said how badly fed they were at St Cyprian's, but dash it all, so was everybody, whether they were at school or anywhere else. Everything was rationed.

And of course, like all schools in those days, we had a cadet corps. I think my father dressed up as a lieutenant. I remember the unhappiness of my parents when old boys of theirs were killed in the war, as a great many of them were. It was a source of great sorrow and grief to both my parents.

John Wilkes and Eric Blair were later fellow students at Eton.

At Eton I always knew him as a boy with a permanent chip on the shoulder, always liking to find everything around him wrong, and giving the impression that he was there to put it right. He was extremely argumentative — about anything — and criticizing the masters and criticizing the other boys, that sort of thing. We enjoyed arguing with him. He would generally win the arguments — or think he had, anyhow. Oh yes, there's no doubt he was very intelligent indeed. But I don't think he tried very hard at Eton, although he certainly read widely. He was very well read. Bernard Shaw was one of his favourite authors, and he saw himself a bit as a future Bernard Shaw, you know.

"Twin Souls"

JACINTHA BUDDICOM never knew George Orwell, but her memories of the young Eric Blair are unique. During his school holidays from St Cyprian's and Eton, so much of Eric's life was spent with Jacintha that he became almost one of the Buddicom family. "We were more or less twin souls," says Buddicom.

Jacintha was two years older than Eric, but the two children shared a holiday world of writing and poetry, of fresh air and flickering fires. Buddicom knew Eric Blair as a happy and stimulating childhood friend. The tortured schoolboy, the "I" of "Such, Such Were the Joys," is, she says, "quite unrecognizable" as the Eric she knew.

Their meeting was a remarkable event in itself. Perhaps out of loneliness, one day in the summer of 1914, the still chubby Eric Blair made a special effort to strike up a friendship with the Buddicom children — Jacintha, her younger sister, Guinevere, and her brother, Prosper. Jacintha was thirteen; Eric was eleven.

> We met him in a field, and he was standing on his head, very ostentatiously, in order to attract our attention when we were playing French Cricket. We said, 'What are you doing there upside down?' and he said you were noticed more if you stood on your head than if you're the right way up. We shall never forget that because it was such a peculiar thing for somebody to do. Anyway, having broken the ice and got to know us by that behaviour, we became friends. It shows, you see, that he wasn't such a shy, retiring boy, or he wouldn't have stood on his head to attract the attention of some strange children!
>
> He was a nice boy, but he wasn't particularly attractive looking. He wasn't an Adonis by any means, but he wasn't as ugly as he tried to make out in some of his later books.

Jacintha often heard Eric and her brother compare life at the prep schools they attended.

He didn't give any terrible accounts of St Cyprian's to Prosper. He seemed to take it as a matter of course, just an ordinary prep school. There were things he didn't like about it, but then boys very often don't care for their prep schools. Very often there's a certain amount of bully-ragging with the big boys and the little boys, but that they take in their turn, and when they get bigger they bully-rag the boys who come after — and so it goes on. No, I think he had a very normal childhood.

His father was a rather difficult old man. His father, of course, was very elderly. They had a habit in the Blair family of marrying very late, because Eric's grandfather would have been a hundred and two when Eric was born if he'd lived that long. And Eric's father married rather late in life, so that to us he was much more like a grandfather. His idea of children was that they should keep out of the way and be seen and not heard. Any children were kept away from Mr Blair. You see, the Blair children mostly played with us at our house because their father didn't like children chasing about and playing in the garden and rampaging round the house.

Books were the common denominator between Eric and me. I was never without a book in my hand and nor was he. He'd tell me what books he was reading and I'd tell him what book I was reading. If he was doing any writing he'd usually talk to me about what he was writing. He was always going to write, and he was always going to be a Famous Writer. He used to say, 'When I'm a famous writer. . .' and I used to say, 'When you're a famous writer . . .' That was his trademark, Eric the Famous Writer.

Eric's holidays with the Buddicom children included a great deal of fishing and shooting with Jacintha's brother, Prosper. Jacintha possesses Prosper's diary for 1920.

Yes, you see: 'August the 27th. Prosper: nine perch, one eel. Eric: eight perch.' 'August 28th — seven perch by Prosper, one perch by Eric.' And he kept a game register too: 'August 28th — one rabbit by Prosper and one crow by Eric.' 'August 29th — six perch by Prosper, nine by Eric.'

I used to go with them on the fishing expeditions, but I don't like catching things and killing them. The time they killed a hedgehog, I was very angry. I wouldn't speak to either of them — Prosper or Eric — for about a week. I thought it was a wicked thing to do. I've always been fond of hedgehogs.

When it was too wet to shoot, they made chemical experiments instead. They blew themselves up on one occasion. I don't know what the experiment was, but they put the chemicals in the fire, thinking they'd have a great explosion, and nothing happened. Then they poked the fire, and of course there *was* an explosion, and they both got into a horrible mess. They lost their eyebrows, I think.

When Jacintha told her schoolmistress that she would be willing to worship the Christian god only if she were also allowed to honour others, Eric wrote a poem, "The Pagan," as a tribute to her independent spirit:

> So here are you, and here am I,
> Where we may thank our gods to be;
> Above the earth, beneath the sky,
> Naked souls alive and free.
> The autumn wind goes rustling by
> And stirs the stubble at our feet;
> Out of the west it whispering blows,
> Stops to caress and onward goes,
> Bringing its earthy odours sweet.
> See with what pride the setting sun
> Kinglike in gold and purple dies,
> And like a robe of rainbow spun
> Tinges the earth with shades divine.
> That mystic light is in your eyes
> And ever in your heart will shine.

"The Pagan" was the first poem he wrote to me. In fact I think it was the first poem anyone wrote me. I remember it was in the mushroom fields, after we had been picking mushrooms, that he wrote it for me. He was definitely fond of me, but we were young then, and I was two years older than he was, and I never thought of him in a romantic way at all. But I think he had, for a child of his age, as romantic a view of me as it was possible for him to have. But it was always highly respectable romance. He never made any attempt to seduce me! He probably hadn't developed in that way at all. I think he was fond of me, but in a romantic and idealistic way. I don't think he ever had the slightest idea of *doing* anything about it.

Eric spent part of the Christmas holidays of 1918 with the Buddicom family. One late afternoon, with a fire blazing in the grate, he composed a sonnet for Jacintha.

Our minds are married, but we are too young
For wedlock by the customs of this age
When parent homes pen each in separate cage
And only supper-earning songs are sung.

Times past, when medieval woods were green,
Babes were betrothed, and that betrothal brief.
Remember Romeo in love and grief —
Those star-crossed lovers — Juliet was fourteen.

Times past, the caveman by his new-found fire
Rested beside his mate in woodsmoke's scent,
By our own fireside we shall rest content
Fifty years hence keep troth with hearts desire.

We shall remember, when our hair is white,
These clouded ways revealed in radiant light.

As far as I remember I think I liked it, though I didn't know we'd be likely to be resting by our own fireside, because I never had any idea of marrying Eric. But it's very sad to think that fifty years hence he wasn't there any more . . .

Eton

In the spring of 1917 Eric Blair became a student at Eton.
CHRISTOPHER EASTWOOD arrived the following January.
His overriding impression was that Blair wasn't trying very
hard to make a mark, either intellectually or at games.

> He just didn't try awfully hard at anything. He was
> always shrewd, though. I think he presumably worked
> hard to get into College, and once he got there he rather
> hung back. Of course, he had a lot of brilliant people in
> his election [i.e, his year] but I shouldn't have thought
> he suffered from an inferiority complex at all. You'd
> never have thought for a minute that he was going to
> make a mark as a writer.

Eastwood remembers Blair as a large and well-built boy,
but "rather soft looking" and casual in appearance.

> He wouldn't have responded well to military discipline.
> He wouldn't have stood up straight and sloped arms
> smartly. He wasn't that sort of person at all. At that
> time, during the war, one more or less had to be in the
> Officers' Training Corps, and he went into the signal
> section because there was less discipline required, less
> marching about and standing to attention, which were
> the things he rather disliked. In the signal section you
> were carried about on trucks — much more convenient
> than going for route marches. I rather think he was a
> sort of commander of the section.
>
> When I went to Eton the war was nearly over, but one
> was conscious of the war all the time. We played war
> games. I remember one called the Road to Berlin, a silly
> little game where you had to pass balls through various
> obstructions and hoped to get them to Berlin. But really,
> apart from the rationing, the war didn't affect our daily
> life much. We never — or very seldom — had jam. We
> had some horrible stuff called 'honey sugar.' Nobody I
> knew had got killed in the war, but it must have affected
> the people two or three years senior to me quite a lot.

Blair felt crossness with the regimentation that went on. It was partly imposed by the boys themselves, partly imposed by the authorities, and partly inevitable because of the rationing and so forth. But really he was more sardonic than rebellious, and standing aside from things a bit, observing — always observing.

Christopher Eastwood and Eric Blair were both King's Scholars at Eton. This meant they were part of a small intellectual elite within the school. The seventy King's Scholars — or "Collegers" — paid twenty-five pounds a year for tuition, board, lodging, and recreational facilities, while the nine hundred ordinary students — called "Oppidans" — paid one hundred pounds. The Captain of the School was always a Colleger, and the Collegers lived in the older Tudor section of the school, whose roots go back to its founding by Henry VI in the fifteenth century.

The question of money didn't affect us at all, really. I wouldn't have known whose parents had money and whose didn't, unless the parents were so foolish as to give them so much pocket money that it was obvious that there was money about. And then, if anything, we'd look down on them rather than admire them.

There were a few boys with titles, but it didn't make any difference to the way one thought about them. You were hardly aware of their titles; they were never used in ordinary conversation. The only time when the title came out was if they were wanted by the headmaster for some offence, and a school official came round to you while you were in class and said, 'Is Lord This-or-that here?' and would he please go to the headmaster's study at 11:45.

As a King's Scholar, Blair played a game that is peculiar to Eton — the Wall Game.

The only people who played this Wall Game were Collegers. A few Oppidans got together a scratch team to play against the Collegers on St Andrew's Day, but the

Oppidans never played it regularly, and of course they were much less expert at it than we Collegers were. I remember Blair, when he got bigger, towards the end of his time at Eton, playing the Wall Game and playing it rather well.

The Wall is a brick wall separating the playing field at Eton from the road. It is about a hundred yards long.

The wall has been there for about two or three hundred years. At one end there was a big elm tree with a painted line on it which was the goal for that end. And at the other end there was another wall sticking out at right angles, which had a door in it, and hitting the door was the goal at that end. It was a much smaller goal, but that didn't seem to make very much difference. And you had a sort of bully, or a scrum, rather like rugger. Somebody put the ball into the middle of this bully. There wasn't much running about, merely pushing other people up against the wall or along the wall. It was a very odd game, but I think it was Blair's sort of game. I think he rather enjoyed getting rather grubby. It all got frightfully muddy if it had been wet, and I remember him coming in once looking rather pleased with himself for having got so very dirty!

SIR ROGER MYNORS and Eric Blair produced a magazine at Eton called *Election Times*. Roger Mynors was the editor, while Blair was business manager. "I wrote it out because I had the best handwriting," remembers Sir Roger. "It was the most dreadful stuff." But the main reason for the friendship between Mynors and Blair was biology.

He and I developed a great passion for biology and got permission to do extra dissection in the biology lab. It was a symptom of a general attempt to explore the world around us. We used to go to the butcher in Windsor and buy organs from animals in order to dissect them and learn some more biology. It seems funny looking back on it that this passion for finding out wasn't encouraged more by the authorities, which might have scented either a distinguished surgeon or an eminent physiologist in one or other of us, but it didn't come to that.

One day Eric Blair killed a jackdaw with a catapult on the roof of the college chapel, which was entirely illegal, and we then took it round to the biology lab and dissected it. Jackdaws haunt medieval buildings, you see. Well, as a scientific exercise the bird met a messy and rather smelly end because we did it all wrong. We made the great mistake of slitting the gall bladder and therefore flooding the place with, er . . . Well, it was an awful mess.

Roger Mynors vividly remembers Eric Blair as a boy who loved arguing.

Endless arguments about all sorts of things, in which he was one of the great leaders. He was one of those boys who thought for himself, and at an age when a good many schoolboys haven't graduated out of thinking the way they'd been taught to think. I remember when we first did Greek and were introduced to Plato and the method of the Platonic dialogue, in which Socrates argues like anything with a lot of other people, proving them endlessly wrong, really in order to get them *thinking*. I remember thinking, 'This man's just like Eric Blair!'

Blair's election followed an earlier one that had the reputation of being conformist.

We inherited a tradition of suppressing our juniors, and we did a lot to modify that. This was because our year was very intelligent, and also the whole world was waking up at the end of the war. It looked as if we were getting into a world in which there was much greater freedom and less prejudice. We got a name for being almost revolutionary. That was extremely untrue. All we were doing was to try and keep tradition and get rid of excessive privilege. That's only one side of George Orwell, but it was, I think, the first side that really matured, and in this way he certainly made a great impression on his contemporaries — this breaking up of prejudices and privileges and so on.

SIR STEVEN RUNCIMAN was an exact contemporary of Eric Blair at Eton and was a particularly close friend in their first year at the school.

I thought he was very good company. He was very bright, and I think he found me a good listener perhaps. He was pleasantly lively in his comments on the masters. They were always amusing — and rather stringent. He was interested in writing and in reading and in words, and that was part of the fascination his fellows felt for him — that he had his own individual way of speaking. But even then he didn't really have many friends. He liked good companions, but if they were out of sight I think he forgot them. I don't think he really felt much sympathy for people's individual character, but he had great observant knowledge of what they were like in the setting.

Later in his life George Orwell liked to give the impression that he had suffered at Eton because his parents were not well off.

I think the idea that he was miserable all the time at Eton because there he was among the grand toffs is absolutely absurd. I think that's where the legend has got it wrong. There were people in College poorer than he, so he had no reason to feel inferior. He wasn't one of the top brains of the year, but I don't think that worried him in the least bit. No, he wasn't this embittered boy at a school where he was the poorest of all the pupils, longing to get away and too poor to go up to university. I think that's all fictitious. I knew him always as a rather sardonically cheerful sort of boy — I mean loving the irony, loving to have a slight grievance against masters and older boys, but enjoying it.

One of the effects of the war was that Runciman, Blair, and their classmates were often taught by temporary teachers as the younger masters went off to the front. For a time Aldous Huxley was a master at Eton.

He was practically blind, poor man, couldn't see what was going on, and everybody treated him appallingly badly, and he'd no idea really how to teach. But we did enjoy his use of *words*, the phrases he used, and that was a thing that Eric Blair very much did appreciate. You felt you were with someone who enjoyed words, and compared to the ordinary Eton master it was a rare, rare joy to listen to him. And it was no intellectual strain; he never asked us questions to see how we were getting on. I don't think you can compare *Brave New World* to *Nineteen Eighty-Four*, but I've often wondered if Aldous had any effect on Eric's later writing, just the sheer *writing*. I think probably he *did* have an effect.

Sir Steven believes that the reasons Eric Blair didn't make the common progression from King's Scholar at Eton to undergraduate at Oxford was simply the allure of the East.

He used to talk about the East a great deal, and I always had the impression he was longing to go back there. I mean it was a sort of romantic idea. He was born there, and I think it was the dream, the wonderful life he had left. I don't know how much it was encouraged by his family, I don't think very much, I think rather discouraged, and that possibly made it more romantic to him. So I wasn't the least bit surprised that he decided to go back there instead of a university, particularly as he used to say he didn't much want to go to a university.

Eric's academic performance at Eton certainly suggests that he didn't try very hard. In the examinations of July 1921 he finished one hundred thirty-eighth out of one hundred sixty-seven — a poor result, and one that would rule out a scholarship. With his father now retired from the

Indian Civil Service and living on his pension, it seemed highly unlikely that the Blair family could afford to pay university fees. Jacintha Buddicom had hoped that she and Eric could continue their friendship at Oxford, but neither of them got there. Jacintha believes, in contrast to Steven Runciman, that Eric did want to go to university but that his family said no.

> How much Eric was enthusiastic about it because I was enthusiastic, and how much he would have felt enthusiastic about it left entirely alone, I really can't say. I think it was probably my enthusiasm for it that fired him. I was crazy to go to Oxford. I was fearfully upset that I couldn't go to Oxford, but you see all the money in our family had to go to educate my brother, Prosper. It would have been very nice if Eric and I had both been up at Oxford at the same time. But I think it was decided fairly early on that he shouldn't attempt to go to Oxford and that he should be going in for the Indian Civil, which turned out to be the Burmese Police. You see his father had been out there, and there was a sort of tradition with his father's family. That was his father's idea for him entirely, and I think that Eric fell in with it.

Burma

Eric Blair left England for Burma on 27 October 1922. He sailed from Birkenhead on the SS *Herefordshire*, and he travelled first class. He had crammed for and passed the necessary examinations to enter the Indian Imperial Police. On his arrival in Burma on 29 November he made a few courtesy calls on British officials in Rangoon before taking the sixteen-hour train journey north to Mandalay, where he would begin his job as an assistant district superintendent. He was still only nineteen.

At the station in Mandalay he was met by a fellow recruit. This was ROGER BEADON (1901-76), who encountered a tall, thin, and "rather lugubrious" young man who seemed pleasant enough but not at all interested in the club life that Beadon was happy to settle into. "I don't think he cared much for the Europeans," Beadon recalled in a BBC interview, "and he thought that most of the Burmese were corrupt . . . He was obviously rather 'agin' everybody." At the police training school, Beadon and Blair saw each other virtually every day. Beadon taught Blair how to ride a motorbike, and the two of them rode out once on a hopeful but fruitless tiger shoot.

George Orwell would write that "the Indian Empire is a despotism, with theft as its final object," but in those first months in Burma he merely took the measure of his new situation, getting his physical and psychological bearings. It is impossible to determine exactly when he began to be uncomfortable in his role as an imperial policeman, but Jacintha Buddicom received three woeful letters from Eric while he was in Burma.

I don't think that when he first went out Eric realized how much he'd hate it when he got there. I don't know really why he did hate it so much, but he did. He thought it was absolutely frightful, but his letters weren't very specific. That's what has always been rather a puzzle to me, and the letters were so vague and guarded that I rather wondered whether they might have been censored. He just said it was frightful and you can't imagine how frightful it was if you hadn't had to go through it yourself. Well, of course, that didn't convey anything to me at all.

George Orwell would write in *The Road to Wigan Pier* of "faces of prisoners in the dock, of men waiting in the condemned cells, of subordinates I had bullied and aged peasants I had snubbed, of servants and coolies I had hit with my fist in moments of rage." But Jacintha Buddicom warns readers not to be oblivious of her friend Eric's well-known penchant for "unpoetic licence."

There is no one alive today who can furnish an accurate first-hand account of Eric Blair's experiences in Burma. Roger Beadon's memories come closest to filling the gap, but another glimpse of Blair the imperial policeman is provided by a fellow Etonian, CHRISTOPHER HOLLIS (1902-77), who met him in Burma in the summer of 1925. Hollis was passing through Burma on his way home from a university debating tour of Australia and New Zealand. The two men had a long talk, and Hollis reported Blair to be wrestling with some "second self." "At this time," he wrote in the BBC publication *The Listener,* "there was a struggle within him of two minds: the policeman who hated the rudeness and insubordination of the native, and the new man who was coming to see Imperialism as the evil thing."

Orwell scarcely wrote a happy word about his Burmese experience. In his novel *Burmese Days*, the fictional but largely autobiographical character John Flory rails against the "life of lies" that has made him "a creature of the despotism, tied tighter than a monk or a savage by an unbreakable system of taboos." And in *The Road to Wigan Pier* Orwell denounces his superior officers as "gin pickled old scoundrels." There is nothing to suggest he enjoyed the challenges his work must have provided, the difficult judgments he was required to make when called in to sort out various crimes in the villages on his beat. Perhaps he comforted himself by tucking away little bits of experience to write about later, gathering raw material for his future career.

Was he stimulated by the contact he had with Burmese culture? The answer to that question at least is fairly certain. When Roger Beadon visited him in Insein, his fourth posting in Burma, Beadon asked Blair if it was true that he had been attending services in the Burmese churches. It was true — and Blair did more than that. He would often talk with Burmese priests in what Beadon claimed was "very high-flow Burmese."

Beadon was surprised to find Blair's house in a mess, with "goats, geese, ducks, and all sorts of things floating about." He interpreted this as a sign of a white man "going native," but Eric Blair always liked to keep livestock around him. He kept animals right through his life.

Blair's service in Burma ended in August 1927, when, because of an unspecified illness, he applied for a leave a few months before his five-year term would have been up. The leave was granted, and he sailed for England. He never returned. In September 1927, while on holiday with his family in Cornwall, he formally resigned from the Imperial Police.

His younger sister, AVRIL DUNN (1908-78), noticed a great change in her brother at this time. Eric had grown a moustache in Burma, and his hair had got much darker. Perhaps because he had become accustomed to having servants in Burma, he had grown very untidy. In a BBC interview Avril remembered that "whenever he smoked a cigarette he threw the end down on the floor and expected other people to sweep it up."

Soon after he returned home, Eric visited his old friends, the Buddicoms. Jacintha was not there, but her aunt gave her a very unfavourable report on the new Eric. "Aunt Lilian said, when I said I was sorry I'd missed Eric, words to the effect that 'you haven't really missed anything, because he's not at all what he used to be, and I don't think you'd like him very much now.' "

Jacintha and Eric never did meet again. But over twenty years later, when Jacintha discovered that the George Orwell who had written *Animal Farm* was none other than her childhood friend Eric, she wrote to congratulate him. The brief correspondence that followed (see Chapter 5) is a very poignant coda to their earlier friendship.

Southwold

Southwold is a small, respectable seaside town on the Suffolk coast. When the Blair family moved there in 1921, it was a resort much favoured by retired Indian civil servants. Orwell wrote later in *The Road to Wigan Pier* that "one sniff of English air" had convinced him not to go back to Burma, yet the stiff breezes blowing off the North Sea onto Southwold's stony beach and promenade were not much more satisfying to his spirit than the Burmese heat had been. Southwold was far too stuffy for his taste.

It was not more than a month or two before Eric went to London on the first of his expeditions among the poor. He had by now told his family that he wanted to be a writer, and he saw these journeys as the way to gain his raw material.

Long-time residents of Southwold NANCY FOX and JOAN MULLOCK had known Eric briefly before he went to Burma, when as a gangly but gentle teenager he would come down from Eton. Now, five years later, they shared with Eric's family some uncertainty about what to make of him.

> NANCY FOX: Eric? Well, I don't know. He was rather difficult, wasn't he, Eric. . .
>
> JOAN MULLOCK: Well, he had socialist ideas, I suppose, hadn't he? And Mr Blair Senior wouldn't really agree with that. Also I think there was a bit of a row when he gave up his job. I mean, young men didn't give up jobs in those days. They did what their fathers wanted them to, more or less. I suppose our parents must have said, 'Fancy coming home, fancy giving up a job. On his parents, and what will he do?' — that sort of thing. Young men were expected to make a go of it and were very lucky to get a job, really.

Eric's sister Avril fitted in far better at Southwold.

> JOAN MULLOCK: I knew Avril when she kept the Copper Kettle Tearooms. She was an awfully good cook. We used to foregather there for a cup of coffee or an ice cream. It wasn't a big place: about five tables. Avril did coffees and ices and teas, afternoon teas. She was rather like a Dutch doll, tiny mouth and big round eyes. Unusual looking.
>
> NANCY FOX: She was famous for that ice cream. It was made out of real fruit and real cream. Just the two things together.

JOAN MULLOCK: And you did, to put it plainly, get a very nice type of visitor here — family people. Some families used to come for summer holidays to Southwold year after year, and we used to get to know them. We used to have mad bicycle games, used to roar around the countryside, and we used to go and 'take' churches by putting up a little sticker outside, and we ended up in Wangford and had tea for sixpence — twenty, thirty young people. Then we used to go over to Walberswick Common, all taking our own picnics and all sitting down and spreading out our food, and then play Go Home. Very innocent fun!

NANCY FOX: I remember Eric used to go on long walks across the marshes, looking for birds and flowers. He was very keen on that. And he was always *talking* to whoever he was with; it was usually only one person. He had his opinions which nobody really took any notice of till just before he died. Sad, wasn't it? His first books were no use. When *Down and Out* was published as George Orwell, everybody here knew it was Eric. We were all rather horrified at it — his being a tramp, you know. We thought it was rather a funny thing to do. I think his parents thought so too.

JOAN MULLOCK: They were an awfully nice family. Mrs Blair had a fringe. She was rather like a doll. Nice looking. Rather spreading figure. And he was sweet, old Mr Blair. He had rosy cheeks like an apple, and he always wore a button hole, a rose or something like that. And he had blue eyes.

NANCY FOX: Always so immaculate, so very well turned out. Splendid to look at, a pleasure to meet.

JOAN MULLOCK: But he wasn't very partial to work. It was Mrs Blair who ran the house and did the cooking and did everything like that. Eric's parents were very hard up, but they always put on a jolly good show.

JACK WILKINSON DENNY, the leading tailor in Southwold,

didn't think the Blair family was particularly hard up. Denny and Sons outfitted Eric Blair with made-to-measure clothes throughout most of his life, and a quick glance through the old, stiff-covered order books confirms that he invariably bought the best cloth. On his return from Burma, Blair had to outfit himself for the English climate.

Nineteen twenty-seven, yes, September: he had a three-piece suit. October: flannel trousers. January: an overcoat. The overcoat was six pounds, and the suit was nine pounds ten shillings. An overcoat like that today would be one hundred eighty to two hundred pounds, depending on the cloth, and his three-piece suit would be about three hundred fifty pounds today. I don't say he was flush with money, but when he talks somewhere about not being able to afford an engagement ring, I think that was tongue-in-cheek stuff.

The order books go back as far as 1922, when Eric was preparing to go to Burma.

E.A. Blair, here we are . . . 1922, May: two pairs of flannel trousers. They were thirty-two shillings and sixpence each. That was quite good, because a general going rate for a normal flannel in those days was about six shillings and sixpence. Thirty-five and six must have been pretty close to a working man's wages for a week. The cloth? It was Hunt and Winterbotham. We never made anything *but* a Hunt and Winterbotham for him. He had one pair of cream and one pair of grey — pleated tops, no belt loops. His riding breeches in 1922 were three guineas. That pair today would be about one hundred sixty to one hundred eighty pounds with buckskin strappings, and we *always* put buckskin strappings on.

He was only a thirty-seven chest man, with thirty-three waist, but long in the leg, you see: thirty-four inside leg. Which gives you some idea of his build. They were always very well-turned-out clothes, but he was one of those people who put on a suit and don't look well-dressed even when they put it on new. I never really saw him looking smart. He always looked pale and a little bit drawn. I should think this TB was lurking about somewhere.

Denny and Sons have been in business in Southwold for over a hundred and thirty years. The firm also has fitting rooms in London's Savile Row. In 1918 there were twenty-five tailors working for the firm, which even had its own soccer team and once hired a cutter because he was a good goalkeeper.

I used to look after Eric, and of course most people unburden themselves while fitting. He used to turn up suddenly and say hello. There was nothing flamboyant about him in any way. In fact, he was shy if anything. He never told me what he was writing, though. He was looked upon here as a little bit eccentric. I remember he was keen on his fishing. He fished from the pier a lot. He joined the badminton club and the tennis club. At one time he tutored a backward boy in Walberswick. When he was fishing he wore a fur hat. He was the first person we ever remembered around here to wear one of those.

Dances and things? Well, he used to appear, usually standing on the outside of the room and not talking to anybody much. He wasn't a drinker. Not someone to stand at the bar the whole evening, or anything of that sort.

As a tradesman in the town, even a "high-class" tradesman, Mr Denny was not considered "society." He remembers how on a Sunday, if he encountered Eric's father taking a walk on Southwold promenade, Mr Blair would walk straight past him with no gesture of recognition.

Old man Blair was terribly autocratic. If anyone got in his way at the golf course they'd get it in no uncertain terms! He felt his weight very much; he was full of his own importance. A typical retired civil servant.

Avril was a bit the same. It was a bit of an honour to be served cakes by her! They'd all got a bit of that. I didn't notice it with Eric so much, though.

Grandma and Grandpa and ''Uncle Eric''

HENRY DAKIN, the son of Eric Blair's sister Marjorie, is the keeper of the Blair family Bible, a huge, leather-bound volume with the family history scrawled in faded ink, by various hands, on the inside cover. His memories of Southwold and of his mother's parents, Dick and Ida Blair, date back to the family holidays he spent in Southwold in the 1930s.

Dick would spend most of his time in the Blythe Club, and Grandma would have her bridge parties. She was very keen on the bridge parties and didn't appear to have all that much time for Dick. But it's sort of a family joke now that Grandma would say, 'All men are brutes.' Mind you, I couldn't think of anyone less of a brute than old Dick. He was a most mild bloke, a gentle old boy. I can't remember his making much comment on *anything*, except that the puddings Ida made were never like those his mother made.

There was a lovely little cinema in Southwold. They had two programs a week, and Dick and my grandma always had the same seats kept for them. Quite often the cinema was nearly empty anyway, but they were always led to their two seats. Dick loved whatever film was on, and he would sit there and watch away, and Grandma couldn't stay awake for more than ten minutes. Her head would get lower and lower and sink on her chest, and all of a sudden she would wake up and watch the film for a few minutes, and then down would go her head. She boasted she had never stayed awake through any film bar one, and that was Robertson Hare in *Pot Luck*.

Jane Morgan, Henry Dakin's elder sister, found Grandma Blair quite formidable.

> I was slightly frightened of her. She did her nails practically every day, and she was fond of rather large jewellery. Jet beads and amber necklaces and earrings — yes, she had amber earrings. And she was *much* younger than my grandfather. And poor old Dick, if he was heard poking the fire it was 'Dick, put that poker down.' But I think her children — I mean my mother and Avril — were terribly fond of her, and also, I think, Eric.

At Eton, Eric Blair had shocked his fellow students by running down his parents in public. He told them his mother was a "frivolous person" and his father "wasn't interested in anything." It would seem that on his return from Burma, jobless and with no apparent prospects, there was some friction in the Blair household in Southwold, since both Henry Dakin and Jane Morgan remember Eric's coming to stay with their family in Leeds, looking for a bit of peace and quiet and perhaps sympathy. Eric may have got a friendly reception from his older sister Marjorie, but Jane remembers there being a certain amount of "feeling" between "Uncle Eric" and her father Humphrey, a civil servant in the National Savings Committee.

> My father didn't exactly brush him off, but my father, you see, was 'hail fellow well met,' and he reckoned if Eric was a socialist he ought to get on well with the working man. But Eric didn't really have a great line in small talk, so I think there was this kind of 'ha, ha, he's a socialist, but he doesn't get on as well as I do with the working man' — that sort of thing.

> HENRY DAKIN: Pubs weren't really his way of life, but they were very much my father's way of life. When Eric stayed with us he would go down to the pub, and my father was very much a pub raconteur, whereas Eric was a far more silent individual, probably taking

it all in and making mental notes, but not actually joining in the conversation. My father felt he understood the working class very well indeed, and he felt that Eric didn't have any idea of what the working class really thought and how they lived.

My mother, Marjorie, had a lot of time for Eric, though, even if he didn't seem to be doing very well at the time. For me then he was just an uncle who appeared on the scene, and he'd spend a lot of time writing. He carried his typewriter with him and then used to disappear.

JANE MORGAN: I remember once we were all going on a holiday to Southwold to stay with my grandmother, and Eric had been staying with us for a time, so we all went down together in the car. There was my mother in the front with my baby sister Lucy, and my brother Henry in the back, and the guinea pigs in a basket, and Blanche, the current kid goat, with her head sticking out of a fish basket — we had a goat because my sister had been ill and they said she had to have goat's milk — and there was the cat, and masses of rugs, because of course cars weren't heated in those days, and food, and hot water bottles, and flasks, and a lot of sort of coming and going, and 'Be quiet, you kids' — you know, getting ready for the great trek. And Eric was sitting in the back seat with my brother, and he was a very tall man and it was a very small car, so that his knees were up round his ears, and he wasn't taking any notice of anything at all, and he was reading a book of *French poetry*! You know, *not involved*. He was there and would be on call if anything was wanted, but he wasn't strictly involved.

CHAPTER TWO

In Search of Poverty

*Socialists don't claim to be able to make the world perfect;
they claim to be able to make it better.*

GEORGE ORWELL
"AS I PLEASE"

Socialism for George Orwell was not a matter of changing human society according to any theoretical or idealistic blueprint. He hated the "slide-rule socialists" of Britain's postwar Labour government, who, he felt, betrayed the spirit of socialist equality as they enacted a sheaf of rules and regulations aimed at levelling incomes and opportunities.

Orwell's socialism sprang from a simple, passionate desire to support the underdog, to right obvious wrongs. If the role of the underdog shifted from the worker to the boss, Orwell was more than likely to switch sides. This made him a contradictory character without the apparent consistency of orthodox reformers who were more willing to adhere to theories long after the supporting facts had changed.

It was Orwell's hatred of injustice that eventually gave him a subject to write about: poverty. And with a straightforward and powerful subject came his equally straightforward and powerful writing style.

Soon after he returned to England from Burma, Orwell was pressed by writers at the *Adelphi* to define his own politics. He replied that he was a "Tory anarchist," and although he may have embraced socialism during the

1930s, he never lost his supicion of organizations and institutions. His book *The Road to Wigan Pier* provided powerful propaganda for his friends of the established Left, but he was often the friend the Left would rather do without — a conscience hovering in the background, willing and able to strike when he felt that the cause of the underdog was being swamped in muddled thinking or irrelevant ideology. He was adamant in his belief that socialism must be sold to the workers. If middle-class socialists weren't interested in doing this, he believed they were doing nothing at all. This suspicion of socialist intellectuals led him to make stinging and sometimes overdrawn attacks on them, notably in *The Road to Wigan Pier*.

Orwell became drawn to socialism at the same time as he was finding his feet as a writer. The two processes were connected, and the mix of Orwell the imaginative writer and Orwell the chronicler of injustice is the key to his development in the years 1927 to 1936. The fascinating thing about his writing in this period is that fact and fiction are never clearly separated. On the face of it, *Down and Out in Paris and London* and *The Road to Wigan Pier* are Orwell's straightforward accounts of his observations. But in fact he rearranged experiences to achieve maximum literary and political effect. If what he wrote was *essentially* true, then he felt his documentary reporting was credible. Similarly, in his novels of this period there are long stretches where "fiction" reads like a political essay (for example, his denunciation of the British Empire in *Burmese Days*).

There is a reason for this mingling of styles. Orwell always felt that he had to write from experience. Like many aspiring young authors, he feared he would run out of things to write about and was constantly stimulating his imagination by going out into the world to find "experiences." And in doing so — as investigator, journalist, and novelist — Orwell always got his hands dirty. If he was to write about tramps, he would live with tramps. If he was to document the poverty of the depressed mining communities of the north of England, he would live among the unemployed and go down into the mines himself. He didn't spend the day observing poverty and the evening recovering from the shock with a good meal and a bottle of wine in the best local hotel.

There is no doubt that Orwell damaged his health by "slumming it" in London and Paris and trudging around Wigan, Barnsley, and Liverpool in February and March 1936, walking long distances, taking public transport, and failing to dress warmly enough. He sought out the dirty and the sordid, and in the process he irritated working people, who wanted him to see their efforts to remain clean and decent in the face of mass poverty and unemployment. Most journalists are quite capable of producing a book or an article about a shocking or brutal subject without damaging their health in the process. But most journalists aren't driven by the guilt that Orwell admitted obsessed him after his five years as a policeman in Burma.

Legally, George Orwell lived and died Eric Blair, but after 1933, when *Down and Out in Paris and London* was published under the pseudonym, new friends came to know him as George while older friends continued to call him Eric. Some of his friends believe that the literary persona of George eventually swallowed most of Eric. In *George Orwell*, Raymond Williams suggests that in this formative period of the early 1930s Eric Blair effectively created "his most successful character, 'Orwell,' who became his shaping presence." Perhaps it should come as no surprise that, in searching out poverty, a young writer might find more than one side of his own self.

"A Man from Another World"

DENNIS COLLINGS was Eric Blair's best friend in Southwold in the years after Blair returned from Burma. Collings's father was a well-known figure in the town, and family doctor to the Blairs. Dennis was two years younger than

Eric, but by the time they became good friends in 1927 they had a lot in common. Eric had spent five years in Burma; Dennis had just come back from three years' growing sisal in Mozambique, and he was planning to go to Cambridge the following year to study anthropology. In the meantime, he and Eric spent long hours talking and taking walks around Southwold.

Dennis maintained a healthy scepticism about Eric's expeditions among the downtrodden of London.

By tramping he was trying to identify himself with the lowest ranks of the working classes, with those who had lost all interest in living what we would call a reasonably normal life. The tramps were people who'd outcast themselves. After all, it wasn't as hard to get a job in those days as it's been made out. I was perfectly aware of the suffering and poverty of a great number of people, but quite a lot of them were playing a game, and I used to wonder what Eric was making all the fuss about. I never took his tramping seriously. His tramping was like his hop picking: it was an anthropological experience he wanted to go through, in the end leading to something that could be written about.

But what I never understood was why he wanted to write about that sort of thing. What made him tick in that direction? He turned himself into an outcast. The most suffering and poorest of coal miners would have looked down on him with scorn. He loved words, yes, but it's a strange thing that he should have put himself through this agony in order to write, when there are so many other things he could have written about.

He never came to Southwold in his tramp's gear, even though the 'Spike' [a tramps' lodging house] was just up the road. He was afraid he'd run into his father, so he never came in his gear to Southwold.

When he was on the road, Eric Blair wrote long letters to Dennis Collings.

Usually he would say, 'Please let me have a return stamp,' which made me laugh. A letter cost three halfpence then, I think. Anyway, I'd put the return stamp on. I mean, supposing he really had run out of money, quite genuinely, and said, 'Could you let me have a fiver?' I would willingly have let him have a fiver, you see, but there was nothing like that.

But one shouldn't criticize him too much; one should treat this as an anthropological study, and that's the way he did it. I think he was trying to atone for something. I mean, why should one go out and walk twenty miles or so, cold, hungry, miserable, shoes worn out, nothing to keep the rain off? It can only have been for self-punishment.

He was a masochist in a way, if by masochism you mean doing harm to yourself in order to try to get some kind of pleasure out of it. I think that fits Eric, yes. You see, he was caught up in a feeling of guilt when he came back from Burma. He felt he had been out there preserving law and order against the will of the people. He talked quite a bit about Burma. He felt we were oppressing the Burmese, that we'd thrust ourselves in there and weren't allowing the Burmese to have a say. He was particularly against the Burmese monks, because so many of them went into politics, which was of course strictly against the Buddhist wishes. I used to say that, as an anthropologist, things didn't seem to be as bad as he said it was. Things were working properly. Burma was doing all right, thank you. But he had no anthropological outlook at all. I saw things in a different light from him.

Actually, I think he just wanted to see *change*. Even if he was in heaven he'd want to change the order of the angels. I don't think it was any deeper than that — just a psychological quirk that he'd got. Things must be *changed*. It might have been something in his subconscious. Something which lies low for years and suddenly comes to the surface. Change, must change.

From time to time Eric would show Dennis some of the things he'd written, but generally he was very secretive about his writing.

> Nobody ever saw him writing anything, because he did that in his little back room in the morning. The routine was, he'd have his breakfast, he'd go to his little back room, and he'd sit down at a table with a pen and paper, and he *wrote*. He didn't mind *what* he wrote at all; he just wrote. And this he looked upon as his training for writing more serious matters later on. He stopped at twelve, and then he went out and had a pint or something, and then he had his lunch, and then he would roam about the countryside with his friends . . .

Southwold was very much a retirement town, but Dennis Collings and Eric Blair found quite a few people their own age to spend time with. Eric became very friendly with Eleanor Jaques (1906-62), who lived next door to him, but it was Dennis Collings who eventually married Eleanor in 1934.

> When I married Eleanor it didn't cause any problem between Eric and me, none whatsoever. Because I don't think he wanted to marry anybody, really, and certainly not someone like Eleanor, because she had her own ideas and she'd stick to them, and if she realized she was wrong she'd say yes, she was wrong, but she wouldn't be browbeaten into pretending to accept an idea she didn't approve of.
>
> In a way, Eric was an intellectual bully; that's not a criticism of him, it's just the way he was. He was very sweet on Eleanor, and they got on very well, but Eleanor realized he wasn't the marrying kind. I mean you can have good friends and not want to marry them. I think he rather had the idea that he should be the boss. I think he rather liked women who were only too glad to have such a wonderful chap over them, if you know what I mean. He was rather a man from another world in that

respect. He was an individual who couldn't *merge* himself. If you're married at all successfully, you've got to merge your feelings.

BRENDA SALKELD was a gym mistress at St Felix School, just outside Southwold. She first met Orwell in 1928, shortly after his return from Burma, and they kept in touch throughout Orwell's life.

Somebody said to me he had a tragic sort of life. I said, 'Not really, in some ways it was a highly successful life.' And I think he felt that too. He wanted to do something and he did it: he became a success. It wasn't money he wanted; he just wanted to be a really successful writer. He felt he had it in him.

We talked about marriage and he said he wouldn't want me to have anything to do with my brothers. I said, 'Don't be ridiculous, I'm devoted to my brothers.' That was the sort of kidding attitude he had.

He was tall, he had a shock of stiff hair and rather drooping shoulders. Very nice hands with spatulate fingers. Very often with artistic people you get spatulate fingers; you know, the top part of the finger is rather broad. He was pale with smallish, rather bright blue eyes. He was good company when he wasn't gloomy and complaining.

We liked to argue and usually took completely opposite views. We used to argue about labour policies and things. And we talked about ideas. He was always trying to shock you, saying some group of people or other were absolute stinkers.

But nothing would come in the way of his writing. Absolutely nothing. I think the words flowed naturally, but in a way he missed a lot of life. I said, 'Never write about people, you don't understand them. Even about yourself you haven't a clue.' He might as well have been in a glass case. He didn't understand people at all.

Like Dennis Collings, Brenda Salkeld was highly sceptical about Orwell's tramping expeditions. Once, when Brenda was at her family home in Bedford, Orwell turned up looking like a tramp.

We said, 'You go up and have a bath.' And while he was up there we said, 'I hope he's not using my loofa!' Our family laughed. They thought this was priceless. He just came in for breakfast and then went off being a tramp again.

You see, what amused us was why someone would want to be a tramp unless they had to be. It's very different if you do really have no money and you haven't anywhere to go. That's very different from someone who just plays at being a tramp. I used to argue with him about this. I said, 'You don't know anything about it, what it feels like to be a tramp. It's almost fun to you.' He was just getting a bit of colour for his writing. But he certainly did look like a tramp; he had a dirty old pair of flannel bags.

His first book was good, though. It was very exciting getting it published. But all his books had a shock line in them. He tried to make you curl up with shock. But he couldn't write about people. He couldn't produce a person that would come to life.

Orwell and Brenda Salkeld often went on walks together in the country.

He'd talk the whole time, you see, unless we were actually birdwatching. We went riding together occasionally.

Once on a walk we were going over a disused railway bridge across the Blythe River, and he dropped my field glasses into the water while we were stepping on the railway sleepers. We were both looking at some bird, and he took the glasses and slipped, and the glasses went into the river. Well, down he went. I spotted the place where they fell, and he waded into the water and found them.

Orwell wrote some of his most interesting letters to Brenda Salkeld.

> He was a great letter writer. Endless letters. And I mean when he wrote you a letter he wrote *pages*. Not a little scribble — *pages*. And he liked to work out his ideas in letters. Then we might discuss them when we met. He wouldn't talk about the theme of a book, exactly, but he'd write about the moral points involved. I never recognized any of the characters in his books, but we didn't talk about people much. It was more ideas, and different writers. Swift he was very enthusiastic about. He thought the existential writers were absolute rubbish.
>
> One evening we discussed *Tropic of Cancer*, and I said I was shocked. And Eric laughed at this. He loved the idea that you were shocked at anything. He always tried to shock you.
>
> He had a sense of the absurd, a sense of the ridiculous. One time I was going to Italy and someone gave me a phrase book which had the most wonderful things in it, like 'Lace my stays but not too tightly' and 'Unhand me, Count.' We laughed over this book, and I think he put something like that into one of his books.

Paris

Blair went to France in the spring of 1928 and rented a cheap room in the fifth arrondissement, a working-class district. It's not clear why he decided to live in Paris, but his intention was apparently to live as cheaply as possible and to write. The presence there of his Aunt Nellie, who would probably offer her nephew the occasional free meal and perhaps even money, may also have influenced him. Nellie Limouzin, Eric's maternal aunt, got on well with him, and throughout her life she appears to have helped him out whenever she could. While Eric was in Paris (April 1928 through the end of 1929), Nellie was living with a colourful Frenchman named Eugène Adam, whom she later married. LOUIS BANNIER met Eric at the house Nellie and Eugène shared. Bannier's description of his encounter with Blair indicates that Eugène Adam may have been an early influence on George Orwell's attitude toward Soviet communism.

> Adam, like me, was involved in the October Revolution in Petrograd in 1917. We were both partisans in that revolution. And when I arrived at his aunt's house, Blair was arguing seriously and noisily with his uncle, monsieur Adam. Blair was praising the revolution, the communist system, while Adam had abandoned that idea at least four years before, perhaps even five or six years before. You see, Adam had gone back to Russia, and there he had learned that instead of it being socialism, it was a future prison. Prominent people in the Party in Moscow had not received Adam very well, and he had come back anticommunist. But Eric Blair didn't know of this change in his uncle. And he, Blair, continued to proclaim that the Soviet system was the definitive socialism. So they were at each other's throats, despite the presence of the aunt.
>
> I heard much later that Blair also became completely changed, just like his uncle, monsieur Adam — furious with the system in Russia.

Nellie Limouzin and Eugène Adam were both committed Esperantists. In 1922 Adam and Louis Bannier had founded, in Prague, the Workers' Esperanto Association of the World.

> Eric Blair had no respect for the Esperanto movement. He didn't believe in the movement or in the principles on which the movement was based — absolutely not. In fact, he criticized his Aunt Nellie on this, she who devoted all her life to the movement. But Adam was only active in the Esperanto movement until his departure from Paris in 1936. He decided to leave because of the lack of harmony with his wife, Nellie Limouzin. The marriage was not happy. She had no character. She was soft, without backbone, without willpower.

She was the daughter of a colonel in the army, and often she told me the story of her life. She had the one sister, who became Mrs Blair, married to Orwell's father. And she told me that her father had lived the life of a prince there (Burma). They had as many as thirty servants, who didn't do much and slept more often than they worked.

Louis Bannier's brief encounter with Orwell in Nellie's house in Paris is one of the very few first-hand accounts of Orwell's activities during his eighteen-month stay in France. From his letters to a literary agent we know he wrote a number of short stories, none of which appears to have been published. He also wrote two novels, unpublished and now lost. On 6 October 1928, however, his first article as a professional writer was published in *Le Monde*. It was about censorship in England. Four other articles — on unemployment in England, a day in the life of a tramp, the beggars of London, and Burma — were printed in the paper *Le Progrès civique*.

In February 1929 Orwell fell ill with pneumonia. His account of his spell in Paris's medieval Hôpital Cochin was published in 1946 by George Woodcock in *Now* magazine under the title "How the Poor Die." In late 1929, apparently because his money and clothes had been stolen, Orwell worked as a dishwasher in a luxury hotel. This experience appears in *Down and Out in Paris and London*.

After Eugène Adam's departure from Paris in 1936, Aunt Nellie returned to England. Louis Bannier met Orwell briefly a second time, in 1945. Orwell had gone to Europe to report for the *Observer* on the immediate post-war situation.

He came to see me at the bank, bringing me canned goods on behalf of his aunt. His Aunt Limouzin had told him you will take monsieur Bannier such and such canned goods. He spoke French quite well. He said he would come and see me again, but he did not come back. Instead he sent another man with more canned goods, but this man unfortunately hardly spoke a word of French. I never saw Orwell again.

"You Must Meet Literary People"

MABEL FIERZ was Orwell's good friend and confidante. She wrote the occasional review for the *Adelphi* but also found great satisfaction in helping young and struggling writers like Eric Blair. It was her faith in Blair, and her tenacity, that would lead to the publication of his first book, *Down and Out in Paris and London*.

Mabel Fierz met Orwell in 1930 while on holiday at Southwold.

He was sketching on the beach, and we met by chance, and we got into conversation. He told me what he was doing, and I said as a literary man it won't help you much to live down here; you must meet literary people who will help you with your work. So I gave him my address in London and said my husband and I would always be pleased to see you, and we would introduce you to people who might be able to help you.

Orwell visited Mabel Fierz frequently after this and seems to have poured out more of his troubles to her than to most of his friends.

He never found anything that was comforting, that brought him any peace and happiness. He was always on edge, always worrying, reaching out for a solution, for an answer on the philosophical side. He was devoted to his family, and he always wanted his father to be proud of him, but they were disappointed that he had thrown up his job in the Burmese Police, which his father had got him into. That was a great sorrow to him, that he never came up to his father's expectations. It always hurt him. His father didn't think he'd ever make money as a writer, and when his father was dying [in 1939] they were able to show him Orwell's latest book, and that was a great comfort to Eric. So his father and he parted friends when his father died. He was very glad about that because he wanted his father to think well of him. That was the reason he changed his name — that if his book was an absolute failure, he didn't want the name Blair, his father's name, to be thought badly of.

As a married woman more than ten years older than Orwell, Fierz was Orwell's chosen sounding board for his thoughts about affairs of the heart.

He used to say the one thing he wished in this world was that he'd been attractive to women. He liked women and had many girlfriends, I think, in Burma. He had a girl in Southwold and another girl in London. He was rather a womanizer, yet he was afraid he wasn't attractive. He told me that in Paris he had a girlfriend and he got very fond of her, and he had a room somewhere, a cheap room in the slums of Paris, and he and this girl were living together, and he was proposing to marry her which would have been very foolish. But one day he came home and he found that she'd gone, with all his clothes and all his luggage. She just disappeared. So that was the end of that girl.

Mabel and Francis Fierz's comfortable house in Hampstead Garden Suburb became a convenient "base camp" for Orwell on his visits to London. There was always a meal and encouragement for him, and he even used the place as a drop-off point where he could store his clothes on his periodic tramping trips. By October 1930 he had finished a draft of the book that would become *Down and Out in Paris and London*. The revised and finished manuscript was then submitted to and rejected by two London publishers, Faber and Cape. A dejected Orwell showed up at Mabel Fierz's house.

He brought his manuscript to us, and he said he had tried various publishers who had returned it. T.S. Eliot was the reader for one of them. T.S. Eliot had said the book was too loosely written, they wouldn't accept it.

He was very disappointed. He said, 'I can't get it published, so throw it away,' and said, 'Keep the paperclips, at least they are valuable.' He needed a lot of encouragement, you see. He was rather a pessimistic person by nature.

Anyway, my husband knew a literary agent in the Strand, through a tennis club, and so I decided to take it to him, to Leonard Moore. So one day I took it to Mr Moore to see if he would read it. And he said, 'Oh no, nobody knows your friend. I'm afraid there's no hope.' So I persuaded him. I said, 'Well, keep it and look at it yourself and see if you can do anything.' Three months later he sold it to Gollancz, and Gollancz brought it out and the book sold well.

Mabel Fierz's influence on Orwell's life didn't stop there. It was through a friend of hers that he met his future wife, Eileen O'Shaughnessy, in 1935.

My friend was renting a room to Orwell in London, and it was in her flat that Orwell and Eileen met. Eileen was an Oxford grad, and they fell in love. And he was very happy. That was the only time in his life when he was really happy. He was devoted to her, and her death [in 1945] was an awful blow.

He was very much a man who was in sympathy with the downtrodden people in this world. His socialism was quite individual, a sort of personal feeling of injustice to the underdog. I think he always felt people should have a fair deal in life. But it's curious: his friends were all upper class, though he was so keen on the underdog. He had no friends except for the upper class. He was very much the Eton boy.

ADRIAN FIERZ is Mabel Fierz's son. Whenever Orwell spent time with the Fierz family in London, he would usually take time to talk to Adrian, who was a boy of eleven when he first got to know Orwell.

He made a very strong impression on me as a very wise and kind person. He would play cricket with us. He was very relaxed with children; I think he liked children. I had a great regard for his opinions and his knowledge on almost any subject, and I remember saying to him, 'Is that a good book?' or 'Do you think the government should do so-and-so?' It became a sort of joke that any statement prefaced by the words 'Eric says' was held to have great authority. For example, 'All scoutmasters are homosexuals' or 'All tobacconists are fascists,' which he just sort of threw off, partly as a joke. And then we would tend to repeat 'Eric says so-and-so' as if it were gospel! He introduced me to P.G. Wodehouse — he was very keen on the Bertie Wooster books — and he also introduced me to the Sherlock Holmes books.

I didn't feel he was a rebel. He had tailor-made clothes — always a brown Harris tweed with a slight check, and grey flannel trousers — and he had typical upper-middle-class English tastes. I don't think he was able to identify himself with the British working man. He would like to have done so, but he couldn't. His interests were intellectual. He wasn't interested in racing, or greyhounds, or pub crawling, or shove-halfpenny. He just didn't have much in common with people who didn't have his intellectual interests. He didn't feel superior to them; he just didn't know what to talk about to people who'd never heard of Thackeray or someone like that.

I find in his essays much the same interest and pleasure that I found as a boy in talking to him. They're sort of thinking aloud about numerous different subjects, from picture postcards to boys' comic papers and so on.

Adrian Fierz believes that his father was instrumental in Eric Blair's choice of the pseudonym 'George Orwell.'

The story goes that he and my father were walking in Suffolk and he said, 'What name shall I use as a *nom de plume*?' And the River Orwell was nearby, so father said, 'Why not take Orwell as the surname?' And then he said, 'What Christian name?' and my father — always as a sort of joke talking to a child he met in a train or something, would say 'Hello, George,' just as Americans say 'Hello, Mac' very often to a stranger — so father said, 'Well, make it George.'

Orwell had a profound effect, as he often did with children, on the young Adrian.

I learned from him the habit of trying to consider all problems and questions in life completely objectively and calmly. Calmness, in fact, is the main memory I have of his whole attitude and way of speaking and way of treating subjects, which is perhaps slightly anomalous because his feelings obviously were very strong. You don't go and live as a tramp when you have the opportunity of living comfortably. He would follow any argument or series of facts through to its logical conclusion, without any attempt to twist that conclusion to fit his own preconceived ideas or prejudices or emotions. He could accept the way the facts or the logic seemed to point.

The *Adelphi*

The *Adelphi* was a literary journal that published the work of new and experimental writers, and it was a natural place for Orwell to go as a young writer trying to get published. He had submitted articles to it from Paris, but it was only after he returned to London in 1929 that he succeeded in having anything of his printed. In fact, two of Orwell's finest essays — "The Spike," an account of a short stay in a tramps' lodging house, and "A Hanging," a description of an execution in Imperial Burma — appeared in the *Adelphi* in 1931.

The journal had been founded by John Middleton Murry (1889-1957), and at the time Orwell was associated with it, it was connected to the British Independent Labour

Party and was critical of the official Labour Party and the active Marxist parties. It went through a series of editorial changes: sometimes its slant was socialist, and sometimes it bordered on mysticism.

EDOUARD RODITI, novelist and poet, met Orwell through the *Adelphi*.

> The *Adelphi* published *marginal* writers; it was open to new ideas and new writers more than other magazines in London. The people who wrote for *Adelphi* were a bit of a group, and we got on well. What kept us together was we were experimental in ideas rather than style.

Edouard Roditi and Orwell often wandered around London together, enjoying a cheap Chinese meal in the East End and then walking back to Roditi's house in Pimlico.

> Once we were in Trafalgar Square, and George Orwell spent a long time listening to the conversations in the Square. And later, when I read his book *A Clergyman's Daughter*, it was like having these conversations played back to me, as if he had recorded them and included them in the novel.

The working-class writer JACK COMMON (1903-68) also met Orwell in the *Adelphi* offices. He knew E.A. Blair (as Orwell remained until 1933 when *Down and Out in Paris and London* was published) by reputation as a rebel, a man to meet. But his first meeting with Orwell, recorded in an unpublished memoir, was a disappointment.

> He looked the real thing — outcast, gifted pauper, kicker against authority, perhaps near-criminal. He rose to acknowledge the introduction with a handshake. Right away, manners, and more than manners — *breeding* — showed through. The public school presence. This man Blair was a letdown to me that day.

Orwell had been familiar with the *Adelphi* for some years. In Burma he had read copies of it, and according to Jack Common, when he disapproved of a particular article he would prop the magazine up against a tree and "fire his rifle at it till the copy was a ruin." But that was when Middleton Murry was editor. When Orwell wrote for the *Adelphi* the editor was a wealthy, idealistic baronet, SIR RICHARD REES (1900-1970). Rees had done already what Orwell wished to do — abandon the world into which he had been born and bred. By 1930, in addition to being editor of the *Adelphi*, Rees was a painter and critic of modest reputation. Orwell and Rees became great friends, and Rees gave a great deal of literary and financial support to Orwell. Richard Rees believed that Orwell's highest ambition was to be a great poet, and he published some of Orwell's better poems, which he recited in a BBC interview.

'And I see the people thronging the street,
The death-marked people, They and I
Goalless, rootless, Like leaves drifting,
Blind to the earth and to the sky . . .'

Rees believed Orwell's poems revealed his basic pessimism.

He looked at the past with horror for its record of injustice and cruelties, but always with a certain nostalgia as well. And he looked to the future with misgivings. He compared himself to Buridan's Ass: 'Between two countries, both-ways torn/ And moveless still, like Buridan's donkey/ Between the water and the corn' [from "On a Ruined Farm near the His Master's Voice Gramophone Factory"].

At first Richard Rees did not find Orwell very passionate or radical. But later, after Orwell's journey to the depressed mining communities of Lancashire and Yorkshire in the north of England, Rees observed that a "smouldering fire" in him seemed to catch light.

Down and Out in Paris and London was published in January 1933 by Victor Gollancz who had demanded savage cuts in the manuscript to prevent charges of libel and obscenity. Even then, Orwell's younger sister, AVRIL DUNN, was surprised at its personal nature.

In his relations with his family, my brother had always been detached and, one might say, impersonal. There was never any discussion of sex or his love affairs or anything. So when all these matters came out in his book it almost seemed it had been written by a different person.

Despite the support of the *Adelphi*, Orwell found it a hard struggle to establish himself as a writer. The constant problem was money. In April 1932 he did what many young, hopeful writers do: he took a teaching job to keep body and soul together.

"The Best Teacher I Remember"

GEOFFREY STEVENS was taught by George Orwell when he took a job as schoolmaster at a very small private school called The Hawthorns. It was located in Hayes, in Middlesex, and it catered to families who were sufficiently ambitious socially to remove their children from the state school system but who couldn't afford to send them to the larger, recognized public schools.

Without a shadow of a doubt he was the best teacher I remember at the school. He was also the oddest man I ever met in my life. Even as a lad of thirteen I could discern he was no ordinary character. He was a man who lived *within himself*. Quite frequently he would suddenly begin to smile; his face would become completely wrinkled with smiles. He wouldn't utter a sound, never said a word, but it was almost uncontrollable. He would have to turn away to do something behind the desk, anything to try and hide his confusion. But he never divulged to anyone what was going through his thoughts.

I never saw him in a smart suit, always in a pair of grey flannels and an old sports jacket, even in class. He never seemed to make use of his full height. He usually had one leg slightly bent, and more often than not one hand was in his pocket.

He completed *Down and Out in Paris and London* just after he joined the school — I think within weeks of coming to the school — and it was at that time that my friend, the proprietor's son, told me that Blair had asked him to post the manuscript, and he told him what it was. So we knew, years before he was known at all as an author. But otherwise in school time he never referred to it at all.

Stevens remembers Eric Blair as a teacher who would take a keen interest in the boys.

Whether it was handwork or natural history, he would wholeheartedly support a boy and try to teach him. He it was who gave me my first lesson in oil painting, setting up small objects like eggs and matchboxes on a table and showing me how to produce the perspective and give light and shade, and how to give roundness to the form of an egg in oils. He used to do quite a bit of oil painting at that time. I remember him showing me a portrait. He did it by artificial light one evening, and when he showed it to me the next morning the face was all yellow.

He was also very keen on essay writing. I think probably some of our essays drove him to despair. I remember him putting remarks like 'bilge' on the foot of them! And the French lessons were only in French, no English. We had no playing fields, so we had to walk to a recreational ground about a mile and a half from here to play football, and he noticed in the window of a house that took in laundry a ludicrous spelling mistake, and he offered sixpence, out of his own pocket, to anyone who spotted it. Well, I was out on my bicycle the very same lunchtime and located it without much problem. Sixpence was a fortune to us boys.

Outside school hours Eric Blair would take any boy who was interested on long country walks. In those days the factories around Hayes hadn't yet eaten up much of the countryside.

We used to walk about two and a half miles to a little stagnant pond, near where the M4 Motorway is now. And we used to probe the bottom of the pond with long sticks and hold jam jars above to catch the marsh gas, as he called it — the methane. Then we used to cork up the top and put a hole through it and set light to the gas. That's the kind of thing he really enjoyed. And a few hundred yards from the school there are quite a few black poplar trees, and he used to take me round and show me where the puss moth caterpillars lived. We used to find their eggs and breed them up in breeding cages. And I don't think I ever think of marsh gas without thinking of Eric Blair. Or if I see a puss moth caterpillar on a poplar tree my mind will go straight back to him as the one who first identified them for me.

There was a rapport between us. I liked him well enough to invite him home for tea. One wouldn't invite a man to tea unless one had a fair regard for him, would one? But I think it was only the one occasion, because the outcome of it was that my homework was increased when he had a chat with my father after tea!

Geoffrey Stevens would, however, occasionally be at the receiving end of Eric Blair's authoritarian streak.

He was pretty strict and rather harsh. We used to have to take our work to the desk, and he kept a rule on his desk. As we stood there he would prod us in the stomach. Well, I used to tighten up the stomach muscles, make them as hard as I could, and one day the rule slipped off, and when I got back to my seat I prodded the boy next to me with my rule, in a rather exaggerated movement. Well, by the end of the session there were two or three of us who were told to stay behind, and we had six of the best. I remember I couldn't sit down on it for at least a week. They were really bad bruises. I had a job to sit in the bath, I remember. But such was the rapport between us boys and Blair that I don't remember any resentment whatever. I never held any ill will for him because of that, although I think it was pretty unjust for such a trivial complaint. But really, he was a kindly man. I think there were two sides to his character, and he was able to show both.

Booklovers' Corner

Shortly before Christmas 1933, Orwell became seriously ill with pneumonia. He left his teaching job and spent the first half of 1934 convalescing at his parents' home in Southwold.

Down and Out in Paris and London had been published in 1933 to generally good reviews, but it had earned Orwell no more than about two hundred pounds. His second book, *Burmese Days*, was published in the United States in October 1934 (the British edition was delayed until 1935 because of changes demanded by Gollancz to avoid libel suits).

Although Orwell was beginning to make a name for himself in the literary world of London, he was not yet earning enough to stop working. Late in 1934 he found a perfect job at a bookshop in Hampstead called Booklovers' Corner. The owners, Francis and Myfanwy Westrope, were socialists, pacifists, and avid drinkers of dandelion coffee. Orwell worked half-days in the afternoons — a schedule that left him time to write. JON KIMCHE worked in the mornings.

Mrs Westrope came to me and said, 'George Orwell has taken a room.' But it was typical of both of us that it was a few weeks before we met; our habits and approach to matters were quite different.

Mr Westrope was tall, slightly stooped, impressive in appearance, rather like a quiet country solicitor. She was much more vivacious, and she was very interested in both of us. We arranged our own food, but they had a very nice sitting room which Orwell was allowed to use, and I used to go in occasionally.

I never saw him *sit* in the bookshop. He always used to stand there in the centre, a slightly forbidding figure. Probably, like myself, he resented the idea of selling anything to people, even books. To me, the only thing of note about him was that he had published a book. I hadn't read it. He also wrote poetry at that time. The picture that remains is of a very tall figure almost like de Gaulle, standing, with a little boy down below looking up at Orwell and buying stamps from him (there were also old stamps in the shop, for stamp collectors).

In the evenings the conversation would almost invariably turn to Roman Catholicism and its influence on public life. I had the impression that was one of his strong 'anti' feelings at the time. Curiously, we never discussed socialism, never discussed current politics. He would *never* discuss his books with anybody; he was quite paranoic about that. He was convinced that someone would steal his ideas. An evening with him was really an evening listening to him. It was interesting, but he didn't draw you out in a discussion.

George Orwell caricatured the bookshop in his novel *Keep the Aspidistra Flying*, which was published in April 1936.

The picture of the bookshop was not at all accurate in *Keep the Aspidistra Flying*, but the picture of the lending library we had there also, was perfect. But when I read his portrayal of the bookshop itself, it sounded all wrong. It just didn't ring true. It sounded false. The bookshop was *not* depressing; the customers were quite normal people. I mean *I* don't remember any 'seedy old gentlemen' coming in and looking for pornography, none of that. And the Westropes were a delightful couple, extremely sincere, truthful, very compassionate, generating an atmosphere of slightly suppressed excitement. But that was the turn of Orwell's mind. He looked at extremes, not at normal things.

KAY EKEVALL met George Orwell in Booklovers' Corner in late 1934. She ran her own secretarial service in Hampstead, enjoyed meeting literary people, and was herself knowledgeable about books and authors.

I saw this new assistant and thought he was a great asset because he was so tall he could reach all the shelves nobody else could without hauling a ladder out!

The bookshop wasn't half as sleazy as he makes out in *Keep the Aspidistra Flying*. It was quite a nice bookshop, actually, and had some interesting stuff in it. It was mainly books we talked about, and then after a month or two of going into the bookshop and talking, he said would I like to meet some of his friends. He was quite a nice-looking fellow, but not all that healthy looking. He had a rather pale dry skin, as if he'd been dried up by the Burma heat.

He considered himself poor and was always talking about money. We used to argue a bit about it, and I said there's loads of folk worse off than us.

I was in the Labour League of Youth. I joined it mainly because I had a boyfriend in it before I met Eric. We were against the whole injustice of things. I think Eric felt that he was one of the victims of injustice because he was poor and couldn't afford the things he felt he ought to have and had to struggle for things, and I said, well, most people have to struggle for things. Anyway, I said, these things are so unimportant as long as you've got a good roof over your head and a warm place and can buy a few second-hand books and entertain your friends to coffee occasionally.

Once or twice we went out to Bertorelli's, which I mean shows that we weren't all that poor, because you couldn't afford to do that if you were. And I used to say, 'We'll go Dutch,' and he would say, 'Oh no, no, I've just had a cheque from So-and-so,' which I didn't

always believe. It was very difficult to make him go
Dutch with you. He had this picture of being a he-man.

And he was so determined to get his point of view
across that he ignored other people's points of view. For
example, some of the sweeping statements he made are
absolutely amazing: Wells is weak, an inadequate
thinker. Shaw's no good. Webb's no good. Henri Bar-
busse is no good. And of course he *hated* the popular
novelists like Priestley, Walpole, and Arnold Bennett —
couldn't *stand* Arnold Bennett. We talked about
Chaucer quite a lot because we both liked him. He
wanted to write an epic on Chaucerian lines about the
history of England from Chaucer's time to the present
day.

He was very, very anti-imperialist. He used to talk
about what horrible people the club people were in
Burma, how they despised the natives although the
natives were doing all the work.

As with so many of his friends, Eric enjoyed taking long
walks with Kay — mainly on Hampstead Heath — staying
out for two or three hours at a time and often ending up at
a café for coffee.

A lot of walks we went on. He knew an awful lot about
the countryside, and he would notice birds or animals
and point them out to me. He'd say, 'Listen!' and he'd
tell me what bird it was singing. By the time I saw them
they were gone! And different trees — he knew the
names of plants. I found it fascinating. I would say to
him, 'What tree is that?' and he would always know
what kind of tree it was. I wasn't very observant that
way, and I didn't know any of the names. I've met a few
people like that who have what I call 'country eyes.'

He did discuss children once or twice. I said did he
ever want any — not that I wanted any by him, just in
general conversation. And he said, 'I don't think I can
have any,' and I said, 'Why do you say that?' and he
thought a moment and said, 'Well, I've never had any.'

I didn't say it at the time, but I felt like saying, 'Well, how do you know? You might have, and they'd never let on.'

Most of my women friends in those days weren't looking for marriage or anything like that. I think we rather despised marriage. I think Eric liked women well enough, but I don't think he ever regarded them as a force in life. They were very secondary. He said, 'Yes, you meet intelligent women who can talk to you, but they aren't the mainstream of things at all.' He had this ultramasculine attitude to them, so that they were just sort of useful appendages to life rather than people. Mind you, he didn't treat you like that when you met him. He was very equalitarian in discussion. Really we were just very good friends, very close in a lot of ways. We were fond of each other. I just thought he was a nice guy.

Kay's friendship with Eric lasted until the spring of 1935, when he met Eileen O'Shaughnessy, the woman who was to become his wife.

I didn't know he wanted to marry. It never occurred to me to even ask him. With most of my boyfriends I said, 'Look, if you find someone else don't hesitate to say so,' because I don't like these dragged-out things. I'd rather have a clean break. And I said the same to Eric. And actually he was the *only one* who ever said, 'I've found someone else.' The others just faded out. Eric was the only one who said, 'Look, I've met a girl I want to marry,' and he told me about Eileen. I met her a couple of times. She was gay and lively and interesting, and much more his level. She was older than me, she'd been to university, and she had an intellectual standing in her own right, and I thought it was rather tragic that she should give it all up. I don't think I would have.

Wigan Pier

More than a year later, when *The Road to Wigan Pier* was published, Kay was horrified by Orwell's slashing attack on middle-class socialists. He wrote of the "prevalence of cranks wherever Socialists are gathered together" and wondered if the mere word "Socialist" attracted "every fruit-juice drinker, nudist, sandal-wearer, sex-maniac, Quaker, 'Nature Cure' quack, pacifist, and feminist in England."

And he was so sweeping about it, that's what annoyed me. It was everybody. Anybody who was at all left was absolutely *damned* by him. It absolutely made me furious. He was maligning all these people. He was insulting them. He made this sort of sweeping state-ment. He condemns people en masse. If he wants to condemn people he doesn't pick out anything good about them, and if he wants to praise them he doesn't pick out anything bad about them. And he had his own prejudices. Fearful prejudices. For example, he claimed that all Scots people were like the whisky-swilling planters he'd met in Burma. Fearful prejudices, and he wouldn't take any argument about them.

I think he had preconceived notions of things, and what he saw he interpreted according to those precon-ceived notions rather than looking at it objectively. I don't think he was a very objective person. There's always two sides, and I think he only saw one side. And he only saw the side he wanted to see — you know, the really depressed, down-and-out workers. He didn't want to see anything positive about them. I felt with the miners in *The Road to Wigan Pier* he was only praising their physical prowess. He wasn't praising their mental commitments, and the miners in those days were the vanguard of the trade union movement — the miners and the railwaymen. I mean, I was meeting trade unionists who'd been out of work on and off for years because they were black-listed by employers. . .

It was the first time I was disappointed in Eric, because I really thought he was more left than he was. He claimed in *Wigan Pier* and *Animal Farm* to be rooting for socialism, but he's so antisocialist that it doesn't come across. And you can't tell me that he wasn't intelligent enough to know that. And even if he wasn't, it was pointed out to him by his friends, what he was doing — and he still went on doing it. So I think he was really expressing personal prejudices rather than understanding what he was talking about.

I think he was a writer first and foremost. This was his sole ambition, to become a famous writer, which of course he did, but to my mind in the wrong way, because he became the darling of the establishment. He became an antisocialist almost unconsciously. I think it was unconscious that he was phony.

Armed with a large advance from Victor Gollancz, Orwell arrived in Wigan early in 1936 to begin his research into poverty. Many of the men and women he met still remember him vividly. Not all of them thank him for effectively making the name Wigan synonymous with poverty and degradation. Some of the residents who feel that Orwell gave their town a bad name do concede, however, that it was in a good cause and that his somewhat overdrawn picture of poverty had a powerful effect on the British public, particularly in the south of England, where even in the Depression life was much easier.

SYDNEY SMITH runs a large bookshop in the centre of Wigan. In 1936 he ran a bookstall in the market, but it was on the street where Orwell found lodgings that the two men first met.

It was on this corner here where I met him. Me and my friends used to gather here before we went off cycling or playing cricket or football, and on one occasion a stranger came along. He was tall, six feet plus, a gentleman with a rather shabby raincoat and a dirty trilby hat. Well, he started to question us about our jobs and what we were doing, and was we fully employed and was we drawing unemployment pay. Fortunately most of us were shop workers and we had jobs, but there were many people who hadn't. Some people were doing jobs and drawing unemployment pay at the same time. Well, we thought this person was a snooper, a snooper for the government, because at that time the means test was prevalent. We were suspicious because he didn't speak in a Lancashire language, so of course we were reluctant to carry on a conversation. He was tall, thin, hollow cheeked, with a sallow complexion and dark hair, but it was the fact that he spoke in different accent to us, a more cultured voice, that impressed us most.

In *The Road to Wigan Pier* Orwell portrays the tripe shop where he lodged as a filthy and degrading place, and its proprietors, Mr and Mrs Brooker, as a lazy couple who enjoy holding petty grievances against the old-age pensioners and travelling salesmen who rent rooms there.

This house here, number thirty-five Sovereign Road, was the shop, the tripe shop that was described in Orwell's book. But I must say, Mr Brooker sold not only tripe but all sorts of bric-a-brac. We knew him by sight. He was a small man, a typical miner, broad shouldered, five foot four in height. The shop wasn't frequented by me or my brothers, because it had a reputation for being a bit on the low side, not quite as clean as you would expect it to be. I understand that previous to keeping this shop he was the licensee of the Foundry Inn, which is not far from here, but he lost the licence through permitting gambling to take part on the premises.

We knew Mr Brooker took in lodgers, and a number of them were men who were canvassing for newspapers. In those days the newspaper proprietors, to increase circulation, offered all sorts of incentives — insurance, for example — if people would take the paper for a period.

We didn't really know Mrs Brooker, because we didn't go into the shop.

Mr Brooker's corner shop has been demolished; only a small triangle of grass marks the spot. The Foundry Inn, however, still stands as a functioning pub, and many of the red-brick terraced houses that Orwell saw in Wigan in 1936 are still lived in today. Sydney Smith maintains that Orwell's descriptions of Wigan tally closely with his own memories of the town.

Prior to Orwell's visit, I remember living in Sovereign Road, and we would be woken up in the early hours of the morning by the miners going to work and the clogs clattering on the cobblestones. And then later would come the factory girls, with more clogs. But when Orwell came to Wigan, I think clogs were declining. Shoes were becoming more prevalent. But clogs were still worn, and in Brooker's shop, besides the tripe which Orwell describes, he sold a number of things like clog irons and clog soles. People couldn't afford to go to the clogger, so they'd do it themselves. Then when iron became a bit pricey they'd go to the leather shops and buy strips of leather to put on the clogs. Shoes were Sunday best.

I was born here at number three Sovereign Road. I was one of a family of six boys and two girls. Our house was very, very cramped. It didn't have a parlour at the front; it wasn't a 'parloured house,' as we called it. Later we moved to number twenty-one, which was a parloured house and had more accommodation. Some of these houses were two up and two down, and some were parloured houses. When Orwell went on to the Wallgate area of Wigan, the houses were in far worse condition than they were here. Most of these houses here are no different now to what they were when Orwell visited, and I think they're a credit to the people living in them.

Between the backs of the houses there's the 'entry,' a cobbled path. The backyards were where the corporation men would remove the night soil. The toilets were adjacent to the houses and as far away from the living accommodation as possible, and that was the end of the backyard. I think Orwell's descriptions were accurate. His descriptions of diet and wages were accurate. I knew of cases where children would wait outside factory gates for any bread the factory girls had left, and they would give it to them. Wages were very, very tight. Oh yes, I think Orwell did his homework well.

CARLTON MELLING worked in Wigan Library in 1936. Orwell visited the library for background facts to support the more anecdotal information he gathered from his conversations and visits to people's houses.

I saw him signing the visitors' book, and my assistant came and pointed out his signature. He said, 'You know him, don't you?' I said, 'I know *of* him.' He struck me as a gentleman, as somebody who'd seen a higher culture. He knew how to use books, he knew what he wanted to find in a book and where to search for it. I helped him research living conditions by giving him some back numbers of newspapers from our files, to show him the dreadful things, the tragedies that had happened. We had the *Wigan Observer* and the *Wigan Examiner*, complete files of them.

There was a kind of personal magnetism about him. I thought, 'Eeh, we don't often see this kind of man in here.'

It was estimated that in 1936 between a third and a quarter of the working population of Wigan was out of work, with many people having exhausted all their benefits.

It was coming to be the time of the Depression in Wigan when it was hitting the coal miners. Many of them were on the dole. They came into the library for a 'warm.'

They certainly didn't come to study. Some of them couldn't read. It was warm in the library.

There was hunger. I know what hunger is myself. My mother brought up thirteen children without a penny from public assistance. For most families, they had to make do with scraps of meat from the butcher. There was no such thing as a Sunday dinner; 'off scourings' they ate — the innards of the animal. Things that the butcher would just throw away. We used to call it 'slink.' Have you ever heard that word?

Actually, we were comparatively well off. We'd got a council house, with bedrooms to sleep four of the girls and a bedroom for my father alone when mother refused to sleep with him because he were drunk. We had a parlour. A parlour was highly thought of even if you had nothing in it. We even had a *piano*, through me mother's saving. And two of my sisters learned the piano.

The toilets very rarely worked — the privies. They were in open backyards. The stench was horrible. There might be twelve families round a more or less open sewer. That was the toilet facilities for those people. I've seen people who had to walk a hundred yards to the toilet. One of my sisters lived in such a house, now of course demolished. The houses were thrown up, the quicker the better — the old story. Primitive, foul conditions.

It wouldn't be tolerated today. It would be shown up on the TV and radio. That's what Orwell did: he showed it up. He was always a man for decency in that way. He was a noble character in many respects.

IRENE GOODLIFFE still lives at number four Agnes Terrace, Barnsley, where in March 1936, at the end of his stint in the north of England, Orwell stayed for two weeks as a lodger in the downstairs front room of the house.

I was ten years of age when he first stayed here. My sister was eleven. Mother always made it clear we didn't bother the people who stayed as guests, so we weren't allowed into his room. It was private. There was a joiner and his son staying at the same time as George Orwell. He says in his book we used to like to stand and watch him typing, but I can't remember that. It's funny because I mean typing in those days was a real novelty, wasn't it.

Orwell's account of his stay at Agnes Terrace is described in detail in *Road to Wigan Pier Diary*, where he refers to Irene, her sister Doreen, and their parents, 'Mr and Mrs G.' Mr G was in fact Albert Gray, whom Orwell described as "a short powerful man, age about forty-five, with coarse features, enlarged nose and a very fatigued, pale look. A bit deaf, but very ready to talk."

George Orwell used to sit and talk to my dad a lot about mining, right until the early hours of the morning. And what he wrote about my father rings true. Every detail. You couldn't have got a better description. It was me father, that. That were me dad.

KEN GOODLIFFE is a miner. He finds Orwell's account of his trip down the Grimethorpe coal mine near Barnsley familiar and accurate.

When I first started down the mine it was very similar to what Orwell was describing. You used to have to bend double along the roadways underground. And I used to do the same sort of travelling underground that Orwell had to do. If you got a face two hundred yards long, you're on your knees from one end to the other. In Orwell's time it was all hand filling, with a pick and shovel, after the coal-cutting machine had cut the face from one end to the other, and the borer had bored the holes, and the shot firer had gone to fire it down. At that period you used to get a lot of falls of ground. People used to get buried. It were quite common. I did notice that Orwell made a suggestion even in 1936 that there ought to be a stretcher trolley made to run on the rail to get injured people out of the mine quicker. In fact that's what we've got now. But it were long after 1936 before these trolleys came out.

Baths? Some pits had them and some didn't. In my forty-one years as a miner I've only done six months without pit baths. I've been lucky. It's still hard work, too. Not all the shovel work has gone out of mining. And it's still hot, depending on the seam where you work.

No, I think Orwell gave a good description of mining here.

"I Was Always Sorry That Eileen Married George"

In June 1936, a few months after he returned from the north of England, George Orwell married Eileen O'Shaughnessy. The wedding took place in the tiny village of Wallington, in Hertfordshire. Orwell had rented a small and rather uncomfortable cottage there and divided his time between writing *The Road to Wigan Pier* and acting as the village shopkeeper. The cottage had once been the local general store, and Orwell reopened it, hoping to provide for himself a small income and some independence from the ups and downs of life as a moderately successful author. The sizable advance that Victor Gollancz had given him for his book on poverty convinced Orwell he was financially secure enough to marry Eileen.

DR LYDIA JACKSON, one of Eileen's best friends, had met her in London in the autumn of 1934, when Eileen was twenty-eight years old. Eileen, who had graduated in English from Oxford University, was studying educational psychology at University College, London.

Lydia Jackson remembers very well the day Eileen met George.

It was in March 1935, towards the end of our summer term, and a fellow student of ours gave a party. George and Richard Rees were there, and I remember looking at the two of them. They were both standing by the fireplace, leaning on it, and I thought what unattractive men they were. Rather faded and worn. That was my impression. I don't think Eileen had read any of George's writing at that time, and to me he was quite an unknown quantity. When we did read his novels, we both thought that some of them were very poor, especially *A Clergyman's Daughter*. I can't say she dismissed them with contempt, but rather with some humour and irony.

Anyway, after that party in London she told me that Eric Blair 'sort of' proposed to her, saying that he wasn't much good, but even so perhaps she would consider him. And I said, 'And did you?' and she said yes. I was rather appalled, I must say, because I felt Eileen really should have someone much more suitable, more attractive, younger perhaps. More physically attractive. Because George didn't look well even at that time. But Eileen had said before that when she reached thirty she would get married. George talked in a way that intrigued her, interested her, because he was an unusual person. I'm very doubtful if she was in love with him. I think it must have been his outspokenness that attracted her.

Eileen was very attractive. She was quite tall and very thin, with dark hair and blue eyes. And her eyes could laugh. Many people were attracted by her. She had curiosity about people. She wanted to know about the people she shared a class with, for example. Her eyes could dance when she was amused, and she would look at you and tell you some story, slightly exaggerating it, in a way that made it more amusing.

I don't know if she was keen on a career. I think she was ambivalent about that. The impression I have is that she was so disappointed at not getting a first-class degree at Oxford — getting a second — that she abandoned her ambition of making a career and just decided to drift. And she did drift, to begin with. She took a job reading to Dame Cadbury, who was old and blind, and after that she did secretarial work and typing for someone. But she was very dissatisfied there, especially with the head of the establishment, and she gave her notice and walked out. She confessed not to be interested in children. When we discussed child psychology, she said she would find it boring playing with children. Also, her health was poor.

That first year of their marriage she expressed some discontent. I think she had hoped to share more in George's creative work, perhaps by typing it or reading and discussing it.

Eileen would expect this because she was used to helping her brother, Lawrence O'Shaughnessy, with his scientific writing. Lawrence was a distinguished chest and heart surgeon, and Eileen would from time to time spend evenings at his flat in London, proofreading and editing his papers and books.

I remember her telling me that she was sure that if anything untoward ever happened to her and she sent an appeal to her brother, he would come at once. She said she wasn't so sure her husband would do this, that his work came before anybody. After her brother's death, she seemed to have less energy. Less sparkle. She seemed to me always tired. She neglected her health. There was perhaps some form of anemia. But I think there was a death wish there as well. Her brother's death [at Dunkirk in 1940] left her with a half-assumed, half-sincere indifference towards her own life, towards herself. . .

I was always sorry that Eileen married George. She deserved someone who would support her. I think his work was all to him, human relationships just a background. She really needed and deserved devotion, I think.

CHAPTER THREE

The Spanish Crucible

No bomb that ever bursts
Shatters the crystal spirit.
GEORGE ORWELL
"LOOKING BACK ON THE SPANISH WAR"

These lines end a poem Orwell wrote in memory of a young Italian militiaman he met briefly in Barcelona the day before he signed on to fight for the Spanish Republican government, under attack from General Franco. The Italian youth was staring, puzzled, at a map. As he left the barrack room he gripped Orwell's hand. It was, Orwell wrote, "as though his spirit and mine had momentarily succeeded in bridging the gulf of language and tradition and meeting in utter intimacy."

In Spain Orwell at last broke through the shell of his class alienation and made real friends among working men. Fighting with a group of mainly British volunteers who, like him, had gone to Spain to combat fascism and prevent the wider war many believed was otherwise inevitable, Orwell felt at one with the working class. He was noting what he saw, and his observations would no doubt end up in print, but he was also fighting shoulder to shoulder with British working men, and for a working-class cause: an elected government that sought to challenge the traditional Spanish elite.

Orwell was inspired by the revolutionary atmosphere in Barcelona, where normal class distinctions had given way to a spirit of equality. The workers were in control, running the factories and redistributing to the peasants land from estates left behind by landowners sympathetic to Franco. Even the waiters, Orwell was amazed to discover, refused to accept tips. The democracy in the militias, where all men earned the same pay, provided Orwell with a concrete example of socialism in action that was to fire his imagination for the rest of his life.

Yet, when Orwell was preparing to leave Spain six months later, he found the atmosphere in Barcelona poisonous. Because it included Trotskyists among its members, his militia had been persecuted by the communists who then controlled the Republican government. Orwell claimed that he was in danger of being arrested, imprisoned or even shot by the communists, working men who had earlier been his comrades. "It was a queer business," he wrote. "We started off by being heroic defenders of democracy, and ended up by slipping over the border with the police on our heels."

Orwell believed that the quick and dramatic collapse of the socialist paradise was the result of communist intolerance of other political groups. He felt that the communists, aided by the Soviet Union, which was channelling arms to the communist-led International Brigade, had totally betrayed the Spanish revolution. He had gone to Spain hardly comprehending the intricacies of continental socialism and was shocked to find that fellow workers would spend more time and energy fighting one another than fighting their common enemy.

Orwell's experience in Spain marked him politically in two very different ways: there was the joyous revelation that the class gulf could be bridged. But there was also the bitter realization that the Soviet Union had become an antirevolutionary force in the world, a force thereafter to be resisted with all his might.

He wrote his account of the Spanish civil war quickly: *Homage to Catalonia* appeared in April 1938. Unfortunately for him, it failed to make an impact in Britain. The British Right continued to lean toward Franco, while the established Left wasn't ready to listen to an account that blamed the communists for the failure to win the war. Orwell's publisher, Victor Gollancz, who was sympathetic to the communists at this time, refused to print the book, even before it was written. The communist *Daily Worker* tried to undermine Orwell's credibility by portraying him as a "disillusioned little middle-class boy," a snob who thought the working class smelled. Orwell would have to wait until 1945 to retaliate with his brilliant anti-Soviet fable, *Animal Farm*.

In literary terms, however, *Homage to Catalonia* stands out as a triumph of reportage. Unlike in his previous documentary writing, Orwell had, this time, tried to tell it *exactly* as he had seen it. Perhaps because he wrote the book when the experience of Spain was still so fresh in his mind, *Homage to Catalonia* captures the spirit of comradeship in the filthy, rat-ridden trenches of the Aragon front as brilliantly as it gives the reader a first-hand account of the dramatic and confusing Barcelona street fighting in the famous "May days" of 1937.

Ironically, it is the very clarity of the book's political message that has led to some criticism by Orwell's friends who also went to Spain during the civil war and witnessed many of the incidents he described. For them, *Homage to Catalonia* presents a simplification, a distortion of the events in Spain in the first six months of 1937. Victor Gollancz goes as far as to argue that Orwell was always "a trifle dishonest" in that he never gave "full play to those doubts, hesitations and searchings about the truth which are the lot of us all but which so many try to stifle."

As with his tramping in London and Paris and his descents into the coal mines of the north of England, the time Orwell spent fighting in Spain was not good for his health. It is possible that his months in the line on the Aragon front led to his first hospitalization for tuberculosis a year later. Some friends believe he never fully recovered from a neck wound inflicted by a sniper's bullet.

Orwell left Spain in June 1937, convalescing from his wound but mentally deeply scarred. Spain completed his political education. It forged him as a revolutionary socialist and gave him a vision of the future to strive for. It also left him with a nightmare image of how quickly and violently working-class solidarity could be undermined and how skilfully and brutally the communists could sweep their opponents out of the way. His hope would find expression, in a lesser-known wartime book, *The Lion and the Unicorn*, as a passionate plea for a revolutionary socialist England. His despair would be poured into his final masterpiece, *Nineteen Eighty-Four*. The seeds of both were sown in Catalonia in 1937.

"I Have Seen Wonderful Things"

LORD FENNER BROCKWAY, then General Secretary of the British Independent Labour Party, was the man who helped Orwell get to Spain in December 1936. The ILP had broken away from the official Labour Party four years earlier, and in 1936 had about four thousand members, many of whom were Marxists, even though the ILP was highly critical of the Soviet government. Fenner Brockway saw the ILP in its origins as a "working class party linking socialists and trade unions, owing more to non-conformity than to Karl Marx."

Orwell went to Brockway for credentials to enter Spain because one of the political groups fighting General Franco, the POUM (the United Workers' Marxist Party), was affiliated with the British ILP. Orwell had already approached the leader of the British Communist Party, Harry Pollitt, but Pollitt had refused to give him a recommendation to join the communist-led International Brigade in Spain. Fenner Brockway, however, did support Orwell and remembers his mood of militancy when the two of them met at the ILP head office in London.

Oh, he intended to fight, there was no doubt about that. He saw it clearly as the beginning of a fascist conflict — Franco supported by Hitler, supported by Mussolini. I remember his saying that it would be an experience that would probably result in a book, but his idea in going was to take part in the struggle against Franco. However, he was a bit troubled as to whom he should join when he got to Spain. There was the International Brigade, and he had a very great admiration for its service and its sacrifice. But at the same time it was very much under communist influence, and he was doubtful of associating himself with the communists.

The ILP had its separate contingent in Spain. We had a representative in Barcelona, John McNair, and I gave George Orwell an introduction to him. When he left he hadn't actually decided whether he would join the International Brigade or the ILP contingent. He said he would look at the position when he was in Barcelona.

When he got to Barcelona, he was very much attracted to John McNair, who had a personality very much like his — very human and very warm, and thinking always of the ethical ideas of socialism rather than of the class-war idea — and McNair and George Orwell took to each other in Barcelona. I would say it was rather characteristic of Orwell that his decision to join the ILP contingent wasn't so much a matter of ideology as of human warmth and human friendship. They were so similar in their enthusiasm for betterment in the world without any doctrinaire views.

JOHN MCNAIR (1887-1968) remembered Orwell's arrival at his office in Barcelona. He was at first rather suspicious of his visitor's drawling Eton accent, but when he realized the man standing before him was George Orwell, two of whose books he had read and admired, the atmosphere warmed up considerably.

"I asked him what I could do to help," McNair wrote later in an unpublished manuscript, "and he replied, 'I have come to Spain to join the militia to fight against Fascism' . . . and added he would like to write about the situation to stir working-class opinion in Britain and

France.'' McNair signed him up and asked a young Catalan journalist and POUM member, VICTOR ALBA, to show Orwell around Barcelona and explain some of the background to the civil war. Alba was not impressed at first by Orwell's revolutionary enthusiasm.

He didn't ask anything especially; he just followed me. He was fairly silent, an introvert man, not expressive in the face, which is a shocking thing for a Spaniard because we speak with the face and with the hands and legs and everything, and we shout. And his voice was low, so I had the feeling he was bored. But you have to remember that I was a kid, expecting from people as much enthusiasm as I had, and as much knowledge, because for me the civil war was my life. I had the feeling he didn't know much about Spain, probably just the normal background of everybody, that's all.

Most of the other foreign journalists I showed round put much more questions than Orwell. But I probably talked a lot and didn't give him time to ask questions! I took him on a 1936-style tour, not a tourist's tour. It was fighting-in-the-streets sort of tourism. I showed him the places where fighting had occurred in Barcelona a few months before, the places where the bourgeois sections and working-class sections were. I remember we went to the fishermen's part of Barcelona.

I had joined the POUM in 1932 because it was not a party that submitted to foreign instructions like the Communist Party. The POUM was best developed, was strongest, in Catalonia, but that was the key part of Spain in terms of the working-class movement because that's where the industry was. Before the civil war the POUM was stronger in Catalonia than the Communist Party was in all Spain.

When I read Orwell's book on Spain, however, I discovered Orwell as Orwell, not as the boring journalist that I had to take around Barcelona. I was in Mexico then, in exile from Spain, having been imprisoned in Spain for six years. I had read a lot of books about the civil war which were full of good intentions, but factually wrong or biased, or just marshmallow. But I was very moved by Orwell's book. He was speaking like somebody who had understood the things in Spain as we try to understand them. He had lived Spain from the inside, and I think what helped him even more than his experiences in the trenches was the several days he spent in Barcelona during the street fighting in May 1937, those crucial days when the power of the revolutionary forces ended and counterrevolutionary forces took over and began to lose the war.

I would say Orwell got the feeling of the country and caught the mood and basic psychological facts of the Catalans at that time much better than many. Even Arthur Koestler's book on Spain and the war is much less perceptive. I would have liked to have written Orwell's book.

Orwell wrote from Spain to his old friend Cyril Connolly: "I have seen wonderful things, and at last really believe in Socialism, which I never did before." In Catalonia Orwell saw for the first time in his life a genuinely egalitarian society. The vision stayed with him and provided a permanent yardstick, an ideal against which to judge socialism in other situations. Most of the other British volunteers were also deeply impressed. BOB EDWARDS, who led an ILP contingent in Spain and became Orwell's commanding officer, found the Catalan revolution, as Orwell did, "worth fighting for."

We were inspired by what we saw in Catalonia. The owners of the factories had left, and workers had to take over the factories. Land owners, always absentees, had left, and the land taken over by the peasants, and cooperatives formed. Hotels were taken over and councils set up to run them. There was workers' control throughout Catalonia, and equality of income. Everyone got ten pesetas a day, the general and the woman sweeping the streets. There was no black market. Prostitution was abolished. Bullfighting was abolished. It was a marvellous country to be in — for socialists.

Another ILP volunteer, FRANK FRANKFORD, was surprised to find that tipping had been abolished and that people called one another "comrade."

You would insult the barber if you offered him a tip. The waiters wouldn't accept tips, and if waiters didn't accept tips that's something! And they didn't. If you asked someone the way, they'd take you on the bus and pay your way. There was this sort of spirit. And when we went to the front for the first time we were marching down to the station to catch the train, and we had this terrific crowd cheering and bands playing. I'll always remember that.

Our ILP contingent was a very mixed group. There was one highlander from Scotland, a huge great man. Bob Smillie was with us, the grandson of the famous Scottish miners leader. One had deserted from the British tank corps, he was so enthusiastic to fight in Spain. I was living in the East End of London at the time and had always been interested in politics and was connected with the unemployed-workers' movement. When the war broke out in Spain, everyone wanted to get in, but it wasn't easy for men to leave their jobs and homes and go out and fight. I spoke at meetings in England about the Spanish civil war, and you only had to put up a platform and people would flock round. You see, Orwell was wrong when he said the British workers were not interested in Spain. They were.

The morning we left England was a Sunday, and on that day the British government brought in regulations preventing British nationals from joining any foreign army. We were threatened with losing our citizenship. It was part of the 'nonintervention' policy. Well, we left from Victoria Station just before the bar came into effect. We went by train to the south of France, then by coach over the mountains and by train to Barcelona, then to the barracks, the POUM militia barracks.

I'd had no military training. The ILP did issue us with a pair of nice high leather boots, though. Everyone at the barracks asked us if we were Russians because of those boots! We did the British military training of advancing, throwing yourself down and firing, and running forward and throwing yourself down again. This highly amused the Spanish. They said, 'You don't lay down and fire, you stand up and fire.' They had to be told to fire lying down. There were even leaflets issued where it showed bullets coming through the air and if a man was standing up it was going to hit him, and if he was laying on the ground the bullet would go over his head. It was as crude a training as that.

At the time we took it for granted that the various political parties in Spain were united against Franco. But of course they were not. It was a centrist, liberal government they'd elected, the Republican government, not really a left-wing government. They were running their own unions, they'd got rid of the burden of capitalism. This atmosphere is what Orwell got so enthusiastic about, but whether he really understood it, I don't know.

Orwell had arrived in Spain before the ILP contingent and found to his dismay "frightful scenes of chaos" and young recruits "full of revolutionary fervour, but completely ignorant of the meaning of war" ("Looking Back on the Spanish War"). RAMON JURADO fought with the POUM and was one of these "eager children" who would shortly be seeing action in the front line.

Orwell got to Barcelona at a bad time for us. Six months of the fighting had gone by, our whole huge mass of volunteers was burned out, and many had died. We had more volunteers, but without the energy or the spirit of the first days. We were manual workers, we were working class. I was a carpenter. Cerdan, he was a blacksmith. Ruiz was a printer. There was another one who worked in a perfume factory, his name was Gamis. We were full of revolutionary spirit. We were fighting the fascists. We knew we were transforming the world.

At the end of January 1937, Bob Edwards' contingent was positioned very close to Orwell on the Aragon front.

They'd linked Orwell up with a small group of juveniles on that same front, well away from the fighting; and probably because of his police experience in Burma, he was made a corporal. All he was doing was training these youngsters how to shoot and take cover. Well, he heard that we'd arrived, and we got a message saying he would like to join us, so I went over to meet him in his little dugout in the mountains.

I'll never forget my first sight of him. A big man, you know, with big boots, the biggest boots I'd ever seen, corduroy trousers, and he had a balaclava hat down over his ears (it was blessed cold up there, and he suffered from bronchitis). He had a scarf round his neck, up to his eyes, and an old Winchester rifle on his shoulder, and two hand grenades hanging from his belt. And running with him, trying to keep up, were two young Spaniards, and they had the same uniform. Behind them was a little shaggy dog with 'POUM' painted on it. It made me roar with laughter. It was comic opera.

Edwards thought that Orwell's courage bordered on recklessness.

He was a bit too brave, I thought. I remember one day when we were being attacked by some Moors — Franco had brought Moors to fight for him — and one of our machine guns got red hot and was useless. It was manned by some of our Spanish anarchists, and they just gave it up and stood there during the attack. And Orwell, who'd been begging of them to take cover, you know, pointing to an olive tree and saying, 'This will save your life, it will cover your heart,' and they used to laugh at him, and they wouldn't get down on their tummies, because they thought it was undignified. So Orwell stood up with them to save their Spanish dignity. I said, 'You silly bugger, why don't you get down on your tummy as you've been telling these people?' That was typical of the man, you see.

One day, during a very quiet period, we were both preparing for an attack — not a major attack, but a small push. Everything was quiet, and all of a sudden there was a terrific explosion. It was Orwell. He'd shot a rat in his dugout. And the noise vibrated all over the front. And the fascists thought this is the attack, you see. Shells came over, bombing planes came at us. They blew up our canteen and blew up our buses and everything. It was a very costly shot at a rat, that was.

When we were besieging the town of Huesca, there was this potato field not far from our lines, and we were desperately short of food. Orwell used to creep out on his tummy and collect potatoes, and he had worked it out, he said they couldn't get him if he did it like that. And I thought it was reckless and I wouldn't let anyone go, but he went. And I thought, well, if they use mortars they'd kill him, but they never did. He was right. A machine gun couldn't get him. And he went quite frequently and brought in potatoes. He was absolutely fearless. But you see, he was always trying to *prove* himself as a member of the working class. I used to call him 'the bloody scribbler' because he was always making notes while we were in the trenches. He wasn't really a good mixer.

Orwell's "scribbling" was probably letter writing. His wife Eileen had come to Spain to be near him and had been given secretarial work by John McNair in the ILP office in Barcelona. Mail from the front to Barcelona seemed to be very reliable, and Orwell's letters, even when written in haste and under difficult circumstances, provided Eileen with raw material with which to type up a basic diary of Orwell's experiences and observations. John McNair later referred to these letters as the "first drafts of *Homage to Catalonia.*"

Orwell was very disappointed with the lack of action on the Aragon front. But there was some excitement. Another member of the ILP contingent, DOUGLAS MOYLE, remembers a night attack on the fascist positions in April 1937.

> We were attacking a troublesome salient, and Orwell wanted a hand grenade and I gave him one. He threw it, and there was a scream from a person being wounded, or perhaps even being killed by it.

Moyle found "leadership and decisiveness" in Orwell's actions.

> I did a night patrol with him. We went out on a brilliant moonlight night. He assured me that although it was a moonlight night there was no need to creep about and that no one would see us even if we stood up and walked naturally. And it was quite true. I felt immediately I could trust him. I knew he had had plenty of experience already of night patrolling. We approached the fascist parapet to within about thirty yards and kept our heads down for the last few paces before dropping into a hollow behind a low ridge. He told me to stay there until he returned but to have a couple of hand grenades ready just in case. Then he moved off into the night and seemed to be getting even closer to the enemy's lines. I was dead scared at first because I could hear the fascists talking quite clearly, but they were completely unaware of our presence. Then, after about fifteen to twenty minutes, he returned, and we walked away without any trouble at all.

But bursts of military action were rare, and Orwell passed a lot of time in the trenches reading.

> I was surprised to find him sitting quietly by himself, sheltering from the cold wind, reading a little volume of Shakespeare's plays. He didn't speak, and I realized he

would rather be left alone. We thought he was rather 'putting it on,' but as a literary man he was doing no more than taking some exercise in the sort of thing he liked doing.

The youngest of the ILP group, eighteen-year-old STAFFORD COTTMAN, was taken aback when Orwell suddenly asked him to sing.

We were doing guard duty, and he said did I remember the Eton boating song, and I sang it for him, just one verse! And he was delighted. In fact I think this was the only time I remember him showing an interest in anything musical.

I thought he had the common touch. He could talk to anyone. He was a natural leader. You had respect for him. He knew what he was talking about, you felt he did. There are people who one is more inclined to listen to than others, and George Orwell was such a man. I think it was his voice, *how* he talked, that was the thing that made you listen.

I liked his direct, forthright 'no messy-mindedness' about things. You were either for something or against it. And if you were for it, you batted hard for it, and if you were against it you didn't have anything to do with it. He didn't have all these 'ifs' and 'buts.' And I think this is why he wasn't really a political animal, in the sense that he wasn't partisan to any particular group. And this probably left him free to analyse things and see them more clearly than the rest of us.

HARRY MILTON, the only American in the British ILP group on the Aragon front, felt that Orwell was "politically virginal." Stafford Cottman remembers Milton as "the one Trotskyist proud to boast of the association, and playing it as a sort of trump card to end all discussion." Milton and Orwell spent hours discussing politics in the trenches in Spain, and the "young American" mentioned in *Homage to Calatonia* is Harry Milton.

Orwell bugged me constantly. He always initiated the conversations. He had no political consciousness at the time. He didn't comprehend the role that the communists were playing in Spain. I think at that time he was ideologically very confused about the role of the International Brigade in relation to the communists. He didn't see the distinction between the communists and the socialists and the role the Russians were playing. Only after he left Spain did he become politically aware.

Our sector of the front was as quiet as a graveyard. We were miserably armed. The majority of the regiment was a bunch of kids. They were shooting each other accidentally. And we had only one real go at the enemy. It was the first time we went into action. It was a hellish business; the whole thing was botched up. I never expected to survive the Spanish experience. It would have been a disaster if we'd really gone into action. [After the ILP contingent had left the Aragon front there was what Bob Edwards calls a "suicidal attempt" to take Huesca. It resulted in the loss of "about seven hundred men."]

It was his intention, when we were going to go on leave, to resign from the POUM militia, the twenty-ninth division, and go and enlist with the International Brigade fighting at Madrid. He said that's where the action is.

Frank Frankford felt that Orwell wanted to join the International Brigade "because he was a journalist."

He didn't like it where he was. He wanted to make a name for himself. We used to have discussions every now and again. Frankly, I was suspicious of him. You always got the impression that he felt socialism was all right as long as the workers didn't run it. I was just as class conscious as he was, probably, but it was his general condescending attitude that got me. He called you 'comrade' and everything, but you weren't. You were a worker. You were a different class to him. He had this middle-class public-school attitude: anybody who was poor, stunk.

When we were out there his book *Road to Wigan Pier* was published, and I took great exception to what he said about the workers in there. And you get a lot of this in his writings, this general attitude of superiority. It's unfortunate that I didn't like him as a man, we just didn't hit it off. But it was definitely *The Road to Wigan Pier* that really annoyed me. I thought it was unfair. I didn't like it.

JACK BRANTHWAITE, whose father was a miner, also remembers copies of *The Road to Wigan Pier* arriving at the front. But the book didn't seem to offend his working-class sensibilities. Branthwaite feels it was Orwell's Old Etonian military style that touched a raw nerve in Frank Frankford.

Eric had occasion very often to tell Frank to smarten up. He told *me* to smarten up too, sometimes! He'd lecture us to stand up straight and act like a soldier and not liked a damned idiot. He'd say, 'You're here to fight a war, not for fun and games.' He'd say, 'If you want to fight for these people, at least make an effort.' He was not, I repeat, *not* a snob. But he was a strict disciplinarian, inasmuch as he wanted things done his way.

And he was disgusted with the 'mañana.' That's what used to get him down. He was a man who wanted to get things done. And he'd always be brushed off with 'mañana, mañana, mañana.' He used to get damned annoyed about it. You see, the Spanish army, if it was siesta time, would just as soon go home and have a sleep as fight a war, and he didn't like that. He thought that we, being British, would have more idea of discipline. He wasn't a snob. No.

We discussed *The Road to Wigan Pier* when his publisher sent it out. Eric said, 'You know, those were the hardest days of my life, meeting those people and working the way they had to work.' He said, 'I wrote about it, but you've got to live it to write it, not for just the few months I was there.' He admired miners. He said whenever he went into any country, the first people he'd look up would be the miners. I thought, 'There's a man who's writing from the heart.' He always used to say it was no good writing unless you can experience it. He said, 'How can you write about the poor unless you become poor yourself, even if it's temporary?' I thought, well, I couldn't do it.

He came to Spain to write. That was his whole object, to find out what it was all about. He had no political leanings at the time, except he was more left than right. Actually, he was leaning slightly towards the communists when I first met him.

I thought he was a wonderful man. He wasn't what you would call a strong type, physically. He used to catch cold easily. I remember he always used to have a 'dew drop' hanging from his nose! Old Eric with his little drip off the end of his nose. We were dirty and lousy on the Aragon front.

And Eric liked his creature comforts. He hated the ersatz coffee we had there and the damn Spanish tobacco, with Rizla cigarette papers to roll it in. And he loved his *tea*. Typhoo tea. He always ensured he had tea delivered to him from Fortnum and Mason's in London. And if he could get biscuits from Fortnum and Mason, he'd get them, and he had other goods sent out from the Army and Navy Store in London, sent up the line. His wife used to look after that. She was in Barcelona.

He and Eileen were meant for each other. Oh yes. She was a mousy kind of a girl, and she worshipped the ground he walked on. She'd do anything for him. Anything Eric did, he was the greatest. And she gave up all her career and centred on Eric.

When we were at the front near Huesca there was all this talk we were going to take Huesca, have coffee in Huesca. That was all we talked about. But we never did get there. Never did get the coffee!

By the end of April 1937, Orwell and his comrades in the ILP contingent were due for leave in Barcelona. Harry Milton travelled down the line with Orwell.

We were on the train from the front going to Barcelona, and he approached me and we got to talking, and I said to him, 'Are you still determined to quit the ILP brigade and go to the Madrid front with the communists?' He said yes. Well, I blew my top. I began to rant and rave like a maniac, and I said to him, 'They won't take you, but if they do, they'll knock you off. You'll curse the day you were born. They'll canonize you.' And that's what they would have done. They would have killed him. I was really vulgar and rude. But he was cool as a cucumber, and he just walked away from me. He was a very disciplined individual.

Bob Edwards also tried to convince him to stay with the ILP group.

I said to him, 'You, you bloody scribbler, you don't know what this war is all about.' If he'd gone to Madrid he'd have been killed, that's for certain. Because in Madrid there was this murderous commissar, a Frenchman, who was political commissar for the whole of the International Brigade, and if anybody had criticism of the war effort, or had any 'Trotskyite tendencies' — that's what they called them, if you were opposed to something that was being done you must be a Trotskyite — he'd have been court-martialled and shot. You see, Orwell had no experience of the working-class movement, and he couldn't understand the conflict and the dialogue that went on between left-wing people in Spain. They were always arguing, and that was true generally of continental socialism. It was their tradition to argue and break away and form new parties. Orwell couldn't understand that.

The big argument, you see, between the communists and the POUM was that we thought this wasn't an ordinary war, it was a social revolution. And if the social revolution was halted and we went back to the old game of inequality, we would lose the war, because the people would lose confidence in us.

Well, I wasn't able to convince Orwell until he'd had his leave and we went back to Barcelona.

"All Hope Gone"

Orwell had spent a hundred and fifteen days at the front when he returned to Barcelona on 20 April 1937. He found that the euphoric atmosphere he had revelled in only months before had dissipated into political infighting between the rival groups of the Republican government. A leading communist was shot in Barcelona the day before Orwell arrived. It was said the anarchists were responsible. The funeral became a massive socialist demonstration. The same day, an anarchist mayor was shot.

Orwell, however, carried on with his plan to enlist in the International Brigade, to go where the real fighting was — around Madrid. He had two weeks of leave to enjoy first, time to be with Eileen and to eat proper food for the first time since January. He also needed new boots. His size-twelve feet wouldn't fit any Spanish army boot, and he wasn't about to go back to the war until a shoemaker in Barcelona had made boots specially for him.

The tension in the city exploded dramatically on 2 May. It began with an incident at the Telephone Exchange building in the large square at the top of the Ramblas, the busy thoroughfare in Barcelona where Orwell and Eileen were staying in the Hotel Continental. The Telephone Exchange was controlled by the anarchists, whose operators tended to listen in to official phone calls and interrupt them to make political points. On 3 May the chief of police in Barcelona decided to take over the Exchange and put an end to the anarchists' harassment. The anarchists resisted, and there was shooting inside the building. Some of the anarchists let off bursts of fire through the windows of the building, and the sound of gunfire was enough to precipitate a wild bout of street fighting among rival political groups.

Jack Branthwaite was with Orwell in the Hotel Continental when the bullets started flying.

> We were sitting there, and a shot came through the window. We all ducked. We didn't know what it was all about. We'd been arguing politics a lot, day and night, before this. The whole problem was that each political party had its own army. The atmosphere was weird. I remember at the hotel there was this fellow we used to call 'Charlie Chan,' and he was looking at us foreigners, and Eric used to say to me, 'You know, I bet he's a Russian.' It was just like a spy film. He looked like a typical Russian KGB man. This was when the POUM was beginning to be suspected.
>
> We were just glad to get out of our uniforms and into some decent clothes. We'd been in the line twelve weeks, and when we got to Barcelona we drew our back pay, about ten pesetas a day, and all settled into the hotel.

At first Orwell didn't take the shooting in the streets very seriously, and on the afternoon of 3 May, a few hours after the bullet had come crashing through the window of his hotel room, he went out for a stroll on the Ramblas. The fighting intensified while he was in the streets, and he was told by an American doctor who had been at the front with him to go farther down the Ramblas to another hotel, which the POUM members were using as a base. Eileen remained at the Hotel Continental.

Harry Milton remembers this period in Barcelona.

> During the 'May days' I was with Orwell round the clock. In *Homage to Catalonia* he describes seeing a

head sticking up from behind a newspaper kiosk on the Ramblas, an American with a head looking like a coconut. That was me! The civil guard were in the Café Moka, next to the Hotel Continental, and they were shooting at me. I'd just dived into the gutter.

Then there was this live grenade on the sidewalk, and Orwell took a pot shot at it and missed. And then Georges Kopp, who was a Belgian and our battalion commander, took a shot and it detonated. It was all a little hair-raising.

The POUM leaders decided that the first consideration was to defend the buildings they occupied in the Ramblas. On the opposite side of the street there was a cinema, the Poliorama, with twin glass domes on its roof. Orwell was told to get to the roof and stand guard, watching out for any attacks on the POUM buildings below. Jack Branthwaite got the same orders.

We were all up in the observatory, and opposite was the cathedral with the flat roof, and the civil guards were on that. Well, the bullets were flying, and our orders were to shoot any civil guard who attacked us.

Orwell was holed up on the roof of the Poliorama cinema for three days and nights. Most of the time it was quiet, with only sporadic shooting in the streets. He must have been astonished when his old friend JON KIMCHE, who had worked with him in Booklovers' Corner in 1934, suddenly joined him on the roof. Kimche had gone to Spain on his own, not to fight but to see what the civil war was all about.

I went to see Orwell on the roof of the cinema. He was sitting there, and when he started talking it was like we were resuming the conversations we had in Hampstead — you know, the same tone, the same approach, and the same attitude. He was making comments about the inefficiency of the militia and the inadequacy of their equipment and of the rifles and ammunition.

Actually, it was like being on guard at a Munich carnival! The Ramblas is this wonderful street — two streets, really — and in the middle this wide pavement full of trees and flowers and flower sellers and women in colourful dresses. When the shooting died down we went across to the Hotel Continental, and the radio was blaring out stirring marching songs. It was an extraordinarily alive scene. There was nothing in the shops, except in the bakeries; you could buy very nice cakes. For some reason they were available. And the result was that conversation, *all* conversation, generally after two or three minutes began to centre on food. I remember there was also Irish stew! Always Irish stew. The fighting was going on a mile or two away.

By now the communist newspapers in Barcelona were denouncing the POUM as sympathetic to the fascists, and Orwell was incensed by the cartoons circulating portraying the POUM as a fifth column for Franco. Frank Frankford was furious, too.

You saw these posters saying, 'Tear the mask.' The mask was marked 'POUM,' and underneath was a brutal fascist face. Well, that struck me as stupid.

Orwell decided that "after this affair I could not join any Communist controlled unit," and he abandoned his plans to join the International Brigade.

On 10 May the ILP contingent returned to the Aragon front. By 20 May Orwell's unit had moved up closer to the fascist lines. Jack Branthwaite was with Orwell on the front.

We were supposed to make an attack on the local lunatic asylum, which the fascists were using. Eric was pretty casual, as always. First thing in the morning he would light up a cigarette and stand there smoking. I said to him, 'Eric, you know, one of these days you're going to get shot.' (You see, Eric was six foot four, and we were building parapets for Spaniards. He was head and shoulders above them.) Well, he just said, 'They couldn't hit a bull in a passage.'

Branthwaite believes that it was from a fascist-occupied church near the POUM lines that a sniper took a very lucky shot at Orwell's exposed head. It was 5:00 in the morning on 20 May. Harry Milton was on guard.

The dawn was rising. It was a beautiful, beautiful sunrise. He came to relieve me. There was a barricade of sandbags, a step of two sandbags. He got on the step, stuck his head over the parapet, which was very dangerous. And then I heard a shot, and he toppled over. I looked for the wound. He was shot through the neck. He had bitten his lips, so I thought he was a goner. The speed of the bullet had seared the entrance of the wound. I put his head in my arms, and when I put my hand under his neck there was a puddle of blood.

Jack Branthwaite was also convinced that Orwell's wound was fatal.

How he lived I don't know, because there are so many vital organs there, the jugular vein and God knows what. When he dropped I thought, 'Oh God, he must be dead,' because I saw the hole there. But he was conscious, and Dougie Moyle said, 'He's breathing.' I think we got him on a donkey first before we got him on a proper conveyance. It was reasonably level ground. If it had been at Alcubierre, we'd have never got him down the line. It would have been donkey rides all over the mountains. There was a doctor there, actually. An American. We were all shaken up by it. In the end we got him to a place called Sietamo.

The hospital at Sietamo was a makeshift affair, a field hospital.

I went to visit him there, and the only thing that had happened was that he had lost his voice completely. Then it came back a bit, and it was three or four tones higher than before, like a woman's voice, very high pitched. And then gradually it came to be *almost* normal, not quite. But I don't think he ever fully recovered from that.

Orwell described the sensation of being shot as "being at the centre of an explosion." From the hospital at Sietamo he was taken by ambulance on very bumpy roads to Barbastro, and eventually to the Sanatorium Maurin, on the outskirts of Barcelona, to convalesce. Here Eileen could visit him easily, and at the end of May she arranged for Georges Kopp, Orwell's battalion commander, to send a full medical report to England to her brother, who was a doctor. Orwell was slowly recovering but had by now realized that, since he was definitely not strong enough to fight any more, he and Eileen would have to return to England. But the political situation in Barcelona had deteriorated even further during May 1937, and it would be difficult for them to leave.

Jack Branthwaite, who was on his way to Barcelona for another period of leave, remembers getting an early warning of the troubles to come.

Before we got into Barcelona station, people along the way, in Lerida, said, 'Get rid of that uniform; throw it away, and destroy any papers of POUM — they've been outlawed.'

I met Eric in Barcelona. By that time he'd left the hospital. He said, 'Well, we're in trouble. Franco's closing in, and all we've got left is this little bit of Catalonia. What are we going to do?' And he said, 'They're after me. I've left my hotel.' I said I hadn't dared to book into any hotel. He said, 'Well don't, because we're known from the last time we came up here, when the fighting was on.' We were the enemy now. According to the communists we were Franco's fifth column. We had to get out quick.

We were almost killed — Eric, his wife Eileen, and myself and Doug Moyle and young Cottman — because we were POUM. It was an awful job. Where I was in bad shape was that I hadn't a passport. I'd gone to Spain on a Cook's weekend ticket, and it was kind of overdue! Eric, he had a passport, and he was reasonably safe. And I told Eric I hadn't got a passport and that the consul had gone. Flipped. There was a vice-consul, but he said he couldn't do anything for me.

In the meantime we heard about Bob Smillie: he'd been arrested and was in prison in Valencia. We heard all kinds of rumours. Bob was supposed to have died there of appendicitis, but he was shot, no question about that. So we had visions of being shot too.

Bob Smillie, as the grandson of a famous Scottish miners' leader, was something of a hero for Orwell. Jack Branthwaite liked him too, and in quiet periods at the front used to wrestle and sing Scottish ballads with him.

Orwell and other members of the ILP contingent now led a hazardous double life in Barcelona. By day they posed as English tourists, trying frantically to get the necessary papers to leave Spain. By night they acted as outlaws, sleeping rough and hiding. At the same time, Stafford Cottman was also trying to get his comrade Harry Milton out of jail in Barcelona.

Harry had decided it was time to go, and he tried to leave a day or two before we did. And he didn't want to waste what money he had on a hotel bill. So he asked me if I would smuggle his luggage out of the hotel, which I did. We got him on a train, but he was picked up because of his POUM card, and two days later he was in Barcelona jail.

Georges Kopp had also been arrested and imprisoned in Barcelona. Orwell tried gallantly to get him out, but without success. The POUM leader Andrés Nin, who had once been an associate of Leon Trotsky, had been taken by the communists and was later killed in jail. Stafford Cottman:

I felt sad and fed up with the whole thing. I thought here we are, all hope gone, and we weren't even winning the war against Franco. I felt especially let down by the communists over the murder of Andrés Nin. The dirty-tricks department had really operated there.

Jack Branthwaite:

What Eric said to me about the communists was this: that he went to Spain to fight against fascism because he thought fascism was going to destroy the world, he felt sure it was. But he said it was the infiltration by the communists in the Republican government that got him annoyed. He got really upset about it — the way the communists took over, the sneaky way they do it. You don't realize what these guys can do, how they can infiltrate and how they can destroy you. Within about eight months, the communists had come to dominate the Spanish parliament. And they took over. It was a great lesson to Eric and me. He said he used to take what people said about the communists as capitalist propaganda, but he said, 'You know, Jack, it's true.' These guys, the communists, had Russian automatics at the front. I had a 1917 Mauser. If I'd shot with it it would have blown my face in. A friend of mine had a Winchester, but no bullets for it. We couldn't understand how the communists were so well armed.

The communists took over the Republican government. First of all one little party, ours, disappears off the face of the earth, then the anarchists. So finally there was only one thing left: PSUC (Partido Socialista Unificado de Catalunã) — the communists. That was the only party left. There was nobody else. And *then* they started to fight the war, to fight Franco. But by then it was too late. After what he saw they'd done to the POUM and the other parties, Eric wanted no more part of communism. He said he didn't come here to fight in a civil war with working people fighting working

people. That's why he didn't join the International
Brigade as he had originally planned to.

Frank Frankford believes that Orwell and some of his
former POUM comrades have exaggerated the danger they
were in during the last days in Barcelona.

Orwell says he was chased up and down, and people
were hiding round corners, and one thing and another.
Well, I walked round those streets on my own, and I
never made any secret of the fact that I was with
POUM, although by then the POUM had more or less
disappeared. I was walking round with POUM identification, and I had to show it to police patrols. No one
ever said anything. I never felt any antagonism.

Jon Kimche holds a similar view.

When I crossed into Spain it was during the time of the
POUM uprising in Barcelona. I was crossing over the
Pyrenees, and a communist border patrol picked me up.
I didn't realize it, but I was actually under arrest. And
when I told the people who'd picked me up I was going
to Barcelona and I knew the POUM people, of course
they were suspicious. But when we got to Barcelona they
released me. I mean, yes, the communists did treat the
POUM badly, but if they were really all that bad they
would surely have shot me and not let me go.
   A lot of the communists in those days weren't Stalin
'apparachiks,' though certainly some of them were. But
most of them had a sense of realism, saying you had to
have power in order to organize an effective army. I
think you can rationalize it like this. You see, I don't
think the Spanish revolution was betrayed, as Orwell
says, by the communists, because if the communists
hadn't taken over the others wouldn't have been able to
hold out as long as they did. Only the anarchists possibly
could have done something on their own against Franco, but even they would have had to do it with the communists. At the time I took the same view of it as

Orwell, but looking back on it now, it was inevitable that the communists wouldn't tolerate other groups.

I mean, all this revolutionary excitement was lovely, it would have been wonderful to have had this excitement prevailing, but it couldn't win the war, not against Franco supported by the Germans and the Italians. These revolutionary armies fought wonderfully in battle and were completely self-sacrificing, but they would have been forced to sacrifice far more than an army could afford to sacrifice. You need a motivated political army, yes, but in a sense the communist army was a political army too. If a revolutionary army is successful, and it produces a revolution on the other side, then it works, but if on the other side you're having to face an army that becomes progressively more efficient and better equipped and supported by great powers, then revolution alone is not enough. If the revolution in Catalonia was betrayed it was by the French and the British, with their nonintervention policy, not by any internal Spanish betrayal.

Orwell, you see, always *reacted* to situations, to people, to individuals. He had certain basic gut attitudes. Very decent but not attuned, I would say, to complicated political or military situations. He was a gut socialist. He was never very analytical, never theoretically searching out how to deal with a situation, or what is the fundamental problem of a situation. That's why he wrote so very clearly and very simply. Because that's how he saw things.

Orwell's exit from Spain on 23 June 1937 was in fact uneventful. Stafford Cottman was with him.

There was John McNair, Eileen, me, and George. The night before we left we all went to a place near the railway station. We had permits by then from the Spanish authorities, but the problem was, if a hotel reported you and they then looked for things like workers' passports and found anything associated with POUM, you could be in trouble. Well John, who spoke French fluently, spoke in French to the proprietors of this place, and they said they wouldn't report us if we were only staying the one night. So the next morning we got up and got on the train.

We each had a corner of the carriage. Orwell was sitting opposite Eileen, and John opposite me. John, who had a literary turn of mind, had a copy of some of John Masefield's poems, and he seemed to think that if I read this book it would create an atmosphere of innocence. I did as he suggested, but I had no faith in it at all! Well, in the end we went through the border with no trouble at all. No funny moments. I think it was the British passports that got us through. They looked impressive compared with some of the informal documents that were around at that time.

At Perpignan, on the French side of the border, Orwell met the man who had helped him get into Spain in the first place. Fenner Brockway was on his way to Barcelona to investigate reports that ILP and POUM members were being badly treated. Brockway was shocked by Orwell's appearance.

In Perpignan I met George Orwell and Stafford Cottman. Orwell was terribly thin. He was hoarse, too, from the bullet that had gone through his throat and just missed his windpipe. I had tea with him and his wife. And Orwell was absolutely shocked by the Stalinist actions of the communists in Barcelona. It was about the only time I saw him really angry. He was usually such a friendly, quiet, warm person. I remember him saying, 'As soon as I've had a brief holiday with my wife on the south coast of France, I'm coming back to England to write about it.' And of course he wrote his book *Homage to Catalonia*.

SAM LESSER is a member of the British Communist Party and a journalist with the communist *Morning Star*. He went to Spain in October 1936 and was involved in the defence of Madrid the next month, fighting with the International Brigade. His version of the reasons for the quarrel between Orwell's POUM and the communists in Spain represents not only the communist defence against Orwell's written attacks but also the position adopted at the time by many among the noncommunist British left.

I met Orwell very briefly on one occasion in Barcelona. I had an argument with him. I'd never heard of him at that time. I don't know that Orwell at that time was all that clear-cut as people now present him to have been. I think in a way he admired the discipline of the International Brigade, and if perhaps someone had argued with him a bit longer and harder than I did with him at the time he might even have joined the International Brigade. But at that time I was perhaps even more impatient and intolerant of POUM people than I am now, although I don't feel very comradely towards them even at this distance in time. There's no doubt that Orwell did a great disservice to Spain, and all the things he claimed he was trying to do he turned against. I don't think his dislike of the communists was justification for doing dirt on the Spanish Republic the way he did.

You see, the International Brigade became very quickly part of the Spanish Republican army, under the command of the General Staff of their army and obeying orders of the government Defence Minister. And what the Soviet Union was doing was supplying arms to the *government*. The government allocated those arms to those units it thought were best able to use them. Because of the high level of discipline of the International Brigade — and they weren't exclusively foreign volunteers, about fifty percent of them were Spaniards — the arms came to us, most of the new weapons came to us.

There was nothing to stop the POUM putting their units, as we did, under the command of the Spanish

Republican army. But the POUM thought as other people did that the Communists were going to seize power. The Communist Party increased its membership enormously during the war, because what they were offering was the perspective of fighting on to victory, and this wasn't just words. People joined the Communist Party because they really believed that the Communists had the possibility of giving the Republican government victory over fascism, and that meant not sitting on your behind in some cushy job in the General Staff, but going and fighting *and dying*, and large numbers of Communists died, were killed. We were convinced that to talk about revolution while fascism was still around was just revolutionary phrase-mongering. And the POUM expected us to say, 'Well, you are the revolutionaries, and we are not the revolutionaries.'

This doesn't mean that there were no revolutionary activities. I remember going into the homes of Spanish peasants and seeing on the wall, framed, a piece of paper, a certificate signed by the then communist Minister of Agriculture, giving the land to them. A great deal of the land had been taken from the absentee landowners and given to ordinary peasants. Take education. A communist Minister of Agriculture began a very active literacy campaign. They were even teaching young Spanish boys, in the intervals between the fighting, how to read and write. You can talk a lot about revolution, but there can be no revolution with an illiterate mass of people. So that very important things were being done.

Now POUM talk a lot about the best weapons always going to the International Brigade. The thing that's always remained in my mind was after I had been badly wounded at the Cordoba front, where I had to crawl on my hands and knees for the best part of a mile before I could find a stretcher — there were no ambulances. When I got back to Barcelona, in *one POUM parade* I saw the most up-to-date ambulances being paraded round Barcelona and being kept there. I saw POUM people going round Barcelona with smart uniforms and fancy black armbands with a red emblem. There were pieces of artillery, too. And when were these weapons to be used? When POUM decided the revolutionary moment had come. And to attack whom in Barcelona? Not the fascists, but the *government*.

So, in time of war, it's understandable that people can turn around and say, 'Well, what you are doing objectively plays into the hands of the fascists,' and there is a very narrow step then to say, 'Well, you in fact maybe *are* a fascist.' But I don't think the differences with the POUM should have been settled in this sort of administrative way, by putting POUM leaders up against a wall, although in time of war differences of political opinion can become life-and-death issues.

I don't think the POUM were fascists. I don't think it should have been dealt with as though they were traitors, although some of the things they did were really very harmful to the cause of the Spanish Republic.

Homage to Catalonia

George Orwell began writing *Homage to Catalonia* in the middle of July 1937, almost as soon as he and Eileen had returned to their cottage at Wallington. Jack Branthwaite, who had managed to get on the last refugee boat from Barcelona to Marseilles, visited the Orwells in Wallington.

I stayed with him and Eileen a month at Wallington. It was the same old Eric, no different. The same drip off his nose, and I remember him on the lawn in the front of the house, milking the goat. I hadn't seen him since we both escaped from hiding in the cemetery in Barcelona.

I remember we always had to dress for dinner at Wallington, Always white shirt, black tie, the whole works, *yes sir!* Of course I didn't have that, I'm just an ordinary Joe, but I had to have a tie on at least. Oh yes, he'd go about looking like a damn tramp during the day, but when dinnertime came he'd go upstairs and he'd wash himself and do his hair and he'd dress, and you'd sit down to the linen and all the rest. And he did a bit of cooking, too.

Another former ILP and POUM comrade, Douglas Moyle, also stayed at the cottage in Wallington and remembers Eileen's cooking "a lovely late dinner, with all the trimmings." Moyle and Orwell went on long walks in the Hertfordshire countryside, usually taking the Orwells' dog along.

He was a lovely French poodle, and he was called Marx. And Eric used to say that sometimes you could tell something about the visitors who came because when they learned the name of the dog they would perhaps ask was he called Marx because of some association with Marks and Spencer, or with Karl Marx, or with Groucho Marx!

Jack Branthwaite commented on the animals around the Orwell's home.

I remarked once, casually, 'Well, I don't know about you, Eric, but I see you've got some animals here. I wonder if we handed over the reins of government to the animals, if they'd do any better?' I was still thinking of the blood and carnage of Spain. He never said a word, but he left dinner and went upstairs and we didn't see him any more that night. It may or may not have started a train of thought which ended up as *Animal Farm*, an idea that he thought might come in handy.

In August 1937 Orwell attended an ILP summer school in Letchworth. Jack Branthwaite, Douglas Moyle, and Stafford Cottman were all there, as was Fenner Brockway, who had returned from his fact-finding trip to Spain.

Orwell lectured on his experiences in Spain, and while we were there I made what I think is perhaps the greatest mistake of my life. I was walking up and down a lawn between beds of red roses with George Orwell in the evening sunlight, and he offered to write for the *New Leader*, the ILP paper, of which I was editor. Well, I made the terrible mistake of thinking that if George Orwell wrote it would be too elitist, too academic, too literary for the paper, which we were producing for sale on the shop floor. And I declined his offer. He wrote instead for the *Tribune,* under Michael Foot's editorship. It was a terrible mistake. George Orwell wrote very simple English, hardly a long word, just simple clarity. I should have understood that he wrote in a way that would appeal to the worker on the shop floor.

It was also while we were at the ILP summer school that he indicated to me his difficulty in getting a publisher for his book on Spain. And I suggested he try Fred Warburg.

Orwell's publisher, Victor Gollancz, had turned down *Homage to Catalonia* without having seen a word of it. On 5 July 1937, only days after Orwell and Eileen had returned to England, Gollancz wrote to him: "I ought never to publish anything which could harm the fight against fascism . . . and I think I should probably feel that your book did do that." Gollancz informed Orwell that he was not a member of the Communist Party and that his decision had nothing to do with "party discipline or anything of that kind." He also reminded Orwell of the agreement that gave him the right to publish Orwell's next three novels, and he made it clear that he wanted to be reinstated as Orwell's publisher for nonfiction once *Homage to Catalonia* was out of the way.

LIVIA GOLLANCZ is Victor's daughter. She still runs the family firm.

My father's relationship with George Orwell was pretty much a business one. I don't think they were ever close friends. Right up to the end of their correspondence they addressed each other as 'Mr Blair' and 'Mr Gollancz.' I don't think my father ever invited Orwell to our house, and they corresponded largely through Orwell's agent, Leonard Moore, except on editorial points. I came across one letter which my father wrote to someone making a study of Orwell, who wrote asking what my father thought of Orwell. My father wrote this in 1956:

'Although I published the great majority of Orwell's books, I had, to be frank, little personal knowledge of him. I am usually a close personal friend of my authors: but, in this case, for some reason or another, our intercourse was almost entirely on a business basis. I never really knew the man as a man: nor do I really know of anyone who could tell you much about him.

'I'm not quite clear what you mean by "literary honesty" ' (The writer of this letter had specifically requested that my father comment on this.) 'If I do understand you aright, I should have thought that his literary honesty was impeccable: I mean, I doubt whether he ever said anything other than he thought he meant, ever used words for mere effect, and so on and so forth. His intellectual honesty is another matter. I should not myself have said that his intellectual honesty was impeccable. I hope you won't think I'm being stupidly paradoxical, and that you will understand my meaning if I say that, in my opinion, he was too desperately anxious to be honest to be really honest. Did he, I am trying to say, give full play to those doubts, hesitations and searchings about the truth which are the lot of all of us, but which so many try to stifle? Didn't he have a certain *simplicité* which, in a man of as high intelligence as his, is really always a trifle dishonest? I think so myself.

'He is an interesting contrast to another of my authors who, in my view, was intellectually dishonest in almost the opposite way. He was always "fudging" a reconciliation between two mutually inconsistent points of view. I'm sorry I can't be more helpful. Yours sincerely, Victor Gollancz. P.S. Incidentally, I think

Orwell is *enormously* overrated.'

Well, I think my father may have been wrong about that!

SIR STEPHEN SPENDER met George Orwell in 1937, shortly after Orwell returned from Spain. They were brought together at a lunch in the Chelsea flat of their mutual friend Cyril Connolly, who had been a school companion of Orwell. Orwell had surprised Spender by attacking, in print, the group of left-wing poets and writers with which Spender was associated. These were British intellectuals who at that time supported Soviet communism. Orwell had called them 'parlour Bolsheviks' and 'pansy pinks.'

Well, he meant that we came from the same homosexual university background, which we certainly made rather clear in our poetry, and he probably considered, quite wrongly I think, that the working class was exclusively heterosexual. He also meant that we were middle-class people who hadn't paid the price of going over to the proletariat. We were continuing to lead rather soft bourgeois lives.

I think he slightly misjudged my position, because while I was in Spain I got into trouble for being anti-communist and for attacking the communists for various things, but on the whole I think that 'pink pansy left' was a fair basis for a rhetorical or polemical kind of attack. I mean, what Orwell was really saying was, 'I fought in Spain, therefore I have the authority to rebuke you who take sides on this issue but who haven't paid the price.'

What I thought was rather misjudged was that Orwell seemed to fail to notice that even if we were rather ineffective poseurs there were very effective and very brave people who took the point of view we did. People like John Cornford, Ralph Fox, Julian Bell, all of whom were killed in Spain. He attacked Auden with particular virulence because Auden, in his poem called 'Spain,' after he had visited Spain, spoke of accepting the 'necessary murder' committed presumably by the Republicans, and Orwell delivered a violent attack on Auden as a person who had never participated in a murder himself and who, if he did, would never have written in this way. In a way I think this was quite an unfair attack on Auden, although it was rather effective, because, after all, if you support any cause that involves fighting you are in effect supporting murder, and I don't see why one shouldn't face that.

Orwell did go in for this kind of rhetoric which was not quite fair, taking things very literally. But we never resented Orwell's attacks in the least. I think we accepted that he had the authority not so much of his rhetoric but of his actual lived life. We thought of Orwell as a kind of secular saint, really. But I think he thought we were dupes and shouldn't have been dupes.

I think Orwell's reasons for coming to conclusions were either the immediate result of his experience within a very limited area, which he then extrapolated, or were sort of intuitive. If you read his works carefully you often think he's arriving at the right conclusions for quite inadequate reasons. For example, in *Homage to Catalonia* there's a striking example of this, when he really doesn't know who's in the right, the Republicans or the POUM, until he happens to see a policeman standing on a roof, firing down from the roof at people in the streets whom he takes to be Trotskyites. Since he believes that the police are, in all occasions, wrong, partly because he himself happened to be a policeman in Burma, he therefore immediately assumes that the POUM were innocent victims. That's the sort of way in which Orwell arrives at his conclusions. It's a very inadequate reason.

But he did happen to be right in his anti-Stalinism. I arrived at the same conclusions as Orwell did, by the time I'd met him — that the International Brigade was being run entirely by the communists. A great many people, especially from England, thought of the

Republic as some kind of liberal multiparty government and then found when they joined the Brigade it was being run entirely by the communists. I did become very anticommunist. Probably Orwell did before I did, and probably Orwell was much clearer about it than I was, but I wouldn't have agreed with him that Stalin was just as bad as Hitler. We still thought that the communists were better than the fascists because communism represented not just an ideology but a system of social justice that, however much it deviated under a Party leader, would ultimately lead to the withering away of the state, and a real socialist society. Whereas fascism clearly didn't do this at all. Fascism was pure tyranny, really.

My poems from Spain are the poems of a pacifist who nevertheless supports military action. Ultimately we thought that we were fighting against war, paradoxically — that victory against fascism in Spain would prevent a second world war.

After their first meeting, Orwell and Spender became friends and would remain friends for the rest of Orwell's life. Spender was slightly amused, however, by Orwell's attempts to be seen as proletarian.

I think it was a bit phony, from his own account of it — living with tramps in hostels and dirtying his own clothes and cutting holes in them with a penknife and so on. It's phony. But even its phoniness is perfectly acceptable, I think. I mean, Orwell had something about him like a character in a Charlie Chaplin movie, if not like Charlie Chaplin himself. He was a person who was always playing a role, but with great pathos and great sincerity. He probably impressed us more than he impressed the working class; in fact, I'm sure he did. I always found him a very nice and rather amusing kind of man to be with.

He always talked in a monotonous kind of growl. I used to think it was like going through a London fog, having a conversation with George Orwell. He talked in this sort of gritty, rambling way. And his prose had a gritty substance, I think, because he refused to use poetic devices in his writing. He distinguished prose very clearly from poetry. I don't think Orwell read very much poetry or liked poetry. He tended to review poetry as though it were ideology. Always seeking for the ideas behind it. He was usually speculating about politics and the political situation.

I always found him rather amusing — like, as I say, watching a Charlie Chaplin movie. I don't mean to be superior about this, but Orwell had a real entertainment value, which I liked very much. But we always come back to the position with Orwell that his integrity lay in the life he led. So it didn't matter very much that some of the things he said were wrong. One always respected he was living out this more or less working-class life. He was really a radical conservative, which has a very respectable English history, going back to the nineteenth-century, to people like Cobbett. What he valued was the old concept of England based on the English countryside, in which to be conservative is to be against changes taking place, especially changes in the direction of producing inequality. He was opposed to the whole hard-faced industrial middle class which arose in the nineteenth century.

I liked him very much. I felt he was extraordinarily sincere and genuine, and always you felt with Orwell the presence of some kind of idea, a rather noble idea. I adored Orwell, really. That's what it comes to.

Preston Hall

In March 1938 Orwell suffered a tubercular lesion in one lung and went for treatment to Preston Hall, an old mansion in Kent run by the British Legion. Eileen's brother, Dr Lawrence O'Shaughnessy, was a consultant surgeon there.

Victor Stacey, then a patient at the sanatorium, remembers Orwell's arrival.

One day somebody told me a patient was coming who was related to the surgeon. Well, the day came. It was teatime, and we were in the dining hall, and in came this tall gentleman, rather roughish looking, I thought. He was wearing great big shoes, a jacket which literally hung on him, and a red pullover, a roll-neck pullover. And I thought, 'Oh, *that's* Eric Blair.'

He was put in a single room, next to me. Some of the boys said 'preferential treatment' — you know, having his breakfast served in his own room — but he wasn't like that. He never said a lot, but he acknowledged everybody. He wasn't stand-offish once he knew you a bit. As time went on, we saw more of him. He used to come in for chats, mainly at milk time at 7:00 in the evening. They made you drink as much milk as you could — it was part of the treatment — and eat as much as you could. Well, he never used to discuss himself, he never *ever* talked about writing papers or books, but he always seemed to get *you* round to talking about yourself. And when he looked at you he had *penetrating eyes*. I've never seen such eyes, especially if he was questioning you on things.

Our walls were very thin, and one night I was on my own in my room, listening to the radio. And I must have been making a noise, and suddenly the door flung open and he said, *'Are you all right? Are you all right?'* You see, he was concerned.

And we used to hear his typewriter going. But never late at night. He was a very quiet man. Sometimes he hardly said a word, because everybody else was talking, but he was *listening*.

I saw his wife Eileen on quite a few occasions, but she didn't seem to come every week or anything like that. She was a very pleasant lady. Very kind. And of course he used to have a number of quite important-looking people coming down. I never knew who they were, of course. Big cars, they had. And then on the other hand there were what I would call 'roughies' — rough working men, probably men who had fought with him in the Spanish war — and they used to come in for a meal. He always seemed at home with the 'gor blimey' types. For instance, we had a stevedore as a patient, a cockney, and Eric Blair seemed to like to chat with him.

Preston Hall was situated just off the main road to London, surrounded by trees and the pleasant rural scenery of Kent.

When you were recovering they used to encourage you to take long walks. I used to go out quite a lot, and on one occasion I was crossing a hayfield and I saw this head, only a head, and it was Eric Blair. He beckoned me over, and he was sitting there cross-legged, laughing to himself. There were these two twigs, with two caterpillars on them, and they were doing all sorts of funny things, and he said, 'Look at this.'

I remember, too, he had a mania for cutting thumbsticks, long sticks you use for walking sticks. I've been out several times and seen him cutting a thumbstick. And he said to me, 'This is the finest thing out for walking.' And he ended up with lots of these, because he used to go out on a walk and forget to take it with him, so he had to cut another one.

On 25 April 1938, *Homage to Catalonia* was published by Fredric Warburg, but it failed to impress the British public. By July Orwell was mapping out another novel, but his doctors forbade him to write anything more taxing than letters or the occasional review. At Preston Hall the conversations often turned to the international situation and the possibility of war with Hitler.

He was interested in Germany very much. And one of my colleagues there, who was quite a cultured gentleman, a war veteran of Gallipoli, used to discuss the coming war with Eric. Somebody said to him, 'Do you think

Germany is going to war almost immediately?' And Eric said, 'No, I can't see that, but I would say in a year's time.' I remembered that, when the war broke out a year later.

Orwell left Preston Hall on 1 September 1938 and on medical advice spent the next six months in a warm, dry climate. He and Eileen accepted a large anonymous loan (from the novelist L.H. Myers) and went to Morocco. Here Orwell was ill again but managed nonetheless to complete the manuscript of his next novel, *Coming Up for Air,* which contains forebodings of war, and covers many themes that would find their full expression in *Nineteen Eighty-Four.*

Orwell and Eileen returned to London on 30 March 1939 and stayed with Eileen's brother, who perhaps wanted to take a good look for himself at Orwell's state of health. Then they went back to Wallington, where Orwell carried on writing, growing vegetables and flowers, and raising small livestock.

At the end of June 1939, Orwell's father, Richard Blair, died of cancer at the age of eighty-two. Orwell wrote to his agent that "curiously enough, his last moment of consciousness was hearing that review [of *Coming Up for Air*] I had in the *Sunday Times.*" That Orwell's father died reconciled, more or less, to his son's career was a great consolation.

At this time Orwell was planning "an enormous novel, sort of saga, which will be published in three parts," to which, in 1940, he gave the title "The Quick and the Dead." Professor Bernard Crick, in *George Orwell: A Life,* writes:

" 'The Quick and the Dead' *could* have been a conception that would have linked the themes of 'revolution betrayed' of *Animal Farm* and of the awful consequences of *Nineteen Eighty-Four* to a family saga of the prior decay of the old order. . . There is also a reference in the notes towards 'The Quick and the Dead' to a horse called 'Boxer' being whipped to his feet by an army officer and driven to death — which strengthens the hypothesis that the two books were planned at the same time, originally part of the same conception.''

CHAPTER FOUR

The Road to Animal Farm

All animals are equal, but some are more equal than others.
GEORGE ORWELL
ANIMAL FARM

In February 1944 Orwell described his nearly finished manuscript of *Animal Farm* as a "little squib." But when the book was published the "little squib" exploded with a bang and a shower of shrapnel. Some of it hit the intended target: *Animal Farm* was a brilliant satire on the Soviet Union and, with its main theme of "revolution betrayed," effectively propagated Orwell's view that the ideals of socialism had been cruelly perverted by Stalin. But to Orwell's dismay the explosion partly backfired when the book was taken up by conservatives as evidence that Orwell the socialist had finally seen the error of his ways and was now convinced that a revolution would *always* be betrayed. Wrap a political message up in a fable, or a "fairy story," as Orwell described *Animal Farm*, and you invite a variety of interpretations.

With *Animal Farm* Orwell showed he had become the master of his craft. The book was beautifully constructed and elegantly written — light years away from his first literary fumblings fifteen years earlier. It was written quickly, and Orwell greatly enjoyed writing it. Some of his friends see in it the hand and the humour of his wife Eileen. Others feel its sunny quality is due to his taking as his characters not people but animals, which he always liked to have around him. (During the war he had to exchange the goats he kept at the cottage in Wallington for a few chickens in the backyard of his London flat.)

Animal Farm brought Orwell worldwide fame and, for the first time in his life, financial security. It is ironic that most of the early income from the book was generated by sales in the United States, where Orwell was commonly misinterpreted as an antisocialist cold warrior. Publication had been greatly delayed as one nervous London publisher after another shied away from handling a book containing such an obvious attack on Britain's wartime ally, the Soviet Union.

It had been a frustrating war for Orwell, ending in March 1945 with the death of Eileen during what was supposed to be a routine gynecological operation. In his bereavement, Orwell was left not only with his own grief but also with the practical problem of coping with a young son less than a year old. Convinced that he was sterile, Orwell had finally persuaded Eileen that they should adopt, and in June 1944 they received a three-week-old boy whom they named Richard, after Orwell's father. Friends remember Orwell's joy in his new fatherhood and, after Eileen's death, his fierce determination to keep the boy and give him the best possible start in life. Anyone who suggested that George might give him up was treated to quite uncharacteristic outbursts of anger.

Orwell ended the war tired and disillusioned with the bureaucratic socialism of Britain's Labour government. Yet he had begun it in high revolutionary spirits, convinced that the sheer effort of mobilizing a nation to fight Hitler could sweep away the old order he so detested. In *The Lion and the Unicorn*, published in 1940, he described England as a "family with the wrong members in charge." Only a revolution, he felt, could save the country, and the moment had come for the "people" to take what was theirs. With his romantic faith in the English character, Orwell seemed to believe that if the downtrodden members of the nation *did* take control, the "family" would somehow hold together. There could be a revolution without a civil war, England would still be England, tradition would be preserved. A lion and a unicorn would still grace the buttons of the uniforms of England's post-revolutionary socialist soldiers.

Orwell was rejected for active military service because of his history of tuberculosis. This was a major disappointment to him, and on top of it the outbreak of war led to financial problems because publishers had little or no paper to print books, and many of the smaller magazines for which Orwell wrote were folding.

Eileen, however, did find a war job, first with the Censorship Department and later with the Ministry of Food. She moved to London, where she lived with her sister-in-law until Orwell joined her in 1940, having found part-time work as theatre and film reviewer for the magazine *Time and Tide*.

During the war Orwell channelled his revolutionary and patriotic feelings in equal part into his service with the London branch of the Home Guard, a defence force quickly put together by the British government to protect the country against invasion. By chance Orwell was assigned to the same unit as his second publisher, Fred Warburg, to whom he confided his suspicions that their fellow volunteers, most of whom were older, middle-class tradesmen, were "either fascists or potential fascists" and certainly not the kind of men to share his view that the Home Guard should become a revolutionary militia modelled after the POUM.

Orwell's notion that the "English genius" would allow for a revolution that did not entail a loss of civil liberties was never put to the test. The war ground on, with no shake-up of the English nation-family — nothing but bombs and shortages, death and destruction.

In 1941 Orwell found war work of a sort at the BBC, broadcasting to India. His scripts were excellent, but he was ineffective at the microphone. If he salvaged anything from his two years as a radio producer, it was a basic training in the developing art of the use of the mass media as propaganda. He told friends that the Ministry of Truth in *Nineteen Eighty-Four* was based in part on his experiences at the BBC.

In 1943 he moved on to the socialist journal *Tribune.* Here he resumed his preferred status as an independent critic. His weekly column, "As I Please," explored any subject that took his fancy. The first piece set the tone: it concerned the heated but suppressed issue of anti-American feeling in wartime Britain. The G.I. invasion had led, Orwell wrote, to the popular feeling that "Britain is now Occupied Territory" and that "the only American soldiers with decent manners are the Negroes."

Tribune paid Orwell to launch well-written broadsides, and he revelled in his much-vaunted ability to "face unpleasant facts." The job was only part-time, even though Orwell was acting as literary editor as well as weekly columnist, and this freed him to work at more serious writing. In particular, he began to put down on paper a book whose theme had been in his mind since his return from Spain in 1937, a book in which the villains were pigs and the lone hero was a carthorse called Boxer. The slogan "All animals are equal, but some are more equal than others" is a perfect example of the malignant distortion of language that Orwell feared would lead to a malignant and distorted society.

Wallington in Wartime

MONICA BALD is a long-time resident of the Hertfordshire village where George Orwell and Eileen had lived since 1936. Her first contact with Orwell had been when she borrowed his telephone book one day, there being only three other people in the village who were 'on the phone.' Later, when war broke out, Monica Bald often had to remind Orwell of the new blackout regulations.

I happened to be a warden, and during the war it was an offence to show any lights in your window, and people in the village were always coming to me and saying, 'It's that man again, he's got lights showing; I'm sure he's a spy.' So I went up to see him, and there he was just writing, quite oblivious to the fact that he hadn't drawn his curtains, quite oblivious. People were quite scared, you see, of what was happening above, scared of a parachute invasion.

He was a nice person, but he was slightly eccentric. You could see he'd got TB. He was gaunt with high cheekbones. But extremely kind, and with a pleasant voice. She [Eileen] was a little short woman and always dressed in a moleskin coat and a moleskin hat when she went to London. Mrs Anderson 'did' for them, and she always used to say she was sure he was a writer because he got money every now and again by cheque, and then she'd say, 'We all got paid.' I wouldn't say they joined in village functions an awful lot, but I used to see him sauntering around. He didn't have a car or a bike.

FRED BATES, a farm worker, remembers Orwell's serving in his shop, which was actually the front room of his cottage.

The counter was in the middle of the room, and you just stood there and got served. There was no end of bacon there; they had a proper bacon slicer. Beautiful bacon they used to have. And sugar and everything else. And he had a goat in the back garden, which Grandfather Hatchett used to go and milk twice a day. They wanted me to taste the goat's milk one day, but I never did. Well, I had just a sip of it, and it was horrible.

OLGA BATES recounted the popular village story of the day in June 1936 when Orwell and Eileen were married in the church at Wallington.

They're supposed to have walked from the cottage to the church. She went in the first gate, up the steps and down the path. He ran around and is supposed to have jumped over the other gate and then met her at the porch of the church. And they both went in together to get married.

ESTHER BROOKES moved into the cottage very soon after Orwell gave up the lease in 1947.

> I found, when I came here in 1948, his old bacon slicer. There were shelves all round the room in which he kept his groceries, and also a lot of correspondence lying on the floor among his boots and scraps. It had disintegrated over the years so I just had to burn it. There was a very tiny pantry here and a very tiny sink there. And the door which connects to the shop has slits in the top so that when he was sitting in the sitting room he could look through the squint and see if there was anyone in the shop. The shop door is about four-foot-six high, and the room is eleven feet square. The farmers here built their barns in units of eleven feet because of a yoke of oxen, and these same dimensions were used for this house. The place is about four to five hundred years old. There's a tiny, twisted staircase here, and upstairs he had two bedrooms and a wide-open landing.

In the small front garden of the cottage one of Orwell's own rose bushes, an Albertine, still flourishes.

> He bought it for sixpence at Woolworths. It really is a magnificent thing. We also still have some of his hollyhocks, a rambler, and the loganberry is his. Oh, and there was also one lilac bush, which I moved and now flowers profusely. A lovely dark mauve lilac.

LETTICE COOPER, the novelist, was one of George and Eileen's friends who used to escape wartime London for the occasional weekend of country peace at Wallington. A stay in such a cottage would normally be a restful, restoring experience, but Lettice Cooper remembers her visits there as something of an ordeal.

> The sink would be blocked. The primus stove wouldn't work. The lavatory plug wouldn't pull. The stairs were very dark, because there were never any bulbs in the lights, and they'd put piles of books on the staircase at odd places, so there were lots of traps, and the place was

rather dusty. But it was a nice cottage, in a lovely part of the country.

You used to have to walk into Baldock three miles away to buy any food [by the outbreak of the war Orwell had stopped running a village store out of his front room], but there was a pub next door. I remember the first time I went, it was harvesting, and it had run out of beer. It had all been drunk by the harvesters, and there was nothing else, of course.

George had an absolute *thing* about beer. He couldn't bear lager. He couldn't believe anyone who was a friend of his or who could be trusted could drink lager. I don't like beer at all, and the only kind I can drink is lager, so when I went to have a drink with them and he used to say, 'What will you have?' and I said lager, he would then go up to the bar and come back with three mugs of dark brown ale, and I couldn't drink it. So in the end I used to have to go up to the bar with him and see what he was getting. Finally it dawned on him, and he didn't hold it against me!

PATRICIA DONAHUE, a London-based journalist at the time, was another frequent visitor to the Wallington cottage. Later in the war, when George and Eileen were both living in London, she and Lydia Jackson moved in for a while after being bombed out during the Blitz. She first visited Wallington after an earlier bomb attack on her block of flats in London.

We had to walk the last three miles from Baldock to Wallington. It was a bombers' moon. You could see the shadows of the bushes lying across the road in the moonlight. These German bombers were purring away up top, you could hear them. They were on their way to Manchester, we found out afterwards. Well, we arrived at the cottage and knocked on the door. We weren't expected, of course. George came to the door and we went in and they were in the middle of supper. They were very welcoming. We shared their supper and had some of Eileen's very nice apple meringue pie; she was an excellent cook. George was very friendly. We stayed there two nights.

They had a dog called Marx who was a very friendly and intelligent animal, a medium-size, grey, unclipped poodle. They had a little Chippendale child's chair, a period piece, and George valued this little chair and later took it up to Scotland with him. I remember the loo was a ramshackle-looking place. The ivy got inside; there was quite a bit of ivy growing there. That amused me. But it was a flush lavatory. At the bottom of the garden there was a toolshed with rusty tools inside and a rusty lawnmower, but there was room for a card table and a chair in the shed. And George did quite a bit of writing there. I myself did some writing there. It was quite pleasant.

There were mice there, too. Eileen said once they had such a plague of mice that they got onto the shelves in the kitchen and she said there were 'battalions of mice, shoulder to shoulder on the shelves, pushing the china off.' That was the kind of exaggerated story she told. She had a good sense of humour and was given to telling funny stories. And funny stories about George, which he didn't seem to mind. In fact I think he rather liked being made fun of by Eileen. I don't think George was an easy man to live with, but they did get on quite well. I had the impression it was a very happy marriage.

One time, when there was a great deal of consternation and alarm about parachute troops, with the Germans dropping parachute troops into country places and knocking at people's doors, there was a knock at the door of the cottage. George immediately picked up his gun, stood behind the door at the ready, tense, while Eileen opened the door, so that if it was an unwelcome visitor he could be shot forthwith!

There were a lot of weapons there — daggers mostly, quite a number of them. I can show you one here.

Altogether it's forty-two inches long and there's gold tracery on the handle, not very visible now, and there's goldwork here too on the scabbard. Perhaps he brought this back from Burma with him. This is the biggest of the swords he had at the cottage.

He made bombs, you know. Probably Molotov cocktails. He was a very enthusiastic member of the Home Guard in London. I remember Eileen used to get fed up with all the weapons around. She said, 'I can put up with bombs on the mantelpiece, but I will not have a machine gun under the bed.'

I think George could hardly have had anyone more suited for him. She had a sort of tolerance, and humour, too, which helped her put up with things some women probably wouldn't have been prepared to put up with. He was a sick man, really. I know that later, when she was at the Ministry of Food, she used to come back quite a long way during the middle of the day to cook a meal for him so that he would have fresh vegetables. She went away occasionally for one or two nights. And once she'd left some cooked fish for George, some quite nice fish for him, and she had boiled some eel for the cat — they had a cat at that time — and she left both these dishes behind. Well, George apparently absent-mindedly ate the eel, and I suppose the cat had the other stuff!

At Wallington George was always pleased to exercise his rights to use the common land. That common land was available to anyone living in the village, and most people just let it grow over with bushes, but no, George exercised his rights as a sort of English peasant, I suppose, and kept these goats up there. He was a country-man at heart. I think he was quite well liked in the village, but he was never one of them. He might have liked to have been, but he was never one of the country-men really, you know.

The Lion and the Unicorn

Orwell left Wallington in 1940 and joined Eileen, who was working in London in the Censorship Department. They did, however, spend weekends in Wallington throughout the war.

While in London Orwell was introduced to TOSCO FYVEL through their mutual publisher Fredric Warburg.

I walked through leafy St John's Wood to Fred Warburg's house, and there I met George Orwell. I must say I was surprised at his appearance. He was tall, gaunt, with deep grooves in his face. Poor hair, poor skin, and a poor little moustache. He looked like a sort of seedy sahib, one of the many British Imperial administrators I'd met in the Middle East.

Fred Warburg wanted to found a group of like-minded people to discuss the war. Well, we talked and we both decided to join Warburg's little group. At the time we all believed you could have both patriotism and socialism. Orwell was trying to identify himself with England in its finest hour.

Out of this meeting came the project for Searchlight Books. I insisted Orwell should write the first one. It was called *The Lion and the Unicorn*. In it Orwell wrote as a patriotic socialist. He hoped for a British revolution, but it had to be a patriotic revolution. So my credit was, I managed to extract from Orwell, with this book, the only really positive, optimistic book he ever wrote.

The Lion and the Unicorn was Orwell's attempt to translate the revolutionary fervour he had experienced in Barcelona to wartime Britain. "When the red militias are billeted in the Ritz," he wrote, "I shall feel that the England I was taught to love so long ago, and for such different reasons, is somehow persisting."

All kinds of people told me afterwards that as young soldiers or even schoolboys they read *The Lion and the Unicorn* and that it made quite an impact. It was an interesting little chapter of both our lives. In a sense *The*

Lion and the Unicorn was the other side of Orwell. It represented his moment of hope — Orwell as he might have been had there been no war, had he not been ill. *The Lion and the Unicorn* inspired John Osborne, whose *Look Back in Anger* has some almost direct quotations from it, as Osborne once told me.

Tosco Fyvel believes that something of the Old Etonian in Orwell came to the fore at this time.

He was always making the point that the number of Old Etonians who fell at the front during the First World War exceeded the national average. And he always said that the British ruling classes might be politically and financially corrupt, but they were not morally corrupt, they were not like the French. I mean, when the hour came, they were all ready to fight and give their lives for the country. He said that was something he always felt people on the left should know about their opponents. He always felt they had a completely wrong idea about their opponents.

The Lion and the Unicorn got Searchlight Books off to a good start, but for Tosco Fyvel, an ardent Zionist, Orwell's vision of a socialist England completely ignored a very important ethnic minority in the country.

If you look carefully at *The Lion and the Unicorn* there is no place in it for the Jews. In his day the Jews were the only real ethnic minority in England. You see, he had been brought up in a class that was inherently anti-Semitic. He knew nothing about Jews in his early life, he told me. He was anti-Semitic by education, though of course in his personal relations it would be unthinkable that he would be prejudiced. When I talked to him about the difficult times for Jewish intellectuals in, say, anti-Semitic Vienna in pre-1914 times, I could see it was a world of which he knew nothing.

It was a great gap in his outlook — a curious gap, I felt, because I had a total obsession with Hitler and

Nazism during the whole war.

Orwell never used the words 'Nazi Germany'; he always took the old-fashioned term 'fascist Germany,' which meant it was some authoritarian version of capitalism. But he never really lived long enough to assimilate the full facts of the Holocaust, the rise of the state of Israel. I remember Warburg once telling me that he had a young German Jewish refugee staying with him who was going to agricultural college, and Orwell said, 'Oh, Jews can never go into agriculture. That's a bad joke, isn't it?'

And after the war he thought that the Jewish refugees could just stay on among the ruins as though nothing had happened. I thought this was fearfully insensitive. I mean he simply didn't know Central Europe or Eastern Europe. He just couldn't understand that at all costs the Jewish survivors in Europe, the wretched survivors, whom the British navy was trying to keep from going to Palestine, should somehow be salvaged. And to him the Zionists were white settlers like the British in India or Burma, and the Arabs were like the native Burmese, which was a crude oversimplification although there was a sliver of truth in it. He was against Jewish nationalism — against all nationalism.

We had a great many arguments, and Arthur Koestler also said he argued with him about Palestine and Zionism, but we both concluded that George had different opinions than ours. It wasn't a *major* theme in our relationship.

Orwell had been refused military service because of his bad health. He was extremely frustrated not to be able to fight and threw a great deal of his energy into the Home Guard, where he became a sergeant in the same St John's Wood company that his publisher Fred Warburg had joined.

I think he was Sergeant Blair, whereas Warburg was Corporal Warburg. Warburg incidentally had fought at Passchendaele so he was an ex-officer. Warburg told me about serving with George in the Home Guard. It sounds like George was an enthusiastic but not frightfully competent member. There was a famous incident when George caused a mortar to fire not a blank but a wooden bolt, and there was this terrible noise and destruction all round.

Fred Warburg later remarked that "there was practically nothing about the Home Guard that didn't suit Orwell's temperament, until it began to be efficient."

At the BBC

While continuing to write freelance reviews and articles, Orwell was hired, in August 1941, as a producer in the Indian Section of the BBC's Eastern Service. The job was a full-time one, and required a short training course. HENRY SWANZY joined the BBC at the same time, and remembers being sent on a rather ineffective training exercise.

We were all supposed to go out in the London streets and come back and do an eyewitness report. I can't remember what we did see, but he and I went on the top of a bus down Park Lane. I'm not absolutely sure he even produced a script, because he didn't take a very close interest in a lot of the BBC activities. At that time I only knew him as E.A. Blair, and I was probably the only person in the training school who didn't know he was Orwell.

The course was held at Bedford College for Women, at the bottom of Regent's Park. There was this fantastic collection of writers and poets and actors, all being given this crash course. It took only ten days, not the usual three months. Hardly any of them knew anything about radio, because before the war intellectuals in England were rather snobbish about radio. They didn't really pay a great deal of attention to it, really.

Well, there we all were on this course. We assembled and looked at each other, and there were certain people who were 'at the top of the court,' you know. Orwell had a name, but he didn't seem to be in the inner circle. He didn't much like the clique. He didn't much like poets, really: he said they were a mutual admiration society.

There was a frightful snobbery in the BBC during the war — a pecking order. And this was something he stayed right outside of. He was awfully nice, not too important to know you, not like some of the others who would always have their eyes roaming over your left shoulder when you were talking to them. He had this curious fluting voice and a dry way of expressing himself. He would sort of drawl out his views, which were often witty and amusing and very critical of the powers that be. The main thing was, he was awfully *personal*. We used to talk over coffee, and I had at this time a hopeless admiration for this member of the opposite sex, and he would be absolutely sweet advising me on the ways of behaving and how one should get over it, or get on with it, or get out of it, or whatever! He was very nice like that.

His reputation was not very great then. I had only read the things he'd written in *Horizon*, these frightfully funny things about dirty postcards at the seaside and children's comic books. And I'd read *The Road to Wigan Pier* and the things he did for the Left Book Club.

We had a lot of things in common, really. He was the product of parents who were not terribly well off. I'd also gone to a prep school in Eastbourne, and I'd also got a scholarship to Wellington, as the son of a hero. You see I come from the Anglo-Irish tradition, and I think the thing to remember about Orwell is that he wasn't English. His father was Scottish — Blair — and his mother was French, and therefore he didn't have the gut reactions of the English. And if you go through this English education system and you don't have quite the right gut reactions about cricket, or anything else, there is a problem, and I think there was in Orwell's case.

I went to tea once at Orwell's flat, this rather impersonal flat just the other side of Lords cricket ground. His wife was there, Eileen, who was a very nice, very tired-looking person. I always remember the extraordinary remark he made about her before I'd met her. He said, 'Well, come along to tea on Sunday, my wife isn't a bad old stick.' Don't you think that was a very odd expression? Of course that is a phrase that was used very much in middle-class circles, really, and I did notice in Orwell a kind of arrogance, or superiority towards materialism and the whole money society, the sort of attitude where it wasn't altogether done to make a lot of money, where to be Left was an antimaterialistic thing.

Orwell had this literary feeling for making a picture and for creating a scenario, which didn't, it seemed to me, sometimes actually coincide with reality. I noticed he made a number of small mistakes when he was literary editor of *Tribune* later in the war. But he had the capacity to turn the world into his own world, really. This is what was delightful, and yet at the same time it didn't actually link entirely onto the reality. In some respects the person I think of most when I think of Orwell is Solzhenitsyn. They have the same wonderful capacity to mould details, and this rather mixed-up basic attitude.

SUNDAY WILSHIN took over George Orwell's job when he left the BBC in 1943. Before then, she used to meet Orwell frequently in the BBC canteen.

You could find anyone in that canteen that you'd ever heard of. It was that sort of place. Everybody met there. The food, for wartime stuff, was quite good, but Orwell thought it was *marvellous*! Terrific stuff. Because it was always there, and it was ninety-nine percent edible, and he could get it whenever he wanted, because it was open for twenty-four hours, of course.

On one occasion somebody said to him, 'You never use any effects in your programs, George.' And he said, 'What are effects?' And they said, 'Well, you know, there's an Effects Department here. You can get music, sounds, background noises.' And he said, 'Oh yes, that's very interesting' and was heard by his secretary to ring up the Effects Department and say, 'I believe you have effects.' And they said, 'Yes, that's right,' and he said, 'Send me a nice mixed lot of effects, would you?' He learned, of course, because he was a very intelligent man, and he picked up various things, but he had no idea of what it was about. He just had to be guided. He had many ideas for programs, and he could write scripts, but when it came to actually being in the studio, he needed someone to guide his hand.

He was rather forbidding in his approach to people, but at the same time you could feel this inner warmth in him, and if you were not the sort of person, and I wasn't, who got put off by a sort of rather sombre, dour approach, you could soon get him to talk to you and even to smile! And everybody used to pull his leg — I don't know why, but I think because of this rather solemn manner — and all sorts of people did this; the Indians, the Thais, the Pakistanis, and ourselves, we all used to pull his leg, and I think he liked it. I'm pretty sure he did, because he found himself among people who knew his worth, knew his background, and at the same time paid no particular attention to it and treated him as an ordinary human being.

He always wore a simple, sombre suit, not very new — a sort of tweedy thing, you know, about ten years old and a bit crinkled. I don't think he had the slightest interest in his appearance whatever. He had a thin face, and he was inclined to look a little ill. But he had a certain kind of luminosity, which, if you could feel it and see it, was there. And it had nothing to do with his external appearance.

DESMOND HAWKINS was a freelance writer and later a producer at the BBC. His first contact with Orwell had been in December 1940, before Orwell joined the BBC, when Hawkins broadcast a scripted talk with Orwell entitled "The Proletarian Writer." In this talk Orwell said that he was sceptical of the currently fashionable concept of a distinct form of writing in which the point of view of the worker got a hearing, arguing that he didn't believe the proletariat could "create an independent literature while they are not the dominant class."

> It was a great thing to discuss with Orwell because in the 1930s there was this awareness of a new kind of writer coming in, the idea that there was some kind of magic quality in a man who'd come up out of a coal mine or off a trampship and had started to write, that such a man was drawing on something outside the tradition of the rest of us. This is what interested Orwell enormously and something that he, like many of his generation, felt he wanted to join. And I think if you look at the poets of that period, the Audens and Spenders, I think they were moving in the same direction, and there was a feeling that the old culture was played out and that there should be some combination of forces with this proletarian movement, if it did exist.

At the BBC Orwell was employed under his real name, Eric Blair. Desmond Hawkins possesses a letter from Orwell that he feels shows that the name "Orwell" had become more than a simple pseudonym for Blair.

> It's on BBC notepaper, and it has a reference up in the corner: 'E.B.' The letter was signed 'George Orwell,' and I think he typed it, since the typing isn't very good. And 'E.B.' was undoubtedly Eric Blair. This was a complex man, you felt. He had these two identities in him all the time, and he was constantly adjusting them, tuning them, and in a small way this illustrated it to me.

In his broadcasts to India, which were aimed at trying to persuade an increasingly anti-British elite to support Britain's war effort, Orwell admitted he had become rapidly "propaganda-minded" and had developed "a cunning one did not previously have." Later, after the publication of *Nineteen Eighty-Four*, he claimed that he had modelled his Ministry of Truth in *Nineteen Eighty-Four* on the BBC. Desmond Hawkins believes that there was more to it than this.

Orwell's 'Minitruth' may have come partly from the BBC itself, but to be fair I think it came also from what we were listening to. After all, we were listening to the full blast of the greatest revolution in propagandist broadcasting that Western Europe had seen — the German propaganda machine. The whole Goebbels technique and method was a total innovation as an arm of warfare. And Orwell's job after all was to unravel it and counter it. I would have thought Orwell would have studied that in terms of a dictatorship of Big Brother and would have filled out the details with our sort of censorship. We were a poor second to that sort of method of conditioning the native population, thank goodness. We were listening to 'Germany Calling,' every kind of distortion of truth and 'doublethink.' So we were seeing how the new mass media could be used, and bear in mind that for Orwell, as for me, we were born into a world where there was no radio.

All sorts of legends grew up about the German intelligence system and how they could put over little truths that people would accept. I mean, a famous one, which I think is quite apocryphal but it had enormous currency, was that Lord Haw-Haw had said that the clock in Lewisham Town Hall had stopped at three minutes past six. Whether that was true or not, it was a new kind of propaganda, and people said, 'Good God, they even know about the clock in Lewisham Town Hall! They must know it all, it must all be true.'

This was very much a new use of the media, and I think what Orwell seized on in *Nineteen Eighty-Four* was to push to extremes what he had observed: that if you once start playing with truth, if you once start conditioning people, if you once start using the loudspeaker in the canteen or whatever, to keep putting over the slightly bent message all the time, and the slightly twisted language, that this is the new potent force. Yes, bless him, he spotted that a generation ahead of many.

"They Led a Pleasant Life Together"

HENRY DAKIN, Orwell's nephew, stayed with his Uncle Eric for three months while Orwell was working at the BBC. At that time George and Eileen were living in a flat in the Maida Vale area of London, while his mother and sister Avril had moved into accommodations in an adjoining street (Orwell's mother, Ida Blair, died of a heart attack at the age of sixty-seven in March 1943). Henry Dakin remembers his uncle's enthusiasm for Charlie Chaplin films.

We went to the cinema together to see Charlie Chaplin in *The Gold Rush*. Eric thought it was all very funny. He guffawed with laughter, more than anyone else in the place. I remember we seemed to pay an enormous amount of money to get in, and I thought it was hardly worth the price, but Eric was very impressed. And he'd seen the film already. It wasn't his first time. In fact it was him who said, 'We must go along and see this, Hen — very, very good.' He thought a lot of Charlie Chaplin!

The routine at that time was that Eric would go off to the BBC, and then in the evenings he would depart to his room, and there'd be the clack of the typewriter. Eileen and I would listen to the radio or chat. Breakfast was always on time, because they had to go to work, but the evening meal would vary.

Eileen's appearance was rather unkempt, but she was extremely nice looking and very pleasant. One of my main impressions of her was that she always had a ciggy dangling from her lips! And she nearly always seemed to wear a black coat. She didn't seem to bother to take her coat off as she got our meals.

But they led a pleasant life together and were very amiable to each other and very amiable towards me.

During this period of the war, Eileen was working at the Ministry of Food. She was involved, with Lettice Cooper, in organizing the BBC's "Kitchen Front" radio talks.

We had a broadcast every morning, about five minutes, about food, and we had different broadcasters, and she wrote the scripts for them. There was one about a thing called 'murkey,' which was turkey without the turkey! You had stuffing and gravy and potatoes and a veg, but you didn't have the turkey. How many people really did that, I don't know! She very much enjoyed the Ministry of Food, and she was always called Emily, and she asked us to call her Emily. I find it difficult now to remember her as Eileen. We used to spend a lot of our time having coffee at a place across the street, which was frowned on by our bosses, but we did it anyway.

Eileen was pretty, very thoughtful and philosophical, and very much interested in everything. She was very good company in a sort of slow-moving way. You used to have to wait a little for her to say things. She was always very fair and honourable. But she used to say that she didn't mind whether she lived or died. She said that all the time. This was after her brother was killed [in 1940]. That was until she got little Richard [the son the Orwells adopted in 1944]. And then she wanted to live.

She was very much afraid at first that, as he was not her own, she might not love Richard enough. But she didn't want to deprive George. George wanted him passionately, and the two things he wanted for the adopted child were to have a cream perambulator with a gold line round it and to have him put down for Eton! In the end Eileen was very happy having him, loving him, and very proud of him. When they got him, he was just three weeks old, in hospital, and the mother hadn't even given him a nightgown to come away in, he had nothing, no clothes except a hospital gown. So Eileen, who'd got all sorts of things ready, had to rush back home before she took him and bring a little suitcase and dress him.

Six months after the adoption Eileen had to take Richard to a local judge to prove that he was thriving and well cared for.

She came round to the Ministry with Richard after she'd been that morning, very proud and pleased. And for the first time in her life she was wearing a hat. She had a neat coat and skirt on — she wasn't generally very neat — and she had bought a yellow felt hat so that the judge should think she was an entirely suitable person to look after Richard.

From November 1943 to February 1944, Orwell was writing *Animal Farm*. It was unique among his books in that he shared its creation with another person. Some people who knew Eileen feel that the simplicity and elegance of *Animal Farm* may be due in part to her influence.

He read it aloud to her every night in bed as he was writing it — the piece that he'd done that day. And she saw at once that it was a winner, the most attractive thing he'd done yet. And she used to tell us about it every morning, and she would quote bits out of it when we were having our coffee at Selfridge's across the road from the office. It was very exciting.

Lettice Cooper also remembers George and Eileen's apparent fearlessness during the London blitz.

They never took any notice of the bombs, unless one actually hit their house. Eileen told me once that a bomb had come down very near to their place, and it had broken a lot of glass in the windows. And she came downstairs, and in the hall she saw an old woman who was very frightened and who was crying, kneeling on the floor. And George, she said, was kneeling on the floor by her, looking, she said, like Christ and putting his hand on her head and his arms round her shoulders and comforting her.

George had a sort of innocence. And integrity, too. He was very English, an English eccentric. I met him first when I was working on *Time and Tide* and he was doing some of the drama criticisms, and I used to give him the tickets for the plays. That was from late 1939 to the spring of 1940. He was tall, dark, and silent — a bit funny, somehow. You wanted rather to laugh at him. He was never quite sure if by being in the BBC he was losing his integrity. I think he felt it was a matter of defending the bad against the worse.

"I'm Writing a Kind of Parable. . ."

MICHAEL MEYER, translator and biographer of Ibsen and Strindberg, was a young man of twenty-two when he decided it was not enough to admire George Orwell from a distance. He wrote a "timid letter" to Orwell at the BBC and got a friendly letter back. Soon after that they had lunch together in Soho, and Meyer quickly became a good friend of Orwell.

I was tremendously in awe of Orwell — terrified of him, to start with. But then, the things one had the courage to do when one was young! A few months after I first met George I thought it would be fun for him and Graham Greene to get to know each other. So I wrote to both of them, saying that the other admired their work and would like to meet them, which wasn't strictly true in either case because Graham thought George was a good writer but not a frightfully good novelist, and George thought any religion was more or less humbug, sort of turning your back on the real thing. He didn't like Greene's *The Power and the Glory,* for example. But anyway, they both said yes they would come, so on my birthday in June, one hot, hot wartime day, I invited them to lunch at a little restaurant in Soho. And I felt very small, because I'm only five foot eight, and Graham Greene is six foot two and Orwell was six foot four. So I felt small in every sense. But they liked each other at once and got on very well. They were both very straight, unaffected men. They hated any kind of affectation, they were both very independent thinkers, and so they appealed to each other. I remember being very disappointed because they talked about politics a lot, which I didn't know anything about. They didn't talk about literature and the novel, as I'd hoped they would. After the lunch we went on to a pub and stayed till closing time. Then George invited Graham and myself to lunch, and later Graham gave a third lunch.

George was eighteen years older than me, and in a way he became a sort of father figure. And Eileen was delightful — Irish and pretty. A good cook and great fun. She was an ideal wife for Orwell, without being cloying or boring. Eileen was unsophisticated and simple. She didn't wear makeup and didn't need to. I never met Sonia, Orwell's second wife, till about twenty years after his death. She was also fun, but totally different. Sonia was smart, hard-drinking, amusing, dangerous, quick-tempered — all the things Eileen was not. With George we never talked about sex. He was shy about sex. And he had a peculiar revulsion towards homosexuality, which I thought was odd in such a liberal-minded man.

George was terrible at describing the plots of his books. He wasn't alone in that. Graham Greene was equally dreadful. Greene once described the plot of a film which sounded the most boring thing ever but turned out to be *The Third Man*! I once asked George what he was doing, and he said, 'I'm writing a kind of parable, about people who are blind to the dangers of totalitarianism.' He described the new book as being about a farm run by people, where the animals take over and make just as bad a job of it so they call in the humans again. And that was *Animal Farm,* which I think ranks with *Gulliver's Travels, Robinson Crusoe* or *Alice in Wonderland*. It's so marvellously simple, one of the wisest and deepest books ever written. When I read it I was staggered and delighted, because it bore no relation to his awful summary . . .

George, like all writers, 'floated' his theories to his friends. He wasn't a monologuist at all; he was never boring. He used to try and bring everybody into a conversation, very much in the tradition of the great talkers like Wilde, Shaw or Chesterton. But if there were a lot of people talking he couldn't raise his voice and force his way into the conversation, and he could easily give the impression of being very silent. He once took me to a lunch with Malcolm Muggeridge and Anthony Powell and others — they used to meet every week in a little French restaurant in Soho — and we all sat at a long table and everybody talked all the time except George and me. George would occasionally try and put in a word, but it was the sort of conversation, the sort of noise, where you just had to sort of bulldoze your way through, and George with his weak voice couldn't do that, so he would just quietly stop in midsentence.

But if there were just a few of you and you drew him out, then he was the *most* rewarding conversationalist, but you had to draw him out. I remember there was this Labour politician called Patrick Gordon Walker, who later became a cabinet minister, and he was very keen to meet Orwell and said would I bring him up to dinner with them. So we went up together and I was greatly looking forward to hearing a debate between these two. Gordon Walker was a nice man but addressed every individual as though they were three hundred people who had paid to listen, and he did so with George. And George just sat there and tried to make a few points, and after a few half-sentences just sat with perfect courtesy, just nodding, and Patrick Gordon Walker spoke for about an hour, and then George and I took the bus home. Some people called him 'gloomy George,' but it was just that he wasn't an interrupter. And he was the most marvellous fun to be with. He was lovely fun. . .

There's a story about George and H.G. Wells. George was a great admirer of H.G. Wells. Well, at the beginning of the war, George and Eileen needed accommodation. I forget if they'd been bombed out or what it was, but anyway, H.G. Wells had a lovely house in the Nash terraces in Regent's Park, and there was a flat above the garage and he said they could have this flat, for which they were very grateful.

Now, Wells was paranoiac. He regarded everyone as friends or enemies, and also, if he thought you'd been talking about him behind his back, he didn't distinguish between fantasy and reality, you *had* been, and you'd get the most *frightful* note from him saying how disloyal you were. Lots of people suffered this way. And suddenly George and Eileen got a note from him saying, 'I've heard what you've been saying about me, you ungrateful swine. Leave my flat by Monday morning. I shall not be in London for the next few weeks, and if you are here when I get back I shall take action,' etc, etc. So, miserable and bewildered, they moved out. And very difficult it was to find other accommodation in wartime London, too.

Well then, about a year or two later Eileen said to George, she told me, 'It's ludicrous you shouldn't be on good terms with H.G., I mean you were such good friends. Why don't I ask him to dinner and see if he's forgotten the whole thing, or anyway whether he'll be ready to forgive and forget?' Well, a letter came back at once from H.G. Wells saying, 'I'm so delighted to hear from you. I don't know what's been happening to you all these months. I thought it was extraordinarily ungrateful of you to leave that flat I gave you above the garage without any notice, but wartime of course is difficult. I forgive you. Yes, of course I shall be delighted to come to dinner.'

So along he came and Eileen had cooked an enormous meal because Wells was famously greedy. And when Wells arrived, he at once said, 'Now you know I'm suffering very badly from an ulcer. I have to be very careful what I eat. What have you cooked for dinner?' And Eileen said, 'Well, I've cooked a curry, an Indian curry.' And Wells said, 'Oh no, I'm forbidden. I couldn't.' And Eileen said, 'Oh dear, I don't know what to do, food is so difficult nowadays.' And he said, 'Oh well, never mind, I'll eat it.' And he ate *enormous* quantities of this curry, and was in the best of humour and drank great quantities of wine, and occasionally rebuked George for having moved out of the flat above the garage without warning him, and was in the best of form.

Then, after dinner, they sat down and began talking and the poet William Plomer arrived, and Eileen said, 'Oh Bill, I love to see you but I'm afraid I've got nothing really to offer you to eat,' because Wells had finished it all up, 'except a plum cake.' And Wells, in full flight of conversation, heard this and said, 'Plum cake? Oh no, I couldn't have that after curry.' And Eileen said, 'It's not for you, H.G., it's for Bill Plomer.' And so along came the cake and Wells said, 'Well that does look very good' and had two large slices and more brandy and went home rather drunk and in the best of humour, saying, 'Don't let it be so long again. Mustn't lose touch.' And George and Eileen thought, well, that's all right.

Well, about five days later they got the most *furious* note from Wells saying, 'You deliberately tried to poison me. I told you I was on a diet. You deliberately cooked me food that you knew would make me ill. You forced extra food on me *and* stuff like plum cake that you knew would be worse for me *and drink*, and I never want to see you again. I was perfectly right to throw you out of that garage.' All that had come back, you see. And I think they never saw him again. . .

My father was a timber importer, and wood was very difficult to get hold of for domestic purposes during the war, and George came to dinner with me and my father in London towards the end of the war, and he was mourning the difficulty of getting wood because he wanted to build some bookcases. George fancied himself as a carpenter. He was a terrible carpenter. There was a most awful chair he'd made which guests were proudly sat in, and you couldn't be comfortable in it in any position! And you would sit having tea in agony in this dreadful chair that George was so proud of.

Anyway, now he wanted to make bookcases. But where to get the wood? So my father said, 'Well, I might be able to get you some wood under the counter.' So George, moral as he was, said, 'Oh, I would be terribly grateful if you would.' Then my father a few days later said to me, 'Your friend Orwell will be very pleased, I've got him some cherry wood,' which is of course the most beautiful wood, and I told George and George said, 'Oh, marvellous!' and gave my father the description of the lengths he needed. And eventually the cherry wood was delivered to his flat. Then, a few weeks later, George said, 'I've made these bookcases. I'd love you to come over and see them. I'm very pleased with them. Would you like to come to dinner?' I went along, and I thank God my father couldn't see them, because firstly he'd *whitewashed* them, and cherry wood has the most beautiful grain, and it's a *sin* to whitewash cherry wood, it really is a wicked thing to do. And secondly, I don't know enough about carpentry to know what he'd done wrong, but he'd done something wrong. The shelves sort of curved like hammocks. And there were these terrible bookcases.

Tribune

In November 1943 Orwell left his job at the BBC and joined the socialist weekly journal, *Tribune*. He had found his broadcasting work increasingly frustrating, and at *Tribune*, where he was hired as literary editor, a job that took up only part of his week, he could devote more of his time to writing. Indeed, very soon after joining the staff he began *Animal Farm*. It was Orwell's friend Tosco Fyvel, with whom he had collaborated in the Searchlight Books series at the outbreak of the war, who was instrumental in getting him his new job.

> I had begun writing for *Tribune* under a pseudonym, and *Tribune* at that time was a focus for critical and dissident opinion during the war. I knew Jon Kimche, who had worked with Orwell in the Hampstead bookshop in 1935, and Kimche was at that time acting deputy editor under Aneurin Bevan. So I brought Orwell along to Jon Kimche, and I said, 'Why don't you make George literary editor?' and Kimche said that was a good idea, and in that way a whole new chapter in George's career was started.

Fyvel remembers that Aneurin Bevan, who was then a Labour M.P. and became, after the war, a minister in the new Labour government, was one of the few British politicians whom Orwell respected.

> He really flowered under Bevan at *Tribune*. Bevan to him was a genuine socialist. George wasn't too interested in Bevan's schemes for nationalization of the mines and railways and so on, but he was fascinated by Bevan's Welsh working-class background, by his self-education. And Bevan gave him complete freedom. He wrote this weekly column called 'As I Please,' and here he could really hold forth, as presumably he would have liked to have held forth on any subject ever since he was at his prep school, St Cyprian's! He became an outspoken and increasingly popular journalist, though I

don't think he was a very good literary editor.

PAUL POTTS, a young, struggling Canadian poet living in London, was reviewing books for *Tribune* when Orwell became literary editor. He believes that Orwell was far too kind a man to be an effective editor.

> The first review of mine, he put my name at the top of it and at the bottom too! I once caught him putting a ten bob (shilling) note into an envelope to send back to someone some poems that even he couldn't publish. When I saw him doing this he looked as guilty as if he'd been a boy caught stealing the jam. We just took to each other. He was such a relief after other left-wing intellectuals. For me he was the quintessence of an English gentleman with his corners rubbed off. In this man's presence there are kings who could have looked parvenus.

Michael Foot, the former leader of the British Labour Party who took over the editorship of *Tribune* from Aneurin Bevan, once characterized Orwell's "As I Please" column as "the only column ever written in Fleet Street by a man who came into the office deliberately every week with the idea of offending as many readers as possible." Foot was not the only one who noticed Orwell's confidence in his own opinions, a confidence that appeared to some to verge on intellectual arrogance. JON KIMCHE remembers him as one of several "prima donnas" in the *Tribune* office at that time.

> Nobody ever shut George up. Ever. I would discuss with him what he had in mind for next week, we would discuss two or three things, and very often he wasn't clear yet, but his copy, when it came, would be in absolutely mint condition. The only thing I had to watch was libel. He was quite careful about libel, but he would sometimes make a kind of crass statement about something, and I would ring him up and say, 'Don't you think it might be more accurate to say this or that . . .'

But by and large it was fairly neutral material in terms of politics. George, like Bevan and Gollancz and the others, had his hobbyhorses and would hold forth with strong conviction. The only thing to do was to listen and say yes and to ignore it. The one thing you can't do when you have four or five prima donnas on an editorial committee is to argue with them!

On the whole, Orwell in his columns didn't deal very much with facts. It was rather generalized statements and opinions. So long as you didn't make it seem you were censoring something he said, facts didn't matter. If you wanted to change them you could, as long as you didn't object to his basic conclusions.

For me, Orwell became progressively more interesting, especially during the *Tribune* association. I hadn't thought him a terribly interesting person when we had first met in the bookshop. I'd read *Homage to Catalonia* and had uneasy feelings about it, the same way I had had over his *Keep the Aspidistra Flying*. Neither account fitted with the way I'd seen those things. Maybe he saw them more sharply, but in some ways I would say what he wrote wasn't the way it was.

Orwell was always pontificating. He wasn't a phony, but he was affected. It was natural for him to play a role, I think. He played it almost semiconsciously, but it was a role all the time. He created the role early on. It wasn't created by a public, because he had no public when he created the role. In some way it was imposed on him by this duality of having been to Eton and then the Burma Police and then down and out and then suddenly coming upon an entirely new world, with Victor Gollancz and the politicos and the literary people. They were something quite different, and I think he realized that if he was to make his way in this world he would have to play the part of 'Orwell.' I always had that feeling.

When Orwell joined *Tribune*, the other editorial director,

with Aneurin Bevan, was a fellow Labour M.P., GEORGE STRAUSS. Strauss wasn't at all perturbed that his new literary editor might range freely in his column over subjects as far apart as the perils of totalitarianism and the mating habits of toads.

It was just what we wanted in the *Tribune*. We didn't want a socialist writer making comments about socialism or antifascism. We wanted someone whose *outlook* was truly radical and liberal, who wanted decent changes to make life more humane. And he did that admirably. Orwell gave the paper very high literary standards. His writing was exceedingly succinct, simple, effective, with a radical feeling going through it all. He didn't enter into politics. He didn't want to; it wasn't his job. With Orwell it was a question of getting rid of the privileges, unfairnesses, injustices of society as it was. His ideas, though, were very vague; there was nothing practical, no 'how to do it.' That wouldn't interest him. He wouldn't think about it. He saw the world full of injustices, and only by major change in society could those injustices be dealt with. That was Orwell's general outlook.

He liked working on the *Tribune* from the word go. Nye Bevan liked him greatly as a person and admired him greatly as a writer. I found him very pleasant too. He never imposed himself on you. He talked very easily, fluently, on a variety of matters and was a most agreeable person to get on with. But you knew that behind this easy person there was an iron will. He was obviously strong, but he would never try to impose his strength on you. He'd discuss; he'd never force a point. Therefore he was a most agreeable companion.

Tribune was widely read in government departments because we used to say things not said elsewhere. It was the paper most likely to expose mistakes and write about them. It was always behind any action likely to improve Britain's war efforts, but it was critical too. There were articles criticizing Churchill's policies very substantially.

That was a freedom we thought necessary during the war.

A critical issue for Orwell was *Tribune*'s official attitude toward Britain's wartime ally, the Soviet Union, which George Strauss and Aneurin Bevan supported.

Aneurin Bevan and I were sceptical about the Soviet government after their public trials, but we still had a belief that this was a socialist country and good things would come out of it. The most important thing was that the Soviet government was the only government in the world to give material support to the Republican government in Spain. Others talked sympathy, Mexico sent a trickle of armaments, but the Soviet government sent a large quantity of armaments to help stem the Franco advance.

While literary editor of *Tribune*, Orwell also contributed regularly to the *Observer*, and he developed a friendship with DAVID ASTOR, the son of the owner of the paper. Astor believes that it was the question of support for the Soviet Union that eventually dampened and then soured Orwell's relationship with *Tribune*.

He got fed up with *Tribune* in the end because he realized they agreed with him completely on the character of the Soviet Union, but they were not prepared to admit that. Aneurin Bevan went to Moscow after the war wearing a revolutionary beret, which Orwell knew was humbug because Bevan dreaded the place and all it stood for. Bevan was his favourite politician, he told me, but he couldn't bear the fact that Bevan wouldn't speak out and say what he really thought of communism.

I'd met Orwell first in 1942; I was introduced to him by Cyril Connolly. I was just beginning at that time to have a say about what went into the *Observer*. I was trying to liven it up a bit, to make it more in touch with what was going on. I had asked Cyril for names of writers of politics, and he gave me only one: George Orwell. I'd only read his *Lion and the Unicorn* then, which I thought masterly.

I remember our first meeting. It was in a restaurant near the BBC building. I didn't know what he was supposed to look like, but there was this tall, slightly detached person standing there, and as soon as I walked in he came up to me and said, 'Are you David Astor?' and began right off like that, as if he'd known you all his life, and you felt he had. We got down to it, chatted and talked quite lightheartedly about what was going on. And he did indeed contribute one or two articles on politics for the *Observer*, the most significant of which he wrote rather quietly, not at all in his usual style, an article saying that political independence had to be given to India immediately the war was over. It was a big thing with him, and it wasn't being said in wartime. Japan was saying we should get out, and we were saying we should stay there and discuss what we should do later. George was very interested in India because of his time in Burma.

He said he always 'stretched it' with any first article in newspapers, testing the newspaper by putting in something which he thought they might not quite like, and if that didn't go into the paper then he'd be disinclined to contribute further. He was establishing the degree of independence he could expect. I know he did it with *Tribune*, giving them an essay on growing roses! He did the same thing in personal relations, too, to establish how he would be able to get on with you. But he was far too independent a person to condemn people. He just liked to know where he stood. He liked to talk, argue, and discuss, but in a very low-pressure way.

The 'As I Please' columns were far more suitable for him than anything the *Observer* could offer. He did do one bit of reporting for us, going to Germany at the end of the war, because he wanted to see the country before all vestiges of dictatorship had vanished, because he had never been in a country under a totalitarian dictatorship and this was a chance to get in. But it didn't work. Eileen died at that very moment, and he had to come back.

He was a much superior animal to us ordinary journalists. It's his critical essays that really stick in my mind. They are really memorable. For instance, the one on boys' magazines. The *Tribune* articles had a nice bit of his style, but I don't think they had the guts of his thinking.

"She Was a Good Old Stick"

Eileen Blair's death was sudden and unexpected. Toward the end of the war her health had begun to deteriorate. She suffered from debilitating internal pains, and finally a growth was diagnosed. Many of her friends suspected cancer. It was decided she should have a hysterectomy, and in March 1945, while Orwell was in Europe writing articles for the *Observer*, she went north to Stockton-on-Tees, County Durham, to stay with her sister-in-law Gwen O'Shaughnessy prior to having the operation in nearby Newcastle-on-Tyne. Shortly before the operation Eileen wrote a letter to her friend and co-worker at the Ministry of Food, Lettice Cooper.

I remember a typing mistake. She'd spelt it 'gwoth,' and she said, 'There, nobody could object to a *gwoth*, could they?' I didn't gather from this letter that it was anything very desperate. But apparently there was something wrong with her heart, because when they did this operation they ought to have found out beforehand something about the walls of her heart, and they didn't, and that was why she died under the anesthetic.

Eileen died on 29 March 1945. Orwell received the news in a telex sent by the *Observer* office in London, and he rushed home for the funeral. Some of his friends found him surprisingly restrained in his grief. STEPHEN SPENDER was one of them.

> When she died I said to Orwell I was very sorry, I liked her very much. And he said, 'Yes, she was a good old stick.' He was acting then his working-class role. He thought that was what a working-class man would say in similar circumstances. He had this attitude towards her which he presumed to be that of a working-class man towards his wife. But I think he was really rather fond of Eileen.

Paul Potts found Orwell openly grieving.

> I spent the next couple of days with him. We didn't talk much about Eileen. He didn't show his feelings to strangers; he wasn't a stage Irishman at all. But I did hear him call another woman by Eileen's name several times after she died. She was a darling, and she loved him very deeply. And he told me that the last time he saw her he wanted to tell her that he loved her much more now since they'd had Richard, and he didn't tell her, and he regretted it immensely.

"There Was Something in Him Which Welcomed Discomfort"

JULIAN SYMONS, crime writer and biographer, remembers Orwell's saying to him after Eileen's death, "My wife died last week. I'm very cut up about it." Symons was surprised that Orwell wouldn't want to talk more about his feelings. The two men had met the year before, shortly after Symons had left the army and taken a job in an advertising agency. He was at the same time a regular contributor to *Tribune*. His friendship with Orwell developed and remained strong until Orwell's death. But when Orwell had first asked him to come into his office at *Tribune*, Symons had not been prepared to like him.

I wasn't predisposed to like him in advance because I had recently read an article that he wrote, one of his 'London Letters' for *Partisan Review* in America, in which he said that I wrote in a fairly 'fascist strain.' To be even slightly linked with fascism in 1944 was no joke. But as soon as I met him, I did actually like him very much, and clearly he must have liked me, because we went round to the Bodega, a pub in the Strand, and sat drinking and chatting.

I was a sort of freewheeling left winger, and Orwell in a sense was the same. We were also both, in the terminology of the time, 'premature anti-Stalinists.' Even in 1944, to be on the left wing and to be opposed to Stalin's Russia was very unusual and very unpopular, and this was something that applied to us both.

Well, after about half an hour or so, he said in a gruff, apologetic tone, 'Very sorry I called you a fascist or pretty well called you a fascist. I shouldn't have said that.' And he actually in a later letter to *Partisan Review* apologized for this. This is a rare thing for a journalist.

You couldn't meet him without being aware that you were in the presence of a kind of 'original,' a character. He was very tall, about three inches taller than me, and I'm six foot. He was very thin, he had dark hair, quite untouched with grey, which bristled upwards untidily. He had a hatchet face with two great lines carved into it very, very deep — deeper than appears in a photograph. And he smiled more than he laughed, smiled in a sort of grim but friendly manner. When he laughed, he showed discoloured teeth. He rolled his own cigarettes, very badly it seemed to me. His fingers were always stained with nicotine, his nails large, and he had calloused workman's hands. He was rather proud of anything he could do with his hands.

He always wore jackets of which the sleeves were much too short. I know it was wartime, but even so, always to be in a jacket where the sleeve came right up, that struck me as unusual. I never saw him wearing a suit. I remember also, a bit later on, when he appeared one day in what was quite obviously an army greatcoat which had been dyed — dark brown, I think. He said to me with pride, 'This is an army greatcoat. You wouldn't know that, would you?' And I said, 'Well I would, as a matter of fact, George.' He was very naïve in many ways. He really did feel it wouldn't be recognizable.

There was something in him which welcomed discomfort, a sense in which he enjoyed hardship. He surprised me very much on one occasion by saying, 'I hate London. I really would like to get out of it, but of course you can't leave while people are being bombed to bits all around you.' Well, I would have been very happy to have got out of London if I could.

Later on we used to go to lunch with Anthony Powell and Malcolm Muggeridge, who were both working in Fleet Street at that time, and on the menu there would always be, as you might say, one fairly decent thing, one real thing, like liver and bacon. George would never order that. He would always order the thing you would normally avoid — the 'Victory Pie,' as you might say. And he would eat this revolting stuff when it came to him, eat it with the greatest relish and then say, again with some relish, 'You won't get anything better than this *anywhere*.' We wouldn't touch the 'Victory Pie.' So yes, there was a strong puritanical streak.

Once my wife and I invited him to dinner, and all we could get were some very dubious pork chops. It wasn't a matter of choosing your meat well or badly; you basically got whatever the butcher could give you. Well, these chops were absolutely appalling. They really were like the rubber chops you can buy in a joke shop. The knife really bounced off them, but this didn't faze Orwell in the least. He hacked away at them with the greatest zest and said, 'Oh very good, oh very good. That was a *very* good dinner.'

By the time Julian Symons came to know Orwell, he had settled very comfortably into the use of his pseudonym.

I'm not sure I even knew his name was Eric Blair. You could divide his friends between those who like myself always called him George and knew him as George, and those older friends who knew him as Eric. I never heard anyone call him Eric, but there were obviously many people who did.

Julian Symons wasn't particularly impressed with Orwell's "As I Please" columns.

I found them often quite amusing, sometimes really infuriating, and sometimes silly, feeling that who cares about elaborate descriptions of whether, when you're cooking potatoes with beef, you ought to put the potatoes under the beef so that the gravy drips on them! But those columns read much better now, and this is the most impressive tribute one can pay to them as works of journalism. They look much better than they did when they were written, and the best of them I think are marvellously good.

When *Coming Up for Air* was reissued he sent me a copy, and in making various comments on it I said that it did seem to me that it wasn't really a novel, that it was very good as what was obviously a concealed autobiographical account of his childhood, but really it didn't exist as a novel. And he wrote to me saying this is all perfectly true, that he wasn't really a novelist at all, and I don't think he was. He didn't have the interest in character and incident that makes a true novelist. But he said, one of the problems is, one's always got masses of experience like the stuff about childhood and fishing in that book, which one wants to use and can't get rid of except in the form of fiction.

For me, almost all the work prior to 1940 is the work of a rather minor writer. If Orwell had died in 1940 he would be remembered now perhaps as the author of a novel or two, quite interesting period pieces, perhaps as the author of *The Road to Wigan Pier*, a very eccentric book, and that would be about all. All the best of his essays — and they are marvellous works, among the best of the twentieth century, for sure — and the two really important works, *Animal Farm* and *Nineteen Eighty-Four*, all of those were the product of his life and thinking after 1940.

In the early spring of 1945 Orwell gave up his post as literary editor of *Tribune*. His successor was Tosco Fyvel, the man who had found him the job sixteen months before.

> George was desperately unhappy and lonely and wanted to end his stint at *Tribune*. And I felt in the mood, after two and a half years abroad, for a part-time job, so I said I would take over from him. And there, in his office, I found a whole drawer full of submitted manuscripts — articles, poems, and stories. And I said, 'What's all this, George?' And he said, 'Oh yes, aren't they all so terribly bad, but somebody or other has written his heart out, and I just didn't have the courage to send them back.' So I saw at that point his famous honesty had deserted him! He always said that somebody might be able to eat if he gave him three pounds for a book review.

Animal Farm

The publication of *Animal Farm* came at last on 17 August 1945. The manuscript had been pushed from one publisher to another for the previous eighteen months, the problem being that its clear anti-Soviet theme made publishers nervous; Stalin was still a vital ally of the British government, and he and other leaders of the Soviet Communist Party were brilliantly satirized as power-hungry pigs who betrayed the revolution at Animal Farm.

When, a year later, *Animal Farm* was selected for the Book-of-the-Month Club in the United States, with a printing of half a million copies, the income gave Orwell a degree of financial security for the first time in his life. But the enthusiastic American reception of *Animal Farm* was double-edged. Orwell the socialist was distressed to see his work taken up by the American right wing and angered when some reviewers concluded that he had, with this book, finally renounced his left-wing views. FENNER BROCKWAY remembers a long discussion he had with Orwell about *Animal Farm*.

> He came to see me, and we talked quite a bit. It was a very personal conversation. And he was emphatic that he remained a libertarian socialist. A great many people thought that *Animal Farm* was an attack on socialism and that he'd gone back on previous convictions. That is not true. His *Animal Farm* was a protest against dictatorship, against Stalinism. It wasn't intended to be a denial of his ultimate aim of democratic libertarian socialism. We had a long talk about whether there was a contradiction between a collectivist society and personal liberty. He said he didn't regard socialism as state nationalization of industry to be administered centrally by bureaucrats. He saw a society which was democracy through life, and because of that it could still be complementary to personal liberties. He wanted industrial democracy, local democracy. He stood for a libertarian form of socialism.

Animal Farm generated misunderstandings even among those who recognized Orwell's continuing commitment to socialism. Because Napoleon (Stalin) banishes Snowball (Trotsky) from the farm as a traitor to the revolution, a superficial reading of the book might suggest that Orwell was a Trotskyist. Julian Symons remembers how keen Orwell was to rebut this charge.

> He pointed out to me that Trotsky, who in the book was Snowball, was potentially just as big a villain as Stalin, who was Napoleon, although he was the victim of Napoleon, because the first note of corruption was struck, Orwell said — and this is so if you look back at the book — when the pigs secretly have the cows' milk

added to their own mash. And Snowball consented to that first act of inequality.

With the huge commercial success of *Animal Farm*, MARY FYVEL, Tosco Fyvel's wife, congratulated Orwell on having "no more money worries."

> I said to him, 'George, it's wonderful, isn't it?' And he answered me, 'Oh Mary, it's fairy gold, fairy gold.' And afterwards Sonia [Orwell's second wife] explained to us what had happened: that he was so naïve in money matters, so unused to having any money, that he had, in that first year when *Animal Farm* sold well, made ten thousand pounds, of which six thousand was taken by the income tax. Before that he paid so little income tax he didn't even bother to open the envelopes, so once he got ten thousand pounds it didn't occur to him that they'd take away all that amount of money.

The publication of *Animal Farm* by Fredric Warburg marked the end of Orwell's relationship with his first publisher, Victor Gollancz; the latter had rejected the manuscript in April 1944, saying that he was "highly critical of many aspects of internal and external Soviet policy" but that he could not publish a "general attack of this nature." George Woodcock maintains that Gollancz not only turned the book down but actively canvassed other London publishers to do the same. Gollancz' loss was Warburg's gain. Warburg himself admitted that publishing Orwell put his "small and very unsuccessful" company on the map.

Orwell's friend MALCOLM MUGGERIDGE is one of many who see *Animal Farm* as a satire worthy of Orwell's hero Jonathan Swift.

> It is a masterpiece. You can't flaw it. That book, like *Gulliver's Travels*, will always be of interest to people. It's beautifully worked out. Actually, I think George was better writing about animals than about human

beings, because the people in his novels aren't really convincing — but the animals were perfectly convincing! I think he had a sympathy with them.

It's a beautiful piece of work, and it was refused by fourteen publishers (twelve in the USA), so that's a good sign! I asked Gollancz once how he felt about turning down *Animal Farm*, and he said, 'Well, I regret it as a publisher, but I don't regret it as a citizen, because at that time it was right not to have something which was an obvious attack on the USSR.' Even that isn't quite true, you know, because although it was the USSR that people had in mind, at the same time I think that George was really making a case against every form of authoritarian government, and it just happened that the model available at that time was the USSR.

What obsessed George in writing *Animal Farm* was that human beings were going to lose their taste for freedom. And I think that was a just fear. This is what he dreaded.

CHAPTER FIVE

Nineteen Eighty-Four

Writing a book is a horrible, exhausting struggle,
like a long bout of some painful illness. One would
never undertake such a thing if one were not driven on
by some demon whom one can neither resist nor understand.
GEORGE ORWELL
"WHY I WRITE"

From the moment Orwell began writing *Nineteen Eighty-Four* in the summer of 1946, he knew there was a danger that the ill health that had shadowed him all his life might prevent him from committing to paper the ideas he had been formulating for several years. He completed the first draft of the book in October 1947, but he had been increasingly unwell throughout the previous months, his tuberculosis having flared up again, and he spent the first half of 1948 in hospital. Immediately after his release, he went to work on the second draft, and he finished it in two months. Then, in a last burst of energy, he typed the final, clean copy of *Nineteen Eighty-Four*. By then he was seriously ill, and in January 1949 he entered a sanatorium. Until his death a year later he remained hospitalized. His publisher, Fred Warburg, believed *Nineteen Eighty-Four* killed him, and in creating the book that remains his most powerful and widely read testament, Orwell certainly contributed to his own demise.

The particular demon that drove him to finish *Nineteen Eighty-Four* was, as he wrote in a letter to Francis Henson of the United Auto Workers of America, the urge to warn his fellow Englishmen, and the wider western world, of the "perversions to which a centralized economy is liable and which have already been partly realized in Communism and Fascism." The book was a satire and a warning. It was not a prophecy. The physical scenery of *Nineteen Eighty-Four* is drawn from images of postwar Britain, with its drabness, its shortages, its bomb-damaged and unrepaired houses and streets. Orwell's purpose was to show that "the English-speaking races are not innately better than anyone else and that totalitarianism, *if not fought against*, could triumph anywhere."

Orwell apparently feared that the political climate of postwar Britain might lead to a far more authoritarian and heavy-handed style of government than English people had ever experienced — even in the war years, when certain freedoms were sacrificed in the interests of security. He felt that the older politicians, including his favourite, Aneurin Bevan, were sufficiently steeped in the liberal tradition to resist this, but if the government failed to satisfy the extremely high postwar hopes and move quickly to solve the country's basic problems, a new, younger, more violent group would take over and force the changes through regardless of individual liberties.

Orwell's working title for *Nineteen Eighty-Four* was "The Last Man in Europe," and there is no doubt that that was very much how he saw himself at the time — a solitary man fighting against the powerful forces of an advancing machine society, a mass society that would drain from the individual the taste for freedom. "I believe also that totalitarian ideas have taken root in the minds of intellectuals everywhere," he wrote to Henson, "and I have tried to draw these ideas out to their logical consequences."

Nineteen Eighty-Four was published in June 1949, and immediately Orwell found himself explaining what it was he was trying to say. The book was, to his dismay, instantly adopted by the right wing in the United States and used as welcome ammunition in the cold war and as antisocialist propaganda generally. The adoption of Orwell by people of all political stripes has gone on ever since, leading to endless debate and scores of scholarly theses. But Orwell's warning was against totalitarianism of the left *or* the right. Big Brother might be in the Pentagon or the Kremlin; thought control remains thought control, whether the technique is torture or the television set; the degradation of language continues on both sides of the Iron Curtain, whether the subject is the "pacification" of Vietnamese villages or the "liquidation" of Soviet dissidents.

It seems ironic that Orwell wrote *Nineteen Eighty-Four*, his grimmest and, according to some of his friends, his most defeatist book, in a physical setting of wild beauty, amid the country peace and solitude for which he had yearned during the hard and dangerous years of the war. In a 1940 diary entry he writes that he is "always thinking of my islands in the Hebrides, which I suppose I shall never possess or even see." But the dream did come true. Thanks to his friend David Astor, in 1946 Orwell rented an old stone farmhouse at the northern end of the tiny, underpopulated island of Jura, in the Inner Hebrides on the Scottish west coast. There, in his stuffy upstairs bedroom, with his hand-rolled cigarette dangling from his lips, he worked on the manuscript of *Nineteen Eighty-Four*, looking up occasionally to watch the ocean waves crashing on the shore a few yards away.

When he'd had enough of the world of Winston Smith and the nightmare torture chamber, Room 101, he would go downstairs and perhaps take his young son, Richard, lobster fishing or, if he felt strong enough, walk over the moorland to visit his nearest neighbours, a mile and a half away. A fisherman on Jura characterized him as "a true communist — by which I mean a true *communalist*." In an old-fashioned setting of independent-minded but interdependent farmers and fishermen, Orwell wrote of a world in which the old and sturdy values he cherished had given way to cold, modern tyranny.

Orwell was conservative in everything except his politics, and his intense love of the English countryside and its firm social fabric surfaced at the very end of his life, when in his will he asked that he be buried in an English churchyard and that roses be planted on his grave. For a man whose father was of Scottish descent and whose mother was half French, Orwell's rather aggressive "Englishness" was a remarkably enduring characteristic.

Perhaps the strongest thread of continuity in Orwell's writing is his endless love of arguing. Everything he wrote was aimed at provoking people to think about things he felt were important, whether it was tea-making or totalitarianism. In the decades since *Nineteen Eighty-Four* was published, the book has excited perpetual argument and discussion. Orwell would surely be pleased.

"Do You Think You Could Care for Me?"

SUSAN WATSON was George Orwell's housekeeper from the early summer of 1945 to the autumn of 1946. Orwell had moved into a flat in Canonbury Square, in a dingy and unfashionable part of London. Susan was twenty-five, recently separated from her husband, and, with a seven-year-old child of her own in boarding school, quite capable of looking after Orwell's adopted boy, Richard, who was less than a year old when Susan moved in.

I'd phoned him up to make an appointment. He said come round on Saturday afternoon. Well, I went to Canonbury and got lost there! The entrance to the flat turned out to be at the back. So I phoned him from the square, and he said he could see me from the window. He said, 'Don't move, I'll come down and fetch you.' It was a long climb up about six flights of stairs, and his flat was right at the top of this sort of tenement building.

I liked him immediately, and he looked so lonely. We went in and sat down and he asked, 'Can you cook?' I said, 'Not very much,' because when I was married we had a cook-general. He said, 'Never mind, we can live on fish and chips.' And then he smiled, and when he smiled he *really* smiled. It was like the sun coming out. Well, I decided I had to learn to cook, so I got friends to give me a cookery book, and I learned how to make steamed puddings and roasts. He loved roasts especially, roast beef mainly, and potatoes in any form. He was very fond of potatoes. He said one day, 'Your hands need never be cold in the winter; you can always put a baked potato in each pocket and put your hands in.'

He was very tall, very thin, and rather large-boned. He had the most enormous hands I'd ever seen — not strong, but gentle and sensitive. They were huge hands! He had short hair, thick on top, with a cheap haircut done with a razor, an ordinary razor, up the back. A hideous haircut, actually! He didn't look very well. He had a greyish type of skin, with a very grooved face, very much lined. His eyes were marvellous. They were absolutely clear and glittering, and they had humour in them. They were the most vital part of his face. He could look amused or serious with his eyes. He's the only person I've ever known who looked absolutely straight and full at you. Sometimes it was a little disconcerting. And he had a little moustache. It might have been clipped with scissors. It wasn't rich or luxuriant.

I hadn't the slightest idea how well known he was. He didn't emphasize it. I only knew he was a writer and that he had recently lost his wife. Maybe I was unobservant, but I didn't notice any grief in him whatsoever. Absolutely not. But later I sometimes thought he was feeling extremely lonely. He said once about Eileen, 'It wasn't an ideal marriage. I don't think I treated her very well sometimes.' I just said I was sorry. Because there was this lovely picture on the mantelpiece of her nursing Richard very tenderly. I always liked this picture.

Richard was a lovely baby. George was very tender with him. . .

I remember Geoffrey Gorer, who was a friend of George's and an anthropologist. He came to tea one day. And do you know why George invited him? He wanted to see whether Richard had got to the same stage as Gorer's chimps! So I bathed Richard, and Geoffrey sat on the loo and said, 'Oh yes, he's *far* beyond my chimps, my chimps can't do that.' When he said this George was absolutely satisfied, very pleased, and went back with Geoffrey to his house.

When he got back to the flat, he had this enormous earthenware urn full of damsons, laid very carefully on cabbage leaves. And he came and dumped them in the kitchen for me to make jam with them. He didn't know whether I could make jam. That's what I liked about him, his extreme confidence in me, so that having done one thing successfully I could go on and do other things as well. You see, at twenty-five I didn't have the stability and confidence I could have. George was a steadying influence on me. I needed it, and I liked him. I mean, the last time I saw my father I was sixteen, and in a way George was slightly a father figure. He treated me as a guardian would a ward. I think in a Dickensian way George was fond of me.

I did a very wicked thing one day. He'd left his typewriter on the table and gone out, and I wanted to lay the table. So I lifted the typewriter off and he'd left a bit of writing in it. So I thought, 'I wonder what he's writing now. I never know.' So I had a little read. And it said, 'I have a *dear* little housekeeper.' So this shows he was fond of me.

He taught me more or less without commands the routine of the house, how he liked it. He didn't give orders or instructions. Never. What was so awfully nice was that a routine developed. I asked him what he liked. It was a gentle thing. After a little while we had a sort of 'knowing' what the other person needed.

High teas were really the high spot of the day. This was what George looked forward to. We had cakes twice a week. I didn't know how to make cakes at first, so I started on rock cakes. I made a fruit cake, and George really liked them. I used to put orange peel and lemon peel and little bits of dates and raisins in them. And chocolate cake. He liked chocolate cake. Once it went sad in the middle, but he liked them sad, you see. He liked things that went wrong a little. Once I was frying some onions. You had to partially boil them until they were soft, then cut them into rings and put them in hot fat, then serve them on mashed potatoes. We had Windsor chairs with arms, one on each end of the table, with Richard in between, and when I brought the food in, he'd say, 'Gosh boys, this looks good!'

He was eccentric and a little quirky. I didn't mind. I'm very used to writers. My mother was a publisher, and our house was always full of musicians and writers, so this wasn't a change. Also, my husband was a mathematician and philosopher. We used to meet people like Wittgenstein, who I liked very much. I knew Epstein too. If George had lived long enough to have a sculpture made of him, Epstein would have been the one to do it, because he didn't harden his clay, and you get all the lines.

George smoked *all* the time. There was never a moment when he wasn't rolling or lighting a cigarette. He liked Dark Shag and Nosegay tobacco. It had a rather nice smell. And he liked stewed tea. The stronger it was, the better he liked it. My daughter says he put eleven teaspoons of tea in this huge teapot he had, but I think it was twelve. Then he would let it stand until it was thick, like treacle!

He *really* liked carpentry. Some people say he was a lousy carpenter, and maybe he was, but he liked doing it so much and was so inventive that I say he was a good one. That was his small bit of leisure.

He used to go out to lunch to meet people, or just round into the local pub. Then he'd come back and work until high tea at six. When Richard was tucked away he would go off and type away until the early morning. The only interruption he had was when I would take him his hot chocolate in a mug with Queen Victoria on the front of it, a portrait done when she was old. He liked his hot chocolate made in a certain way, too.

He wasn't dour. He was gloomy at times, but he wasn't dour. In fact he had a boyish sense of humour. He asked me if I'd dye his Home Guard beret, and I did, but it shrank. I took it in at teatime to show him, and he got up and put it on his head and took his Burmese sword from the wall and did a sort of waltz. People say he was clumsy in movement. That's not altogether true. When he moved, he moved with agility and consciousness of movement. I also dyed the sitting-room curtains. We had some terribly tasteless and rather dirty curtains, and I said would you like me either to wash or dye them? And he said, 'Would you *really*?' So I dyed them from beige to scarlet, and I said, 'What about you having a divan cover, for a change?' I said it would have to be hessian, and what colour would he like. To my horror he said he wanted emerald green. I said, 'What about your cushions?' And he said, 'Black satin, because they're so sensual.'

I met George's sister Avril while I was at Canonbury Square. Immediately, we didn't like each other. It was nothing that either of us did. She looked at me with extreme disapproval. She was very sour. Although she was a guest, and I'd made a nice special tea with extra cake and all, she looked sour and disapproving. She came with her sister Marjorie, who was a nice, friendly, open, warm-hearted type of person. They were utterly different.

One night Susan was wakened by a commotion in the passage outside her room. Orwell was having a tubercular hemorrhage.

It was a Monday night. He was walking towards the kitchen. I said, 'Can I help?' and he said, 'Yes you can. Get a jug of iced water, a block of ice, and wrap it and put it on my head.' I said, 'You go back to bed, *immediately*, at once!' And he said, 'Thank you.' So I got the ice from the ice-chest, wrapped it and put it on his head, sat by him and held his hand until the hemorrhage had disappeared.

And you know, the strange thing about this was, he never told me he was tubercular. Neither did he go into any detail after this. And because I felt his sensitivity and awkwardness, I didn't either. This was the strange thing about how we got on. Even when he started to tell me something about his relationship with Eileen, or his need to buy new clothes, I just heard a little bit and then I felt awkward, and so I said 'I'm sorry' or 'I must go and do something.' He was very private and very concealing. I mean, think how concealing he was about his health.

I made him stay in bed a whole fortnight. And I got the doctor to him against his request, too. I thought of a ruse. I rang the doctor up and said, 'Look, I'm on my own here and a bit worried about young Richard. He seems to have a bad cold on his chest, so as you're round the corner, could you just call in?' When the doctor came, I buttonholed him and said, 'It's not Richard, he's a very healthy boy. It's George I'm worried about.' And I said I was keeping him in bed because he'd been extremely ill. But I didn't think it was up to me to explain that it was tuberculosis. I thought George should do that, and so I took the doctor in, and the doctor failed to diagnose it, and George didn't tell him. I don't know why this was. I would really like to know.

After that hemorrhage I think he felt his life span was shortening. I think he was worried. And he just started proposing to girls without any real confidence of being accepted. He proposed to them because he felt desperately lonely and disoriented. His working life was very successful and the baby was extremely fine, but as a person his needs were not being replenished. I think he would have loved a wife.

Orwell's first proposal was to Sonia Brownell. Four years later she would become his second wife, but in the winter of 1945, when she was working with Cyril Connolly on the literary magazine *Horizon*, she said no. Susan Watson remembers that Sonia first visited the Canonbury Square flat with Cyril Connolly.

That was the time I bought a bottle of sherry so that he would have something to offer Sonia. Because he never had any drink in the house. It didn't occur to him to drink alone. And tea was a magnificent beverage as far as he was concerned. You could not better it. So when he invited people, it was tea.

Later on I remember Sonia coming again, when we all sat round and listened to the radio. George had a very old mahogany wireless set at the flat. We listened to Darwin's 'Voyage of the Beagle.' George had adapted it for radio. He invited me in that day, I think (a) to meet her and (b) to listen. And he never told me then that he'd scripted it.

CELIA GOODMAN was another of the young, attractive women Orwell proposed to in the first year after Eileen's death. He met Celia just before Christmas 1945, when she and Orwell had accepted invitations from Arthur Koestler to spend Christmas at a farmhouse in Wales. Celia was the twin sister of Koestler's then wife, Mamaine.

We arranged to go up on the same train. So we met at Paddington Station. Well, there he was on the platform, easy to recognize even if you'd never seen him before or had no idea what he looked like. A tall, slightly shaggy figure, with his upright brushlike hair, carrying this baby on one arm and his suitcase in another. We got into the train, sitting opposite one another, and he put Richard down next to him, and after a while I said, 'I wonder if Richard will come and sit next to me.' And George said, 'You'd better try it out.' So I got Richard over to my side and showed him a few books, and we had a perfectly happy time all the way up to Wales.

It's difficult to describe what's special about someone, but I do remember that I was immediately struck by this quality George had. And I was already thinking, by the time we were halfway up to Wales, I would really like George and me to become friends. When we got there George looked after Richard perfectly, as he always did. He used to look after Richard as to the manner born. How he did it I don't know, because he'd never had a baby before. But he'd somehow learned how to bath Richard, how to dress and feed him and everything else. In those days it was very unusual. But he really loved doing it, and Richard simply loved George. If George showed any signs of going off without Richard, Richard used to howl and go on howling until George came back for him. He really loved him.

George didn't have the sort of obvious sex appeal. He wasn't a sort of glamour boy or anything of that sort. But he had this terrific quality which one just spotted. Over Christmas we had a game of Truth and a discussion about what qualities one would like to have if you could choose, and George said, 'If I could choose mine, I should like to be irresistible to women,' which was rather a surprise, somehow. I think George liked me very much because I loved small children, and I loved Richard because he was a very sweet small child. So I think that's what made George feel interested in me. He wanted someone to look after Richard because he didn't have a wife, you see.

What he actually said was that he would like me to marry him, and if I wouldn't agree to marry him would I have an affair with him, and that was it. Well, I didn't know what to do about this, because I mean, if I say I loved George, I wasn't 'in love' with him. But because of this quality, I felt a feeling that I call love. So when I got this letter I didn't know quite what to do, because I didn't want to marry George and I didn't want to have an affair with him either, not because I didn't think George was attractive, but because he was such a serious person that you couldn't have an affair with him without getting involved with him, and if you were going to get involved with him you might as well marry him, and I didn't want to marry him! So, I was in a real dilemma about the whole thing.

Arthur [Koestler] practically went on his knees and implored me to marry George because he simply loved George, and he would have loved to have had George as a brother-in-law. He thought that was a wonderful idea.

Anyway, I wrote back to George some rather ambiguous letter, and George said even so, he'd like to go on being friends with me, so we went on seeing each other.

Arthur Koestler, who had once been a member of the Comintern, admired Orwell partly because he spoke out strongly against communism and totalitarianism.

Arthur recognized George's qualities simply years before anybody else did. I mean, at the PEN club meeting about 1942, he said in ten years' time he'd bet that George would be a most famous English writer, and the bet was twelve bottles of burgundy. Arthur was so clever himself that he spotted how clever and original George was. And of course they both had the same enlightened view of the Soviet Union, which George had never been taken in about, and he was one of the few socialist intellectuals who never had. So that was another bond between them. Arthur once said usually if you meet a writer you've always admired it's a great disillusionment because they're different from their books. But he said there's one person that didn't apply to: it didn't apply to George Orwell, because he was exactly like his books. Which is true, I think.

Arthur also tried to persuade me to get George to wear a dinner jacket, and what he called 'pep him up a bit.' Which is a terribly funny idea, because you couldn't possibly imagine George wearing a dinner jacket. Arthur was rather a hedonist himself, which George disapproved of because George wasn't at all like that. He even wrote in an essay about Arthur that he disapproved of Arthur's hedonism. But Arthur thought George should be pepped up and not live on strong tea and sardines and shaggy suits. He should go out, not to night clubs but to snappy restaurants. Which didn't really fit George's style of life at all.

Celia Goodman knew Sonia Brownell through her work at *Horizon*.

We all knew Sonia very well. She was a lovely person, and she was unbelievably generous. Also she was rather lovely looking. She had enormous shining blue eyes, fair hair — a lovely, rather voluptuous, luscious-looking woman; but the kind of life she led didn't quite go with the kind of person she looked as though she was. She elected to lead an intellectual's life when she wasn't really an intellectual, although she loved literature. She was a person of feeling, that's what she really was, and I should imagine that's what George saw in her, someone with a warm heart. She was a very unhappy person, always. She was basically unbelievably unhappy. She kept up always a smiling façade with her friends because she wanted her friends to have a good time. She was a very good and generous hostess.

ANNE POPHAM lived in the same block of flats as Orwell in Canonbury Square. She was another of the women Orwell proposed to.

My flat was on the floor below George's. We'd met often enough and said hello on the stairs, and once he came to a dinner with V.S. Pritchett, and he and V.S. Pritchett talked *at* each other all the time.

I was working in Germany for the Control Commission. I'd gone there in the winter or autumn of 1945. I came back to London on leave in March 1946, and the day or two before I was due to return to Germany I met George Orwell on the stairs, by my door, and he said, 'What are you doing now?' And I said, 'Governing Germany,' and he said, 'Oh, is it interesting?' I told him I was going back tomorrow. Well, a little while later there was a 'plop' through the door and I found a note which said, 'Dear Miss Popham, I was sorry I did not discover earlier you were back, because there was something I wanted to say to you . . . I wonder if you could look in and have a cup of tea about four, or any time really. I shall be in all day.'

I was a little disquieted by this, but I went to tea and sat with Susan Watson and the little boy Richard at the tea table and had nice brown bread and honey and mugs of tea. He dismissed Susan and Richard and said, 'Go along, now.' Then he said to me, 'Come and sit here. It will be more comfortable on the bed in the corner.' I think he embraced me, and said, 'You're very attractive,' and he said, 'Do you think you could care for me?' I found it all very embarrassing because it was so precipitate, so calculated. I disengaged myself; neither of us had behaved at all badly, but I said, 'I'm sorry, I'm going.' And he said, 'Can I write to you?' And we said goodbye and that was it.

Orwell did write to Anne Popham in Germany, saying that "there isn't really anything left in my life except my work and seeing that Richard gets a good start." He asked Anne to write and tell him if she felt she could "take an interest" in him.

I wrote back and told him that I didn't *know* him. And I was in Germany and he in England, and therefore there was really no prospect of getting to know him. He wrote again, a longer and moving letter. He began, 'I wonder if I committed a crime in approaching you.' Well, I wonder what I'd said to him? And then he says, 'What I am really asking you is whether you would like to be the widow of a literary man.'

I wrote back again, and he said, 'I've thought over your letter a lot, and I expect you're right. Anyway, let's say no more about it.' I think I met him again, but no more was said about it.

I was never at ease with him. He was more than a dozen years older than me. My field was the visual arts. My knowledge and understanding of literature and politics was superficial, if willing, and I felt considerable awe and respect for someone so committed to both, though I didn't find his person or his personality attractive. But his letters to me are, I think, very moving, interesting, and illuminating about his state of mind and feeling at that period.

SIR ALFRED AYER and George Orwell became quite closely associated in 1946 when they were both on the editorial board of a short-lived literary journal, *Polemic*. Ayer was already an acclaimed philosopher, his famous book, *Language, Truth, and Logic*, having been published ten years earlier.

Polemic was fun to write for while it lasted. And it was there of course that Orwell wrote his famous pieces about the misuse of the English language. They first of all appeared in *Polemic*. It was edited by a man called Humphrey Slater, who'd been a commissar for the International Brigade in Spain and then turned very much against the communists because of what he saw in Spain, very much in the same way as Orwell had. And Slater had got some money out of a rich Australian, a man called Rodney Phillips, who didn't mind what his money was used for. Bertrand Russell was also on the editorial board with Orwell and me. It ran to about six issues, and then our angel decided that he could lose his money in more amusing ways and decided to back musical comedies, where at least he could get to know some chorus girls, and so *Polemic* folded.

Orwell and I shared a common outlook — politically, for one thing. We were both radicals, but he wasn't interested in academic philosophy in the very least. I think he thought it was rather a waste of time, that if people were going to philosophize they ought to apply their philosophy to political and social questions. I think the kind of abstract philosophy I went in for didn't appeal to him, and we didn't talk much about it. And he didn't hold it against me that I indulged in it!

Ayer had met Orwell briefly in the Hotel Scribe in Paris in March 1945. Orwell was there to report on the last stages of the war for the *Observer*.

He seemed to like me, and we took to each other at once and saw a great deal of each other. He disappeared for a time because his first wife died and he went back to England. Then he returned, and he never told me anything about it, although by then we were quite close friends. He never mentioned his private affairs at all, although I think I knew he'd adopted a small child.

I remember he talked a lot about *Animal Farm* because it was coming out about the time I was in Paris. And I think he was a little afraid it would play into the hands of people he disliked almost as much as, or even more than, the communists — namely, the English conservatives. And of course it did. I mean, people like Winston Churchill praised it very highly.

There is a legend that Orwell was a very austere man, very much of a puritan. It's not borne out at all by my experience of him in Paris. He used to like going to good restaurants. He liked good food, liked drink. In fact he was a lively, gay companion.

The substantial income from *Animal Farm* enabled Orwell to give up his routine journalism and realize his dream of retreating to a Scottish island to write and bring up Richard in a healthy country environment.

Even today the island of Jura, in the Inner Hebrides off the western coast of Scotland, is a barren and isolated place, supporting a population of no more than two hundred. One single-lane road runs for some seventeen miles along the eastern coast of the island, where most of the settlement is. The deer far outnumber the people. The main village, Craighouse, boasts a hotel, a post office and store, a café and gift shop, a whisky distillery, and not much else. On Jura Orwell rented Barnhill, a large, previously uninhabited farmhouse at the northern end of the island. Here he settled down to write *Nineteen Eighty-Four*.

It was DAVID ASTOR who found Jura for George Orwell by arranging a holiday there for him in September 1945.

I never knew that Orwell was interested in Scotland. He was embarrassed by the name Blair; he thought it made him sound Scottish. He had been brought up in England and felt more English than Scottish. Well, at the end of the war he was obviously exhausted, and I wanted to do something for him, to try and help him have a complete break and a rest. He'd never left London all through the war.

I knew Jura because my family had a property in the central part of the island. I used to walk to the northern part. It's the most beautiful part of the island and certainly the most lonely and remote. So I said to George, I knew this place, and one or two families, and asked him if he would like me to try and get him in. He was attracted by the idea and asked me to do so. I started correspondence with the McKinnon family, who'd been there for generations. I knew Janet McKinnon because she'd helped out in our house in Jura. I wrote, mentioning a friend who wouldn't want a fancy room, and said, 'Could you possibly let him stay in your house?' At first they said no, they couldn't do it. I decided not to take no for an answer and wrote again, and again, and finally Janet agreed.

George went off. I heard nothing from him. Then I discovered he had found an empty farmhouse while he was there and had applied to the landowner asking if he could rent it. I was horrified when I heard this. It was an extremely uncomfortable place to live. There was only one doctor on the island, no telephone, and no proper road. For a person in delicate health it was a crazy place to go, but he was very independent; I would never have dared to advise him against settling there. But then I didn't know how ill he was. If I had, I think I would have said, 'This is crazy.'

The "empty farmhouse" — Barnhill — was owned by the laird of the northern part of Jura, Robin Fletcher, and his wife, Margaret, who operated the estate from their large and gracious stone house at Ardlussa, where the paved road ended and the seven-mile track to Barnhill began. Orwell arrived to set up his new home in late May 1946. MARGARET FLETCHER NELSON (she remarried after Robin Fletcher's death) agreed to put him up at her house for his first night on the island.

He arrived at the front door looking very thin and gaunt and worn. I was immediately struck by the very sad face he had. He'd had a long journey, up to Glasgow from London, then a boat down the Clyde, then buses and boats to Craighouse on Jura, which is seventeen miles from here, and he'd done that last seventeen miles in the post van. He was tall and dark and very haggard looking and a very sick-looking man. He looked as if he'd been through a great deal.

I remember being extremely anxious about letting him be in Barnhill on his own. It was just after the war, and things were very difficult to get. We were miles from a telephone. Food was rationed; there was only one shop on the island, and they kept our ration books and sent up our rations once a week. It was very, very difficult to housekeep. Barnhill had been empty quite a while during the war, so we had done quite a bit of work getting it straight, cleaning it, putting back slates, and generally trying to tidy it up and make it respectable for him before he came. We went up there a number of days doing it before he arrived. It was quite a job. Building materials were hard to get. Everything wanted repair, and there were a lot of urgent jobs to do. But we rather enjoyed the challenge of trying to get it ready. We were very enthusiastic about getting the estate going, getting people back to work here. My husband had met him in London before he came, and explained the isolation and the difficulties, but Eric wasn't put off. He decided it was what he wanted to do and where he wanted to come.

Well, we put him up that one night, and then we took him up to Barnhill. I remember driving along this bumpy track with him and coming to the top of this last hill and looking down on Barnhill. It's just open moorland, really, open hill moorland with very few trees. Very few. There's grazing now for a few deer and a few wild goats. In the summertime the cattle have the run of the place; they're pushed outside from May and stay out on the hills until October. People talk about isolation, but they don't realize until they get here what it's like.

I think he was determined that Richard should have a country life because he was worried Richard would get TB. I think Richard was uppermost in his concern — Richard and his book. He was determined the little boy should have a country life and as healthy a life as possible.

You can see Barnhill down there near the sea. It's a fairly substantial farmhouse with outbuildings, which used to have horses, a cow for milk, and sheep. There's a place at the back where we used to clip sheep in the summer. There's a sheep tank. I think this house was built originally when people had sheep here in a big way.

This is the house. It's got four bedrooms and three rooms downstairs and a kitchen. The first time we came here with Eric, we opened this door and came into a scullery place, a sort of outhouse, through into the kitchen where there was an old-fashioned kitchen range with an open fire and an oven at the side, as houses used to have then, and a fender around. I don't think the fire was lit, but we lit it quite quickly, and there was a table and a chair we'd brought up. I think we'd brought a bed and one or two other things, like mats for the floor.

I remember we showed him round the house, and then we thought we'd leave him once he'd got his cases in. I remember turning to him and saying, 'Look, Eric, if there's anything we can do to help over getting food or anything, you will let me know, won't you, because I'm always ready to help.' And I remember him saying — I remember being quite hurt at the time — he said, 'Oh no, don't worry, I'll manage myself. I'll manage myself,' in a rather abrupt sort of way. He didn't want to cause any fuss, really. I suppose that was quite understandable. I got the impression he didn't mind doing it on his own, as long as he had a roof over his head and a loaf of bread to chew. Anyway, he was completely his own master here. He could do what he liked, when he liked. He had complete independence from other people.

The first few weeks for Eric must have been very difficult and very lonely. But I suppose it was what he was looking for and what he wanted. In a small community like this everybody is dependent on everybody else. Everybody shows their worth, and each person has something to offer. Actually at that time, just after the war, we were all excited. Life was beginning again, with hope for the future.

Often he used to come down to us, to collect his box of groceries which had come from the shop, and he'd say, 'Oh dear, there's no flour, could you lend me some, and I'll repay you when I get some more.' And every week we'd come up to Barnhill to bring up the mail. Every Thursday. We had a farm a bit beyond here, so we'd call in on our way back in case Eric had some letters that were to go out. The only way to order groceries was by post, from the shop at Craighouse. It could take a week or ten days before you got the stuff. Everything was a very difficult operation.

Sometimes we'd be going along up the track to Barnhill and we'd see him sitting by the road fiddling with his motorbicycle. It was constantly breaking down. He'd be sitting on the roadside with bits of motorbicycle around him. He'd sit there in the sun and fiddle for about an hour; then he'd find the sparking plug or whatever still wasn't working, so he'd abandon the bicycle and walk to our house at Ardlussa to see if he could find someone who'd come and help. At that time we had two men, one of whom had been in the Eighth Army and one in the navy, and both were very good with engines and making things go when nobody else could manage. They would come along and get him going again, and he'd chug off or chug back to the house, pick up whatever he was going to pick up, his rations and things, and then depart up to Barnhill. He wasn't very good with engines, although I think he probably thought he was!

This was their dining room. I think he did a bit of writing in here in the beginning. Then, with other people about and people staying and Richard playing, he went to one of the rooms upstairs. It's quite a cold room, too, with a window to the north, a window to the south, and just a small fireplace. Fuel was quite difficult. Either they had to cut wood or get some coal from us, which was quite a job. You see, the first year he wouldn't have cut any peat, it was too late to cut any peat, so I don't think he used this room very much. They're good-sized rooms, aren't they? Very nice and light for an old house like this.

This is the bathroom. Their water supply wasn't very good. They had a tank up on the hill, and if it was dry for several days the water supply became very intermittent. But they managed.

And this is the bedroom that Eric wrote in. It's above the kitchen, and as they had a kitchen fire going, it got a bit of warmth, though it was pretty cold and uncomfortable. He had this Valor stove which smoked very much and smelled horrible. And oil lamps because there was no electricity, of course. This is the desk he wrote on, and this is the filing cabinet. Nobody came up here much, except Richard Rees, perhaps, when he came to stay with Eric. It's quite a big room. I suppose he could work out his thoughts here.

I never asked him what he was writing. When he was here we had small children, and they'd be playing with Richard and so I didn't really have much conversation with him at any time. It was mainly about mundane things like groceries or journeys or people coming up to visit. Just the day-to-day things. But he had this great urge to get this book [*Nineteen Eighty-Four*] finished. An incredible spirit he had, wasn't it, to battle on against all those odds and get it done. I'd read one or two of his novels, and I was amazed how gloomy they were. But one didn't think of him as a gloomy person. *Nineteen Eighty-Four* is terribly depressing. Certainly not bedtime reading.

Orwell's nearest neighbours at Barnhill were Donald and Katie Darroch, who were tenant farmers, or 'crofters,' at a small house a mile and a half farther north, almost at the tip of Jura. KATIE DARROCH remembers Orwell as "a very good neighbour."

He came up quite often to our house and made himself at home. He'd sit round the table and draw in his chair and say, 'I can't resist your scones, Katie!' We always had scones. I still bake.

I wouldn't say he was a very good-looking man. He was tall, and you could tell he wasn't very well. But otherwise he was cheery and happy in his own way. He knew he wasn't well, but he never complained, at least not to us. He came up for milk at first, nearly every day until they got the cow for Richard. Richard didn't come up with him very much; it was over a mile journey. I went down to Barnhill occasionally, but not very often. My brother Donald was very friendly with him. He was a good neighbour and would help you in any way he could. He was one of those who are willing to help anyone.

About a week after Orwell moved into Barnhill, his younger sister arrived to stay. Both their parents were now dead, and Barnhill had perhaps become in her mind the new Blair family home. Margaret Nelson was impressed with Avril's very practical attitude toward life at Barnhill.

She had wonderful qualities. Able to pick out the essentials and leave the unessentials. Maybe the house wasn't very tidy, but at least everybody had good meals. She did what she could to make sure everybody was looked after. There was always a pot of tea, and she was a very good baker. And an admirable housekeeper.

In July 1946 Orwell made a quick trip to London to fetch Susan Watson and young Richard. Immediately there was friction in the house.

Obviously some sort of friction after Susan came. But one didn't ask about it. I suppose there was bound to be, with two women in one house, miles from anywhere. I remember the little boy when he first came was quite slow, just starting to walk. I suppose he'd been cooped up in a flat in London. Eric was terribly proud of him, wanting to show him off. Very proud and obviously very pleased to have him here.

Susan Watson was surprised to find Avril already ensconced at Barnhill. Perhaps fearing an adverse reaction, Orwell had failed to tell her that his sister was living with him.

He didn't tell you things that other people would. He might have told me she was there. After all, it was a forty-eight-hour journey up to Jura. But then he didn't tell me to bring some nice dresses either, only trousers, boots, and sweaters. And one day Mrs Fletcher [Nelson] invited Richard and me to a party and we had no form of transport, so he'd arranged with Donald [Darroch] to bring a carthorse to fetch us. Well, along came the carthorse, and Avril had lent me her brown woollen dress. I was lifted up onto this carthorse, and Richard with me, and at five they came to take us back.

I'm used to cottages and things. I don't mind remoteness. I like to get away. I loved this sort of romantic, magical quality of Jura. It was really beautiful. I'm half Scots, but I'd never been to Scotland. I liked Barnhill. It was made of lovely stone — thick white stone.

I brought my own daughter up to Jura, and George told her the most awful witch stories. We passed a lovely wood, very dark but nice, and he told her a witch lived in the wood on piles of money. (I think George suffered very much when a little boy from a feeling of dire poverty, and he put too much stress on money in my opinion.) Anyway, he told her this money was in little chamois leather bags, and the witch sat on it in this very dark wood. She was only eight or nine and was quite scared to pass the wood. He took her out fishing once and told her more stories about Jura. He was utterly unaware. He wouldn't have frightened her deliberately.

Quite soon it became obvious that Susan and Avril weren't going to get on. According to Susan, it was "a clash of personalities."

One day I was dressing Richard. Avril was sitting watching. His jersey had shrunk a bit, and he yelled when I put it over his head. Avril said, 'You should smack him,' and I said, 'Nobody will smack Richard, it's George's job.' And Avril said, 'Furthermore, it's quite unsuitable you should be living on this island, because you're disabled and you can't get around.' [Susan was slightly lame in one leg.] Avril also said, 'You're not to call George "George." ' And I said, 'He asked me to do it.' She said, 'His proper name is *Eric.*'

One day I was darning a sock, and I'm not very good because my co-ordination is a bit odd, and she said, 'Call yourself a nurse and you can't darn socks.' And it flashed across my mind that she spent so much time knitting that she might darn a few for me. But it obviously didn't flash across *her* mind. So I decided to take this to George one evening. Avril was out helping Katie milk the cow. I went to George and said, 'I *can't* get on with your sister.' I told him I would try, and I respected her as his sister, but she interfered so much, and that we thought so completely differently, and I said, 'I'm not having her smack Richard.' And he said, 'Oh, no.' He wouldn't. He always treated Richard as an equal.

At this time Orwell asked Susan to stay on, and the crisis passed for the moment. The primitive life at Barnhill continued.

George used to shoot rabbits on Jura and saltpetre the skins. He made himself a tobacco pouch of rabbit skin lined with an old piece of inner tube. Talk about old-fashioned craftsmanship! Also he had this awful idea we would like carrageen pudding. You go onto the seashore and pick up the [carrageen] seaweed; then you wash it and peg it on the line to dry; then you stew it. I thought it was disgusting stuff. I wouldn't eat it, but he thought it was good and healthy. He also shot geese on Jura, which shocked the Scottish fishermen like anything because it doesn't do any good to the meat. And Avril used to sit there in the barn, plucking the goose, looking witchlike. Once every three weeks we had a gorgeous goose. I was quite pleased to get rid of them because Richard was afraid of them, although I taught him to go after them with the yard broom and drive them away, because they used to peck his bottom. And they were noisy, filthy creatures. I was always slopping about in goose muck.

Once he had settled into Barnhill, Orwell began to invite some of his London friends to visit. MICHAEL MEYER received one of the first invitations.

I thought it would be enormous fun until I got his letter telling me how to get there. First I had to get to Glasgow, which was about four hundred miles from London, and from there, he said, 'it isn't a formidable journey.'

The journey actually involved getting a train from Glasgow to the port of Gourock, a boat from Gourock to Tarbert East, a bus to Tarbert West, a boat from Tarbert West to Craighouse on the Isle of Jura, and then a seventeen-mile taxi ride along a rough road to the northern part of the island. After that, Orwell informed Meyer, "the final walk can't generally be avoided.' The walk was seven miles along a lonely track across open moorland.

Altogether it was a forty-eight-hour trip from London, and George ended his letter by telling me he was 'chronically short of bread and flour.' I figured if *George* said Jura was a bit primitive, it might be the end of a friendship if I went there! George liked to live in spartan conditions, although he did like good food, but I think Jura sounded not the best place for a chap with TB. George drove himself hard. He regarded any kind of self-pampering as immoral.

One person who did make the journey in 1946 was Susan Watson's boyfriend, DAVID HOLBROOK. Holbrook had been a tank commander in the army during the war, then gone on to Cambridge University. During his vacations he worked on a left-wing monthly paper of the arts called *Our Time*, which fostered interest in socialist culture and was owned by a group of Communists. Holbrook himself was a Communist at that time.

We all knew Orwell was maddening, didn't fit in, kept needling the Left, and was particularly hostile to the communists, but he'd had a good deal of success and was well known and respected as a writer, and I thought it would be fascinating to go and stay with them and have all this brilliant conversation and talk to him about writing and culture.

I'd never been to a place like Jura before. It was marvellous crossing the water on a steamer; that was quite an adventure. But then I got to Craighouse and was rather bewildered how to get to this house up at the north of the island. So I got some bloke with a car who said he'd take me as far as the road went for twenty-five shillings. So we drive up this bumpy track, seven miles I suppose, and we stopped in the middle of nowhere, and he said, 'Well, there it is.' So I gave him the money and he drove away leaving me in open moor. It was an August day, with lots of midges. Then, as he left, this taxi driver said, 'It's the ruttin' season.' And I said, 'What's that?' He said, 'Well, the stags — they're mating. They get rather peculiar this time of year. But you'll be all right. If you're lucky they'll take no notice of you.'

So I set off walking. These great stags with antlers, clashing their antlers and fighting and making this terrible noise — *wooooo* — across the hills. It put the wind up me. I kept walking and half-running and then walking, and eventually I came over a little hill and there was this fellow shooting this goose! He was wearing sort of dismal oilskins, and he greeted me, shall we say, with suspicion and rather cold resentment. I think he thought I'd been sent by the Communist Party. He knew I was a communist, or he'd gathered it, and was very much on his guard.

When I first arrived, Orwell and his sister would have long conversations, with a lot of space between the sentences, of a very gloomy kind, without any reference to me at all. I mean, I just sat in a corner, and there would be this slow, miserable conversation about when he would go over to try and rescue the motorcycle, how Donald [Darroch] or somebody would be brought over to mend the boat. It was as if in the interstices they were thinking how miserably they could form the next sentence. It was certainly not a jolly occasion at all.

Normally we all sat together in this rather dismal kitchen and got on as adults do, but then the laird was going to come with his retinue. I think they were looking over the game, or perhaps they were on a shoot — I don't know. But the funny thing was that Orwell suddenly became very 'Burma Police,' very snobbish, and made it plain to Susan and I that we were 'below stairs.' The laird was going to be entertained in the sitting room, which was not very often used, and they were going to have tea there, and we were not to appear. I think there was some retinue, beaters and so on, and Susan and I had tea in the kitchen with the beaters, and Orwell and his sister had tea in the sitting room with the laird, which we thought was very comic.

I think he was very absorbed in writing *Nineteen Eighty-Four* upstairs on his old typewriter, and we used to tiptoe up and read a bit, and that was pretty depressing stuff. There was this man Winston, which puzzled me, and these dismal sexual episodes. It just seemed depressingly lacking in hope, as he was in everything. In London at the time, after 1945, there was this feeling of hope. A lot of things were happening in theatre, a lot of things coming back to life, the social program of the government was being pushed forward, and everything was opening up. That was what was so strange by contrast, to go into this remoteness and find this man expressing a loss of hope for the future of the world. A man who was ill, rather grumpy, and had altogether fled the world because he feared atomic war, and there with his sister, who was a very dismal woman. It was disturbing to see this man shrinking away from humanity and pouring out all this very bitter hopelessness.

Susan and I kept our relationship very dark. We didn't let on to Orwell and his sister that we were living together. But I think he suspected it. What Susan and I developed was a very jokey, self-protective, ironic attitude to him and his sister, and I think he detected that we were taking the mickey out of him a bit, because he was a very solemn man. If you asked him about the seagulls, he would go on and tell you all about twenty-four different sorts until you could die of boredom. And he'd let everything go, let the boat be stove in, the motorbike had blown its big end, the van had knocked its differential out on some rocks.

He was in a sort of self-destructive mood and used to grumble. He had this wound in his throat which used to whistle, and there was this dismal whistling sound as he went about, and this droopy moustache. And instead of this very lively and entertaining mind, there was this miserable, hostile old bugger that we just had to put up with. It was a great relief when he went out, and even more a relief when his sister went out. We used to go out, of course, to the moors to get away. The sister and Susan used to quarrel about the little boy, and the sister used to ruin all this good food, like she absolutely blackened the goose so it was almost inedible. There were lobsters, but nothing was ever cooked right. Altogether it was a depressing experience.

With other people who weren't carrying on with his nursemaid, and who weren't members of the Communist Party, he was probably quite different. But to me as a young man it was shattering in a way. He was a literary idol, though we regarded him as a sore thumb on the left. But I certainly thought it was going to be more rewarding than it turned out to be.

Orwell and David Holbrook never argued openly, but the hints that Holbrook wasn't welcome at Barnhill were so clear that after a short while he left. Susan Watson, who had come to find Avril's attitude unbearable, left with him. They walked together back down the rough, seven-mile track to Ardlussa, once again running the gauntlet of the mating stags with their clashing antlers. Margaret Nelson remembers the two of them "suddenly arriving with their suitcases." She put them up for the night at her house, and they left the next evening for Craighouse.

Orwell's harsh treatment of David Holbrook is in complete contrast to his brotherly attitude to his friend, the poet PAUL POTTS, another visitor at Barnhill in the summer of 1946. Potts remembers:

> I once went out to collect some wood, and I chopped down the only nut tree on the place. Orwell took great care at dinner that night to be kind to me. I had extra roast beef.

Potts, however, also left Barnhill suddenly, after a falling-out with Avril.

Orwell returned to London in October 1946 and spent the winter at his flat in Canonbury Square. His friend Tosco Fyvel, who had taken over as literary editor of *Tribune*, asked him to resume his weekly "As I Please" columns, which he did until April of the following year. During the winter of 1946 he also resumed his friendship with Sonia Brownell. In the spring of 1947 he returned to Jura. There had been some changes while he was away. A young Scotsman named BILL DUNN had moved in as a lodger with the Darrochs in their cottage at Kinuachdrach, north of Barnhill. He would later marry Avril.

> I'd just come out of the army, and I'd lost a limb, but I could get about all right. I'd always wanted to farm, but I thought perhaps I wasn't fit to farm, so I went to Glasgow University during that awful winter of 1946 and did a term there studying for a B.Sc. in Agriculture. But I couldn't stick it, so I put an ad in the *Oban Times* saying I was available to anyone interested and I wanted

to do some farming. I had no money at all. I got a reply from Robin Fletcher at Ardlussa, Jura, and he invited me to stay for a couple of days and have a look over the place. Well, I liked it, and I liked Fletcher, so I decided to return, and I spent the summer of 1947 working for Fletcher's estate, not being paid but getting fed. It was sort of reconnaissance, you might say.

Jura isn't much different now from then. It's fairly derelict. It's hopeless farming country. In fact, apart from deer, the only thing worth bothering with would be sheep, hill sheep, and even they don't do all that well.

I remember first meeting Eric. I had to go down to Barnhill to get some grass seed which was stored in the byre at Barnhill. It was in May 1947, and Eric and Avril came out of the house. He didn't look at all well. I had heard he'd been shot in the neck in the Spanish war, and I thought that was what was wrong. It wasn't till some time later that I found out it was worse than that. We didn't get on badly. But I don't think we got on on particularly friendly lines. As a matter of fact it was Avril I was more friendly with. We used to go fishing. I was just a friend of the family.

Richard Rees came to stay that summer. He had a certain amount of money, and he sent me a note suggesting I might like to farm at Barnhill, and he would put up a thousand pounds in a partnership, with Rees as a sleeping partner. Well, I grabbed the opportunity to get started. It was suggested I should go and live at Barnhill, and I went in about October or November that year. It was a lovely house, a big, well-built house. I knew him then as 'Eric' or 'Mr Blair.' I don't know what he thought of me moving in with him and Avril. There was no suggestion of disapproval. In fact it was with his approval that I went there. It seemed the obvious thing to do. Orwell was the tenant at Barnhill. But I leased land from the Fletchers.

I remember one surprising little incident. He, Avril, young Richard, and I went for a picnic to Scarba in a boat that was subsequently shipwrecked in the gulf of Corryvreckan. Well, the first live thing we met on stepping ashore was an adder. Eric put his foot on it, just behind its head. I expected him to bash it with the other foot or a stone or stick or something, but surprisingly he deliberately took out his penknife and opened it and slit the snake from top to bottom. He degutted it, filleted it.

Eric was keen on practical things apart from gardening, and he had a small workroom at Barnhill, with a vice and a bench and quite a lot of tools. One day I remember we were making hay at the back of the house, and we broke a hay rake — one of those wooden hand rakes with wooden teeth — and we thought, well, if we take it into the farmhouse, maybe Eric will have a hammer and a few nails and we could splice it. When Eric came out and saw the rake, he was delighted and took over. He got hold of the rake and took it into his workroom, very businesslike, to fix it up in a vice. And then he said, 'Ah yes, let's see, *copper* nails, I think.' And he mended it with copper nails! It was quite impressive.

By May 1947 Orwell had told Fred Warburg, his publisher, that he was about a third of the way through the first draft of a new book that he had first conceived under the working title "The Last Man in Europe." This was the book that would become *Nineteen Eighty-Four*, and Bill Dunn remembers Orwell's early work on the manuscript.

I would hear him typing, but I never knew anything about what he was doing. I didn't go up to his room often, but occasionally I'd go up with a cup of tea. It was the end room, a fairly big room, and it had a window on the south side, looking onto the sea. And it had a fireplace, so I suppose some air could get in or out there, but as you know he smoked very heavily and that awful, thick, black tobacco which he rolled into cigarettes. And he had this black paraffin stove in the middle of the floor, and the window was tight shut and the door was tight shut, and it must have been terribly bad for him.

Occasionally he would come down and would seem to be a wee bit hungry, but he wouldn't really eat anything substantial. He would eat something like brown bread and marmite, and he would seem to enjoy it. Then he would go back upstairs and go on writing away. Sometimes in the day he would go out and do some fishing — not a great deal, because it made him tired. But always in the evening — about five, at teatime — he would chat for a bit and maybe discuss the news on the wireless, and then he'd say, 'Gosh, I should go and do some work.' And that would be the last time we'd see him that day. Ricky [Richard] would only really see him during the day.

Bill Dunn was not the only newcomer to the small community of northern Jura in 1947. A young Polish ex-serviceman and his Scottish wife had moved into a cottage near Donald and Katie Darroch. Like Bill Dunn, TONY ROZGA found his retreat through an advertisement in the *Oban Times*.

There was a job advertised, and I applied and was interviewed by Robin Fletcher. I come from a farming community and loved to work on the land, and after the war I wanted a house and peace and quiet. I loved the place when I saw it. The salary was five pounds a week and free house and two cows for milking. I got the job after two Scottish boys refused it. I worked for Robin Fletcher for eleven years.

When I first came I was on my own — my wife came later — and the Blairs would invite me to tea sometimes. He talked (my English was very poor then), and he offered me one of his books, *Animal Farm*. He gave it to me as a present. I didn't ask him why he came to Jura, but the impression I got was that he came for much the same reasons as I did: hiding from people, fed up with the war, fed up with people. Hiding oneself in a corner and enjoying life . . .

I remember one time — I shouldn't say this, really, because I was poaching in a way — I shot a duck, and with a strong tide running the duck was floating away, so I took my clothes off, and off I went after it. And when I got to the shore, I found I couldn't walk, I was shaking. I was frozen, paralysed, the water was so cold. We had no drink in our house, so my wife said, 'You'd better run to Barnhill, maybe Eric Blair will have some.' So I explained to Eric what had happened, and he poured me a good double black rum, and I was normal immediately. It was marvellous.

Everything was rationed, of course, and occasionally I'd run out of cigarettes. So I'd walk to Barnhill, and Eric just produced a big packet of shag tobacco, which you have to roll yourself, and some black Spanish tobacco. You took one draw, and that's all you would need. That would last you for an hour. It was terrible strong stuff. I offered to pay, but he wouldn't have it. He really enjoyed communal living. When we passed each other in the fields, we'd wave. We only lived a mile apart, but we both felt it was wonderful to see each other. I think he was very happy at Barnhill. He was ill, but I think he was happy there.

JEANNIE ROZGA, Tony's wife, remembers one particular incident that amused Orwell.

The only time I really saw Eric laugh was when Ricky got up to a bit of devilment. Eric was putting in a field drain, and it had taken him months to get the permit to put it in. And the tiles themselves, it took ages to get them to Jura. And when they got to Craighouse they had to be unloaded off the boat carefully, by hand, thousands of tiles, red tiles, and very easily broken. But the day finally came, the tiles were all laid out across the field ready to be put in, and Bill Dunn went off for his lunch. And Ricky was out with his hammer and smashed the lot. About half a mile of tiles, twelve-inch tiles. Ricky — you know, 'ding dong' — smashed the lot. He was only three or four. I couldn't repeat what Bill said; the air was absolutely blue! But Eric howled. He laughed, he laughed when he heard about it. He saw the funny side of it. Bill didn't, of course.

Eric had this big marquee in the garden where he used to sleep sometimes. We went over maybe twice a week, and he would hear us and come in, and if he'd had a bad day we wouldn't see him, but if he'd had a good day he'd come in and join in. He liked company. He had a huge number of friends, and they were real friends, believe you me, to come all that way to see him, even in the middle of winter. I don't think there was a week went past without someone coming up there. And they would stay for ages. Richard Rees was one of his favourites.

Jura is a place for healthy people. I don't think anyone that's sick should live there, not if they want medical attention. But at that time I don't think it mattered where he stayed. He was obviously far better staying where he liked to stay. I think he knew there was no cure for him. He was so ill. I was absolutely amazed he lived as long as he did, because he always looked as though he didn't have long to live. And he made such an effort when people came. I think he was so pleased we came. Even to come in and say hello and pass the time of day was an effort sometimes.

We never knew what he was writing. He didn't even tell us he was a writer. When we knew he'd written *Animal Farm*, then we knew he was a writer. But we didn't think of him as a 'famous person.' He didn't come across that way. To me George Orwell was a tall, quiet, gentle man. I was quite surprised when I read *Nineteen Eighty-Four*. I couldn't believe it; he didn't seem that sort of person. I thought, 'Fancy him writing that sort of book.' I would have imagined something gentler.

In the summer of 1947 the three children of Orwell's recently deceased sister Marjorie came to stay at Barnhill. The DAKIN children were HENRY, who was then an officer in the army; JANE (now Jane Morgan), who had just finished six years with the Women's Land Army; and LUCY (now Lucy Bestley), still a teenager. Their father, Orwell's brother-in-law Humphrey Dakin, had seen quite a bit of Orwell years before when he periodically turned up at his sister's house in Leeds. Lucy remembers that her father "always considered Eric a fool." But the children greatly enjoyed their uncle's company and the chance to have a summer holiday on a remote Scottish island in the Inner Hebrides.

JANE: Barnhill was a lovely house, with a lovely kitchen, a proper farm kitchen with an old-fashioned range. It was cosy because Avril was a very relaxed sort of person, really, and had the knack of making a place seem cosy, even though she wasn't a neat and tidy person. But she created a welcoming atmosphere.

Eric always came in for meals, but he worked hard and had his routine. He'd have his breakfast, and then he'd go up and write; then he always came down at lunchtime, and we had the main meal in the middle of the day. Meals were always fun. There always seemed to be plenty of chat. Eric didn't exactly hold forth; he used to listen. But he liked to have lots of chat going on. He would usually interpolate some funny little thing, and laugh. Like all of us, he liked his own jokes. He liked pudding, I remember. And so did his father. I think Eric must have inherited that. He liked steamed puds, and he'd make nice appreciative noises when he was eating them, which I always thought rather funny because my father hated puddings.

There were fearful adders that summer. I remember Eric once putting one of his enormous feet on a snake and cutting its head off and tossing the body away. I was terrified of these awful snakes. And especially at haymaking, because you never knew what you were going to find underneath. It was lovely and peaceful there. Those islands have a special magic.

Eric looked hellish. But then he always looked hellish, with the graven lines down his face. And he always smoked, and he always had this little cough. But he didn't talk about his health. He didn't complain.

HENRY: Really, most of the time we talked to Avril. She was a chatty individual. She talked our kind of language. Eric would only appear at mealtimes. He obviously wasn't very well, but he was determined to do all the things he felt he should be doing. You know, his gardening and his fishing and going out with a gun to look for rabbits and his pottering with the upturned boat. All this between the colossal amount of typing he seemed to be getting through.

In August 1947 Orwell nearly drowned Henry, Lucy, young Richard, and himself in a boating accident in the infamous Corryvreckan whirlpool, which forms in the tide race between the northern coast of Jura and the adjacent island. The whirlpool is recognized by the British Navy as one of the most dangerous in Europe.

LUCY: There was this talk of going over to the other side of the island, because the Barnhill side is typical Scottish things like stones and seaweed, but not very much nice sand. And everybody said over the other side there were these lovely beaches, and there was supposed to be this abandoned cottage we could stay in, so there was this great expedition. I remember Bill [Dunn], who knew all about the tides, kept saying, 'Well, are you sure you know about the tides? Very dangerous, Corryvreckan, very dangerous.' And Eric said airily, 'Oh yes, yes, I've looked it all up.'

Anyhow, we all piled into the boat, and we had blankets and things. We got to the other side of the island and had a super two or three days. I remember Jane and Av [Avril] were bathing nude. I don't know where the others were, and I was very shocked at this. Then suddenly round the headland came one of the navy ships, and everybody sort of scuttled off!

Then came the time to go back. Jane and Av said they were going to walk over, and Hen [Henry] and Eric and Rick and I were going in the boat. And again there was this great discussion about the tides, whether they were right. So it was all decided, yes, it was OK. Eric knew what he was about. So we all got in, and this boat had got an outboard engine on the back of it. And we had all the gear, the blankets and stuff, and we went off. I forget how long we'd been going, but anyhow, we suddenly realized that the waves seemed to be getting bigger. And the outboard engine was labouring away, and we weren't making any headway. Hen said, 'I think we must be in the edge of the whirlpool.'

HENRY: And round the edges of the whirlpool were dozens of smaller whirlpools. We weren't in the main surge. We were flung this way and that way. Eric was at the tiller. There was a cracking noise, and the engine came straight off its mountings and disappeared into the sea. And Eric said, 'I think you'd better get the oars out, Henry.' And he patted his chest and sort of said, 'I can't help you, Hen, of course.' And so the oars were fished out in this wildly swaying and swinging boat. Everybody was fairly calm. The kids were thinking it was a bit of adventure. I think Eric and I thought it was a little more than that.

LUCY: However much Hen rowed, nothing happened. And at that point a seal popped its head up and looked at us. And Eric said, 'Curious thing about seals, very inquisitive creatures.' And I thought, 'I honestly don't think this is the sort of time to be talking about seals,' because it was really getting to be a bit frightening by that time.

HENRY: I can't say I really rowed, but we steadied the boat, and luckily the whirlpool was going down rather than increasing. He'd only misread the tide tables by half an hour or so. And we edged our way towards an island that was about half a mile off Jura. We finally got under lea of it, but even then we weren't completely out of trouble because it was Atlantic rollers, and they were rising and falling. I'd taken my boots off, actually — I had my army boots on — so that if we did have to swim for it we'd have a better chance.

As we got close to the cliff I clambered up with the painter, leaped from the boat onto a ledge, and unfortunately as the boat went down it rolled against the edge of the cliff and turned over. To my horror, all I saw was upturned boat. But then first Lucy appeared from under it, and then Eric, and he dragged out, from under the boat, Ricky. He must have dived as it went over — a quick bit of thinking. Gradually all three of them were hauled up onto the rock, soaking wet. Very little of the equipment could be rescued from the boat, apart from a fishing rod and one or two bits of clothing.

Anyway, there we sat, and we hadn't been there very long — about a quarter of an hour — and Eric said, 'Oh, we must have something to eat,' which seemed a little extraordinary because we'd only had breakfast an hour and a half before. Obviously that's what happens when you get onto desert islands, you have something to eat! He got his lighter and flicked it a few times, and it actually worked. He tramped off in search of something to eat. The rest of us just sat there. He came back in about half an hour and said, 'Extraordinary birds, puffins. They make their nests in burrows.' And then on the subject of food he said, 'I did see some baby seagulls, but I didn't have the heart to do anything about it.' So food was forgotten for the time being. And he also did say, when the others were out of earshot, that he thought we'd had it. And I agreed, I thought we were lucky to get out of it, really.

LUCY: I suppose we must have been on this island about two hours, and we were debating how we could attract anybody's attention. Then, much to our joy, a lobster boat came round purely by chance. I think they were taking some visitors round. So we all stood up and waved and cheered, and they came along and more or less told us what fools we were to have been there at that state of the tide. They took us off, and they were going to offer to take us round to Barnhill. I'd lost one shoe in all this, and scraped my ankle, and Henry hadn't got any shoes, but Eric, who had got both *his* shoes, said, 'Oh no, it's all right, we'll walk back.' I remember being furious.

So we were landed back on Jura and had to walk over. Well, it was four or five miles over the island. Eric was striding off all right with Rick on his back, but we were staggering along. Anyway, we finally got back, and there were Jane and Av making hay. And they looked up and said, 'I thought you were coming back by boat.' And Eric said, 'Oh, we lost the boat,' without any mention of the drama that had taken place, with a calm acceptance of things that was typical of Uncle Eric. He was sweet and kind, but in another world.

HENRY: They simply didn't believe we'd been wrecked in the Corryvreckan. They really took a bit of convincing. Much later somebody said to me about this incident, 'Of course it was a deathwish on Eric's part.' And I said I hardly thought so; if he'd had a deathwish he'd hardly have taken three other people with him. He wasn't that kind of chap at all.

"Ricky"

RICHARD BLAIR, or "Ricky" as he was known by many, was nearly three and a half years old at the time of the Corryvreckan incident. Today, an agricultural engineer and a married man with a family of his own, Richard is able to remember a few details of that plunge into the water in the summer of 1947.

> Prior to the accident I'd been saying, 'Up-down, splish-splosh,' so I had evidently been enjoying the scene up to that point. I suppose this ceased abruptly when we were dumped into the water! I don't remember there being much talk about the whole thing afterwards, although we came fairly close to drowning. It certainly didn't do my father's health much good, because his lungs flared up again and he was not at all well later on.

The problem of living so far from any professional medical help affected not only Orwell but also Richard, who fell and gashed his head that same summer.

> I was watching my father making a wooden toy for me, and I was standing on a wooden three-legged stool. I must have leaned too far, because I went crash-bang-wallop onto a large Victorian jug. I split the jug wide open and my head as well. There were blood and tears, and I still have the scar. The problem was how much damage had I done to myself, and what was my father going to do about it, since the nearest doctor was on [the island of] Islay, thirty miles away, a two- or three-hour journey. As it happened, it wasn't that serious. The doctor came and stitched me up. But it was quite a nasty cut.
>
> I liked living at Barnhill. It was marvellous for a child, with acres of land to roam on. Nobody minded too much where I went. The only thing to worry about was the occasional adder that came into the garden. There were quite a few around. We had a boat, and we'd go lobster fishing. We'd catch fish and a few lobsters.

My father and Avril used to read to me when I was a child of three or four; Beatrix Potter was a great favourite. I was not aware of being lonely. There were always things to do, messing around on the farm. My father was concerned that my speech development was slow, perhaps because I wasn't able to play with children of my own age. I used to go down to Ardlussa House, which was fun. I played with other children there, and there were always floods of tears when the time came to leave. But we always had people trooping in and out of the house during the summer. Lots of visitors. Richard Rees came, and my aunt, Gwen O'Shaughnessy, with her adopted daughter, Catherine. Catherine and I made ourselves sick one day hiding in the bushes, eating peas, pods and all, and strawberries. Anything we could find!

We had a pig, I remember, a sort of family pet, really, which we fed on scraps and fattened. Then the day came when it was time for the pig to be killed. I was told to go into the house, and I knew something awful was going to happen and that it had something to do with the pig. A little later I heard terrible shouts and awful squeals. There was a lot of drama that day. Then, once the pig was dead, we ate it quite cheerfully. We had it smoked for bacon. It fed us for quite a long time.

My abiding memory of my father is in that summer of 1947. I found a revolting old pipe in the garden one day. I took this new-found object into the dining room. My father used to throw his cigarette ends in the fireplace, so I took all the cigarette ends out of the fireplace, put them in the pipe, and then asked him for a light. Nothing was said, my father just passed down his lighter, and I tried to light the pipe. I couldn't get it going, because it was packed so tight. Later, though, I did get it going, and I was sick. On reflection it was obvious my father was laughing his head off. He thought, 'Let's see what will happen if he gets this thing going. With a bit of luck it will put him off smoking for life.'

"His One Desire Is to Get This Book Finished"

Orwell finished the first draft of *Nineteen Eighty-Four* in October 1947. The effort had exhausted him, and he was now suffering from inflammation of the lungs. A chest specialist was called from Glasgow. Accompanied by his friend Richard Rees, Orwell made the journey down the track to Ardlussa House, where Margaret Nelson had prepared a room for his examination by the doctor.

We had him in bed for the specialist to see him. It was too difficult for the specialist to go up to Barnhill. And when the doctor came he said to us, 'Look, keep him here, he may have a severe hemorrhage any moment. On no account must he go on that bumpy road to Barnhill.' But of course Eric wouldn't hear of it. We had small children, he had TB, and anyway he wanted to get back to Avril and little Richard. We urged him to stay, explaining that we had been keeping his things separate and would destroy his bedding, etc. We said a few more days wouldn't make any difference.

During this time he had long talks with my husband Robin. They had both been to Eton, but Robin twelve years after Eric. Robin used to go and sit with him in the evenings. One time I remember him saying to me, 'You know, he *knows*. His one desire is to get this book finished while his health holds out. He realizes his health is very bad.' Eric knew he hadn't very long to live. Once I thoughtlessly left painkiller tablets for toothache by the bed he was using. I was in the garden when I remembered and hurried back in. But I needn't have worried. Eric's concern was to have enough strength left to finish his book. I think he knew he was racing against time. Anyway, he wouldn't stay. So Richard Rees came down in the lorry from Barnhill and off they went, luckily without any adverse effects.

After tuberculosis had been diagnosed again, Orwell became terrified that he would pass his disease on to

Richard. He had been boiling Richard's milk for some time, and now he tried to find a TB-tested cow. At that time Richard Blair didn't know why his father was trying to keep him away.

He was very concerned about not being able to see me as much as he ought to. His biggest concern was that the relationship wouldn't develop properly between father and son. As far as he was concerned it was fully developed, but he was more concerned about son-to-father relationships. He'd formed a bond with me, but it wasn't as strong the other way around. I don't know if at that age a child is aware of love. Three square meals a day are probably more important. I remember at Barnhill at that time he would spend days at a time in bed. But he would still be working with his typewriter at night. I would hear it clattering away. But when he played with me, he treated me as if he were quite fit and healthy. I was always happy when he'd appear to play or just to talk. I think he bore his illness with great fortitude.

It's a strange feeling having George Orwell for a father. I can be on the outside looking in, seeing George Orwell simply as a well-known figure. But I also feel that I was his son, and part of him. He was my father — there was no question about it, although I'd been adopted by him. He was my father.

Lettice Cooper saw Richard long after Orwell died.

When I saw Richard again a few years ago he told me that he'd never known if either of his parents loved him. You see she died before he was a year old, and George, as soon as he knew he had TB, was terrified to let Richard come near him, and he would hold out his hand and push him away — and George would do it very abruptly because he was abrupt in his manner and movements. And he wouldn't let the child sit on his knee or anything. And I suppose Richard had never asked. Children don't, do they? And he said, did they love him? And I said they both did, so much. It was very hard, that, wasn't it?

PROFESSOR JAMES WILLIAMSON was a junior doctor at Hairmyres Hospital near Glasgow, where George Orwell was treated for tuberculosis in 1948. Orwell had entered the hospital five days before Christmas 1947. Dr Williamson joined the Thoracic Unit in February 1948 and saw Orwell virtually every day until he left to go back to Jura in July. Although by then the new Labour government in Britain had instituted its National Health Service, Orwell was, Dr Williamson believes, a private patient. Because of this he occupied a room with only two beds, although most of the time the second bed was empty.

His disease was of a very chronic nature. It was confined to the upper part of both lungs, mostly his left lung, and he had positive sputum. There were tubercle bacilli in his sputum, which means he was infectious. But he wasn't the sort of classical consumptive of nineteenth-century fame, coughing up lots of sputum and continually disappearing and using sputum mugs and that sort of thing. Most patients had sputum mugs on their bedside lockers. I don't remember him with that at all. Mind you, I don't think there was any room for anything on his bedside locker because there were always books everywhere. So he was never very ill with severe wasting and drenching night sweats. But he'd probably forgotten, almost, what it was like to feel completely well.

There wasn't much 'cavitation.' It was what we call fibrotic tuberculosis. His lung would have been tough, like leather. With chronic fibrotic TB you could live for quite a long while, although at a lower level of health and fitness and comfort, as he did. He lived for many years with TB.

In 1948 there was not yet a cure for TB. The treatment Orwell received at Hairmyres Hospital was designed to rest the lung and give tubercular lesions a better chance to heal. The technique employed involved paralysing the phrenic nerve, which controls the expansion and contraction of the lung.

It was a fairly trivial operation: you could do it in five minutes. You just pull the muscle aside, expose the nerve, and tweak it with a pair of forceps. The patient would get one sudden pain, and the diaphragm would jump, and that was the diaphragm paralysed for three to six months, until the nerve recovered again. Then we pumped air into his abdomen. The diaphragm was pushed up by this, and the lungs were collapsed. You put anything from four hundred to seven hundred cc of air in, under low pressure, with a special machine, through a needle which was a fairly elephantine-looking thing, a hollow needle about three inches long, actually. The first time you did it, you used a local anesthetic, because you had to go very cautiously and advance it very slowly. But after that you just stuck it in, because patients agreed that if it was done expertly, one sharp jab was better than all this fiddling about with anesthetics and things.

I remember he used to dread each 'refill' and couldn't relax at all when he was on the table. But he never complained. In fact we all noticed how much self-control he had. There was never a gasp, or any kind of noise from him when we did this.

I don't think he would ever have been terribly infectious. The person who is highly infectious is the person who is coughing a lot, whose sputum has a lot of TB bacilli in it. He wasn't coughing a lot, nor was his sputum, as I remember it, terribly strongly positive. But he would still be a potential danger to other people, particularly to young people like his son.

It was a very long trek from London to Glasgow, but Orwell's friend David Astor made the journey to Hairmyres Hospital several times.

I spent a bit of time with him there. He'd become much thinner, but he was always a person who had a 'presence,' whether he was dying or not, and you couldn't help treating him as himself. He didn't ask for pity. The really awful part of the treatment was they put a sort of rod down his throat, slithered it down, to look at his lungs. In those days it was the only way they could find out. It was a hideously painful thing, and very frightening. He spoke of this with a fair amount of horror. I felt in *Nineteen Eighty-Four* the torture scenes could have derived from the sensations of this experience.

One funny thing was that Orwell discovered that the doctor [Dr Bruce Dick, Williamson's senior colleague] had been on the opposite side to him on the Spanish civil war, and he decided not to engage in political talk. He was half amused that he'd fallen into the hands of a doctor who was politically completely disapproving of him. The doctor asked me to come and tell me what I knew of Orwell. He was obviously struck by him. I said, 'Can I do anything?' and he said that streptomycin from America would be the only thing that could be of use. [Streptomycin had been discovered in the USA in 1944 and would prove to be extremely effective against tuberculosis. It was still being tested in Britain and was therefore not available for use.]

I applied to the then Minister of Health, Nye Bevan — I knew him as a friend — and he didn't hesitate to get me permission. You needed exchange-control permission to import the drug, and I had connections in America, so I could do it. It was a desperate attempt. Streptomycin was very experimental then, but George was willing to take any chance. He knew he was in a bad spot.

Dr Williamson remembers the arrival of the streptomycin at Hairmyres Hospital.

I think it was a hundred grams we got, which would have been enough to start him off. He got, I think, one injection a day, an intramuscular injection. Or it may have been half a gram twice a day. Anyway, he seemed to be perking up, but within a short space of time he developed this fearful allergic reaction. He came out in a generalized skin rash; his whole skin became red and inflamed and itching, and his mouth became inflamed, and ulcers appeared and his eyes were all red, and his hair started to come out. But he was very stoical about it. I mean, most people would have been round the bend with that.

Subsequently we learned that if somebody got an allergic reaction, you could desensitize them by going back and starting with a tiny dose, and giving a slightly larger dose the next day, and so on, just verging on an allergic reaction. But we didn't know that at the time. So his drugs were given to two other patients at the hospital. If it had been two or three years later, it would have been pretty easy to cure his TB. But you see, he might still have died from a hemorrhage because the hemorrhage was really a sort of indirect result of the TB. You can actually die of a hemorrhage although the TB is cured, because if you have an area of the lung where there is an artery crossing, and that area is exposed and eroded because of the damage done by the old TB, then you can bleed to death from that. In the end, when he left us, he was in fact a bit better. We did get his sputum negative, you see.

Bill Dunn had visited Orwell during his seven months in Hairmyres Hospital and, by the summer of 1948, thought he "looked better, quite well."

When he came back to Jura he had explicit instructions not to do any physical work, but Avril frequently had to grab a barrow or a rake out of his hands to stop him. Then he began typing the second draft of *Nineteen*

Eighty-Four. He worked at it all the time. And his health began going down. I think he felt pretty ill.

Orwell completed the revised draft in November 1948.

He came down from his room and said, 'Well, I've finished it.' And we celebrated by opening the last bottle of wine we had in the place. And Avril said to him, 'What's the title, what are you going to call it?' And he said, 'I think *Nineteen Eighty-Four*.'

The revised manuscript was a mess. Orwell had scrawled corrections and cuts all over his original typescript. He wrote to his publisher Fred Warburg, asking if Warburg could send someone to Jura to help him. "A skilled typist under my eye," he wrote, "could do it easily enough." But Warburg failed to find anyone willing to go, and Orwell typed it out himself, averaging an exhausting five thousand words a day. Warburg later said in a BBC radio interview that "by the time he'd finished it, he was all through. I think *Nineteen Eighty-Four* killed him."

Orwell was confined to bed throughout December 1948. Bill Dunn and Avril were becoming quite alarmed about the fact that any slight exertion would send his temperature up. Plans were made for him to leave Jura and go, once again, into hospital. The last entry in the domestic diary he kept while on Jura is for Christmas Eve 1948: "Snowdrops up all over the place, a few tulips showing, the wallflowers are still trying to flower." It was the isolation of his Scottish retreat that was the potential danger, not the weather, which was actually quite mild.

In January 1949 Orwell made his last trek down the stony, potholed track to Ardlussa, the first and most hazardous stage in the long journey south to the sanatorium he had arranged to enter, in Gloucestershire. Bill Dunn remembers that final trip.

It was January, and at night, and in order to get the steamer the following morning he had to get down to Ardlussa that night and stay with one of the villagers.

Then he'd get the mail van about 8:00 in the morning, and it would take him down to the boat. Well, we started off in my Austin 12. It was basically a good car, but it was messed up by the awful roads. And halfway between Barnhill and Ardlussa it got bogged. Just sank into a soft bit on the road, and no way could you get it out. At that time we had a lorry at Barnhill, which Richard Rees had bought for the farming, and it was a bit of a white elephant, but it did some good that night because Avril and I walked back to Barnhill and got this lorry out, leaving Eric and young Richard sitting in the car waiting.

Richard Blair, by then a boy of five, also remembers the incident well.

We just sat there together, talking. It was raining. It was cold, and I do remember my father giving me boiled sweets. He was a very sick man, but he was quite cheerful with me, trying to pretend that nothing was wrong. It was getting dark by the time Avril and Bill got back with the lorry.

Bill Dunn:

We had ropes and things, and we tried to pull the car out backwards because we didn't think for a second we'd be able to get past, it was such a narrow track. And she wouldn't come out at all. So we tried to get round. And it must have been the only place on the whole road which was firm just off the road, and we just got past. And of course, once past, we just got them into the lorry and went down to Ardlussa. I remember Eric saying, when we'd failed to pull the car out backwards and took the risk of getting round on this awful boggy land, it was a chance in a million of getting past, and he said, 'It was like staking your all on zero.' That's what he said. And we got down to Ardlussa about ten at night.

The new sanatorium was at Cranham, in the Cotswold Hills, not far from Gloucester. Fresh air and rest were the 'treatments.' Orwell lived in a wooden chalet. "The most persistent sound," he wrote, "is the song of birds." Bill Dunn:

> Eric wrote to Avril from Cranham saying he wanted Rick to come down to see him. I think it was the following summer. He wanted Rick to see him before he looked too terrible, too horrible. That was pretty frightening, you know. Rick did go down and stayed near the sanatorium.

Richard Blair:

> I was sent to stay with Mrs Wolf at a place called Whiteway, which was an anarchist colony. I was there some time, because I remember going to school down there. When I saw my father at Cranham I used to say, 'Where does it hurt, Daddy?' because I couldn't understand why he said it didn't hurt, but he was in bed. I couldn't relate to that at all.

Orwell's niece Jane Morgan travelled down to Gloucestershire with her father, Humphrey Dakin.

> We went down in a motor bike and sidecar. It was a very pleasant, slow journey. When we got there I was rather horrified, really; it seemed rather stuffy and untidy and cluttered, not airy and bracing as one would suppose. Anyway, Eric was very pleased to see us. I don't think he was expecting us. I remember him saying, 'Hello, Hump, how nice to see you, come in and have a drink.' And he reached out and got this bottle of rum from his locker, which again horrified me: I thought you weren't supposed to have alcohol if you were tubercular. We had a nice little chat. I think TB has this effect on you, you sort of have this ebullient attitude, not that Eric was ever ebullient really, but people who have TB don't

always seem to realize quite how ill they are. He did look terribly ill, and cadaverous, and worn.

Brenda Salkeld, Orwell's friend from his Southwold days, also visited him. She came away convinced that he knew he was going to die and that his main wish was to be told exactly how long he'd got left, whether it was "six months or a year."

"Nothing Ever Dies"

In February 1949 an old friendship was suddenly revived. Orwell's childhood companion JACINTHA BUDDICOM wrote to him, having found out that the Eric Blair who had written romantic poems to her as a teenager was none other than the author of *Animal Farm*, one of the best books she'd ever read. For years she had been disappointed that her friend "Eric the Famous Writer" had apparently not managed to fulfil his ambition since she had never seen his name on the cover of any book. They had lost touch when Orwell went to Burma nearly thirty years earlier, and Jacintha had no idea that Eric had adopted a pseudonym.

It was Auntie Lilian who wrote and told me. She'd seen in some literary magazine an article saying that Eric Blair was George Orwell, and I was very pleasantly surprised. I was terribly impressed with *Animal Farm*; I thought it was a miraculous book. I rang up the publishers, and someone there told me Eric was very ill in Cranham and gave me the address, and I wrote to Eric there.

A week later Jacintha received two letters from Orwell, both in the same envelope, the first written on Valentine's Day 1949 and the second the following day. The first was straightforward and factual. The second was more personal.

He starts, 'Hail and Farewell my dear Jacintha,' and then he says, 'Ever since I got your letter I've been remembering. I can't stop thinking about the young days with you and Guin and Prosper and things put out of mind for twenty or thirty years. I am so wanting to see you. We must meet when I get out of this place.' His last paragraph, you see, begins, 'Are you fond of children?' Well, that rather unnerved me because if he'd got a motherless child that he wanted to find a new mother for, well, I didn't feel it was up to me. I didn't want to encourage him in any ideas of that sort. I didn't want to put ideas into his head.

Jacintha didn't visit Orwell at the sanatorium. Instead she began reading all his books, discovering what "Eric the Famous Writer" had written. She liked *Burmese Days* and the essays, but was shocked that Eric had taken up arms and fought for a foreign cause in Spain. She enjoyed seeing how much of Henley-on-Thames she could find in Orwell's description of Lower Binfield in *Coming up for Air* but wondered why his heroines all seemed to end up dowdy and defeated. She exchanged several more letters with Orwell: "The last letter of all from him was the one he wrote on June eighth, 1949, saying, 'Nothing ever dies.' " This letter coincided exactly with the publication of *Nineteen Eighty-Four*. Jacintha read the new book immediately and was horrified.

I thought *Nineteen Eighty-Four* was a frightful, miserable, defeatist book, and I couldn't think why he'd written it, so I didn't write to him at all. I didn't answer his last letter, because all I could have said about *Nineteen Eighty-Four* was that I thought it was unspeakable, and it didn't seem at all the thing to write and say that to him. So I lost touch with him completely again. It never occurred to me to go up to Cranham and see him. I don't know, I never did seem to treat Eric perhaps as I might have.

Not long after *Nineteen Eighty-Four* was published, Tosco Fyvel and his wife made the trip to see Orwell at the sanatorium.

George was flat on his back, looking pale and thin. It was a terrible shock to us to see how ill he was. I'd done a talk about *Nineteen Eighty-Four* on the BBC Third Programme with Malcolm Muggeridge, and George told us he had listened to it and enjoyed it. Because he was so ill, we had tried to make it a light-hearted discussion, and I remember we said the famous scene in Room 101 looked to us rather like the sort of talk that small boys at a boarding school might indulge in in a dormitory, where one says, 'What's the worst thing in life you can imagine?' and the other says, 'Well, a cage full of rats is put over your face and the rat first eats your nose and then your lip and so on.' And then the prefect shouts, 'Silence all of you, lights out,' and that's the end of it. George told us he'd laughed loudly when he heard that.

Anthony West has written a rather neat essay about Orwell in which he showed that *Nineteen Eighty-Four* is in a way a reflection of Orwell's experiences at his prep school, St Cyprian's, and that the rules of the Party which had to be obeyed were like the rules of the prep school. Well, the point is of course that Orwell drew on his own psychological traumas in writing *Nineteen Eighty-Four*, and probably, without the neuroses of Eric Blair, the works of George Orwell would never have been written. But to reduce the works to these neuroses is, I think, a rather naïve reduction. I think to say that Orwell, in writing *Nineteen Eighty-Four*, was preoccupied or even obsessed with sadomasochism is quite absurd. He was writing, after all, about dictatorship in an age of real dictatorship, when Hitler and all his horrors were only destroyed two years or so previously, and Stalin was still in full control. And *that* was what he was writing about.

When *Nineteen Eighty-Four* was first published in the United States it was taken up by the extreme right, to George's distress because he did not mean it to be an attack on socialism. Indeed, in his definition of 'Newspeak' he says quite explicitly that the Party of *Nineteen Eighty-Four* called its system 'Ingsoc' because they had taken over the name of British socialism as Hitler called his followers 'National Socialists.' One of the criticisms of *Nineteen Eighty-Four* was that he made his totalitarian party have no ideology. It was not communist, it was not nationalist, not racist; it wielded power for power's sake. This was a very good forecast of the Moscow of the 1980s, where the old ideology and its fervour of Marxism/Leninism is long dead.

What he felt really was that we were facing a great social change in society in which the old bourgeois institution of the landed gentry, and the local trades union branch, and the local government, and the individualism in arts and letters were all either disappearing or on the retreat, and a new mass society was taking over. Although he died before he could have seen the mass audiences looking at television advertising, in a sense that was already in his mind. *Nineteen Eighty-Four* is in a way prophetic of a world in which, to many television viewers, the stars are for the moment more real than the people they know. And he felt a society like that could very easily be abused. Although *Nineteen Eighty-Four* was directly an attack on Stalin's communism, it also was, in a faint way, an attack on American big business, mass entertainment, the society where elections are decided by political slogans and everything becomes show business. What he felt was the old bourgeois culture in which he had grown up and which he no longer supported was coming to an end. But he was sad at its passing. And he felt that the new collective society that was coming held grave dangers.

Orwell told his friend JULIAN SYMONS that the title of *Nineteen Eighty-Four* was not meant to convey what life was going to be like in the year 1984; it was simply an inversion of the last two digits in 1948, the year he finished the book.

Hence all the things that people say now about whether the predictions made in *Nineteen Eighty-Four* have come true, or might come true, or don't they now look rather absurd, are beside the point, because it isn't a book of prediction, it is a book which is largely about the problems in Britain in 1948. You can see, if you read the first thirty to forty pages of *Nineteen Eighty-Four*, the similarity between the atmosphere in the book and the general atmosphere of life in Britain in 1948.

Orwell, in the last five years of his life, after the coming to power of the Labour Party, became more and more disillusioned with the sort of practical socialism that tried to measure everything out, and that in measuring everything out, and endeavouring to do it fairly, also involved certain erosions of freedom, individual freedom. He came to feel that there was too much bureaucratic operation at the top of the Labour Party. And so he felt perhaps more sympathy with the anarchists he met at this time than he did with the Labour Party. But he never denied the idea that the state had to have authority, which is, of course, the basic difference between any socialist and an actual believer in anarchism. He would have thought there must be authority to preserve the essential decencies of most people.

It upset him at the time that the book was being seen as being written by a man who was disillusioned with socialism and that socialist beliefs would lead to the world of *Nineteen Eighty-Four*. In Britain at the time this wasn't stressed so much, but it was in America, and Orwell issued a statement saying this was not so, the book is not an attack on socialism. It is a book, he said, about what the possible perversions of socialism might create in the future, and by the perversions of socialism he meant primarily of course those in the Soviet Union. In fact Orwell remained a libertarian socialist until the day he died.

On 3 September 1949 Orwell left Cranham for a bed in a London hospital, where, his friends felt, he could be given first-class care. Room 65, at University College Hospital, would be George Orwell's last home. The head nurse of his ward was AUDREY DAWSON.

His room was quite small, with just one window in it and standard hospital furnishings: a high bed which could be tipped, a bedside table with a telephone, a dressing table, a wardrobe, an armchair, one or two upright chairs, and of course the commode. Because he was a severe case of tubercle, with positive sputum, he had special white china, a heavy china because it had to be boiled every time. Everything he used had to be boiled.

He was always, as I recall, sitting up in bed in a rather old camel-coloured woollen cardigan. He was always courteous, but not very communicative. He didn't complain a great deal. I wouldn't call it resentment, but there was a feeling that he railed against being ill and being confined to bed. I felt that. I remember his hands. He had long fingers. Nice hands — sallow coloured, like himself.

He showed a lot of enthusiasm when his little boy came. He seemed quite excited at the thought of him coming. But I don't think the boy would have been allowed in regularly, because of his condition. It was a special concession, and he would have been told not to kiss his child. The tubercle is transmitted through the sputum in the breath. The child wouldn't be allowed to sit on the bed or get too close.

It was 'Mr Blair' on his door, not 'Orwell.' Sometimes visitors would ask for Mr Orwell. It was confusing.

David Astor called in frequently, since University College Hospital was on his route home from his office at the *Observer*.

He was always talking of the things he was going to do. He said to me casually, 'Do you think one can die if one has a book in one's mind one wants to write?' I was taken aback. I couldn't imagine the answer. He answered it for me by saying, 'I've asked the doctor here, who has looked after other writing people, and he says, "Yes, you can have a book in your mind and still die," but I don't think that's so.' He was trying to give himself hope.

"I Suppose Everyone Will Be Horrified"

Even before he had left the sanatorium in Cranham, Orwell had been mentioning the possibility that he might, though very ill, get married again soon. "I suppose everyone will be horrified," he'd written to Fred Warburg in August, "but apart from other considerations I really think I should stay alive longer if I were married." On 13 October 1949, in a special bedside wedding, Orwell married Sonia Brownell, the woman who had turned down his first proposal shortly after Eileen's death in 1945. Astor was a witness at the ceremony.

I can't help saying it was an embarrassing occasion. We were in this tiny room, like a small cubicle, with a very sick man. There was Sonia, Sonia's girlfriend and her husband, me, and the chaplain and the doctor. He wanted the doctor there too because he thought the doctor was a friend, he was looking after him. We just about packed the place.

Orwell looked like Gandhi. He was skin and bone. But he entertained us in a way. He made a joke of the fact that they couldn't give him injections any more, he was too thin. We were his guests, you see. He talked to us as best he could. The chaplain did the minimum for a marriage, and then we went away. I'd arranged to take them to lunch after, to have some kind of celebration. So we trooped off to the Ritz Hotel.

Sonia was a very handsome, fine-looking, delightful person. In *Nineteen Eighty-Four* there's a girl called Julia who seems too good to be true; she never becomes a real person. I think he saw Sonia that way. Eileen was his workaday wife; Sonia was an idealized female he dreamt of. He thought to keep alive he must marry her. It was a gesture to say he wasn't going to die. She admired writers, but I think she didn't contract marital relations with people easily, and I think when this man who was obviously very feeble asked her to marry, it may have suited her to marry somebody rather 'non-operational,' as it were. But I don't think she thought he was dying. I'm sure she didn't from what she said to me. I think both of them were acting in some sort of fantasy way.

STEPHEN SPENDER, whose friendship with Orwell had continued since their first meeting in 1937, believes that Sonia did realize Orwell would soon die.

I think he was very much in love with Sonia and had been for some time. She was fond of him, and she was in a position to make him happy. She also knew he was going to die. Therefore it seemed a rational proposition. But decisions arrived at on that sort of rational basis never turn out how you think they will, and when he died Sonia felt intensely unhappy. She blamed herself and thought she had done the wrong thing, and so took over the cause of George Orwell for the rest of her life, and she never really recovered from this.

You see, I think Sonia always wanted to have a genius in her life. She had a romantic conception of genius. Orwell, to some extent, fitted her idea of the solitary genius who needed backing. She was always in search of her genius. She looked on a relationship with a man as a kind of a crusade where she was marrying someone and defending him against the rest of the world and making it possible for him to fulfil his talents. I think she was quite disinterested, in marrying Orwell. She laid herself open to the accusation that she married him for his money. This is totally unjust.

One of Sonia's closest friends was DIANA WITHERBY (now Diana Cooke), who worked with her and Cyril Connolly on *Horizon*. Diana Witherby agrees that Sonia's motives for marrying Orwell were not in the least mercenary.

It isn't at all true to say that she married him for money and his royalties, because that wasn't the position when she married him. It all began rolling in suddenly, and it was, I would have thought, a very unexpected thing. She had no idea he'd become so famous. He was quite famous as a writer, but nobody had any idea it was all going to become as it is today. Sonia certainly didn't realize. And she was totally conscientious about keeping the inheritance money for Richard.

She did marry him possibly for her own security, and to have a future, because it was rather a blank future. *Horizon* was going to fold up, and I do remember her saying, 'When *Horizon* folds up, I'll marry George,' and I said, 'Well, I hope it'll be all right,' and she said, 'Yes, it will.' She didn't fancy the idea of going back and starting typing again after all those years with *Horizon*, so it's possible she married him for those reasons as well as feeling great affection for him and wanting to buoy him up as he was so fond of her, so much in love with her. He was absolutely dotty on her and adored having her as his wife, proud and pleased to have her as his wife. And she certainly didn't think she was marrying someone who was dying. She knew he was ill, but there was always this plan: when he was out they were going to go somewhere. I think they'd both got this hope he'd get out of hospital and they'd live somewhere. It wasn't regarded as a hopeless case.

Sonia, in those early days, looked very much like a painting by Renoir. She had a pink and white skin, blonde hair, and beautiful features, and she was rather shy, a characteristic she shed later on. Her father, I think, had been in the army. He had died, and her mother, who remarried, was a very typically jolly sort of English person who played bridge and was nice-natured.

She went to this convent school where you weren't allowed to have a bath without clothes; you had to wear some sort of robes. It was rather a fashionable, smart sort of place. But she threw over Catholicism completely, and she *really* threw it over. In fact, she always said, 'I always spit if I see a nun,' and when we were walking along the street she'd spit, and I'd say, 'what are you doing?' and she said, 'I just saw a nun.' I hadn't seen any nun, but she had. She took jobs as a secretary, and she was very, very clever. She had a wonderful brain. She took up typing and of course typed faster than anyone that ever typed; she could take down typing at shorthand dictating speed. Then she went in some ministry, and that's where I first met her, in the war.

She had lots of admirers and followers. But she didn't to my knowledge have any long-standing affairs with anyone at that stage. She flirted and went out with men, but underneath it all I think she did have a feeling against them which was deep-seated. She would always be criticizing, saying, 'Oh, men!' A lot of us used to do that, as a sort of joke, but with her I think it was more deep-seated, because she really *did* used to give them the brush-off directly they started getting very keen on her, and she was attractive to many men. At the same time she was very generous. She was always obsessed with her friends' difficulties. She'd lend money when she had any, and she'd ask rich friends for money for other people. Her main characteristic all her life was that she was passionately interested in her friends' troubles.

She talked to me a lot about George, usually with great affection. She thought he was frightfully *English*, as she called it, and in those days when we said somebody was English we didn't regard it as a total compliment. But she was very loyal, really. I wouldn't like to give the impression she was anything but that. She used to joke with George, and I think her laughing away all the time was one of the most endearing characteristics about Sonia. She would have laughed at him, and he would have liked that. When he became really keen on her, she told me he wanted to marry her. I really didn't feel when she first told me that it was a good idea. But when it actually happened I could see the motive for it, when she told me how happy he was when she went to see him. He was absolutely longing to marry her. She thought she could make him happy, and she did.

After the wedding to Sonia, Orwell's health improved briefly, but in November and December 1949 he grew progressively weaker and thinner. One of the junior chest doctors at University College Hospital at that time was DR HOWARD NICHOLSON.

There was no medical treatment, really, just resting and being well looked after. He had quite extensive bilateral pulmonary tuberculosis. He was really very ill indeed. I have no doubt he suffered greatly — not pain, I don't think he had any pain, but general misery and awareness of what was happening. I'm sure it was terrible.

I only saw him a few times. I went down to his room with the nursing sister. My memory of him is of rather a poor little man, sitting in a chair in a corner. He was shrunken and seemed miserable and obviously very ill. He would spend a little time in the morning tipped up with his head down, to help his sputum, to make him more comfortable, and of course he would spend all day in the room. There was a constant procession of people going in to see him. A lot of visitors.

By early January 1950 the senior doctor in charge of Orwell, Dr Andrew Morland, decided that he should be taken to Switzerland. Orwell seemed keen on the idea, even getting his fishing rod ready and laying it across his hospital bed. Dr Nicholson was rather sceptical about the trip.

We younger doctors regarded the idea of patients' going to Switzerland with a certain amount of suspicion. There wasn't really anything to be done there. It was put across that it was a good thing to be in a higher altitude, with pure air, but really I don't think it made the least difference. I think it was mainly a method of letting the patients die comfortably, in a place where they were really used to dealing with that sort of thing.

Orwell's friend JON KIMCHE remembers Tosco Fyvel's asking him for help in arranging a special flight to Switzerland.

Tosco came to me about ten days before he died and said, 'The doctors say it's very important that he should be taken to Switzerland' and could I organize a special flight through the Swiss embassy — I'm Swiss, and I knew people at the embassy, or the delegation I think it was then. I said yes, and I got onto their press man, who knew Orwell and was a rather literary figure. So we fixed it up and made arrangements for the flight.

Many of Orwell's friends called in to say goodbye before he made the trip. STAFFORD COTTMAN, who had fought with Orwell in Spain in 1937, telephoned to find out when it would be convenient to come in and visit.

I spoke to him on the phone, and he said, 'I'm frightful. I look just like a skeleton.' And I honestly thought from the strength and tone of his voice that I would see him when he got back.'

Celia Goodman also tried to visit Orwell at this time.

I rang him up and said, 'When can I come and see you, George?' And he said, 'Well, I'm going off next Wednesday with Sonia to Switzerland.' And I said, 'Oh, that's wonderful news, George. They must think you're going to get better.' And he said, 'Either that or they don't want a corpse on their hands.' Well, then he said, 'Come next Monday,' and then the next morning a friend of Cyril Connolly rang me up to say that George had died the night before, the very night of the day I'd rung him up.

It's possible that Paul Potts was the last person to see Orwell alive. He knew Orwell had been worrying about getting the right kind of Ceylonese tea in Switzerland, and he brought him some as a parting present.

He loved tea, very strong tea. He used to have people in for high tea with anchovy paste and Cooper's Oxford marmalade. Like all civilized people who'd been poor, he loved entertaining. Anyway, tea was rationed then, so I'd brought him some. There was a window in the door and you could look in, and I saw he was asleep, and I knew he had a great deal of difficulty in getting to sleep, so I didn't wake him up, and I left the tea at the door. But he died just after that. I often wonder who got the tea.

Orwell was an unusual man. A rebel. It's hard to put it into words. He had this fantasy that if he'd lived in a peaceful age he'd have just watched his walnuts grow and written novels. But in fact he thrived on trouble. The only time he liked London was during the Blitz. And he couldn't take up his pen without disagreeing with somebody. And then when he met them he found that he liked them. For me, along with Bertrand Russell and Churchill he was one of the three great Englishmen of his time. He had this ability to treat people as equals. He might have been my father; he was the same kind of Englishman. It's hard for me to realize he's been dead for so long. It feels like I saw him six weeks ago.

"Here Lies Eric Arthur Blair"

Orwell died, as the doctors had feared he would, from a massive hemorrhage of the lung. It was the night of 21 January 1950, and he died alone. The BBC broadcast a short obituary. There was a funeral service, even though Orwell was very much a lapsed Anglican. It was held at a large church in Albany Street, not far from Regent's Park in London. Orwell's friend MALCOLM MUGGERIDGE arranged it.

I felt very sad when he died and very sad when I visited him before he died. He was someone for whom I had, and I think most of his friends had, a very big affection. He was lovable. And he was lovable in the deep sincerity of his disposition, which was a very beautiful thing. I mean he was utterly sincere. If he took a position and then the position was challenged in some way, and he felt it was faulty, then he would abandon it. He always wanted to be sincere. From the very beginning I thought of him as a Don Quixote. He had a certain melancholy in the face, like Don Quixote, and the same tendency of identifying himself with various out-of-the-way causes which he felt very strongly about. Actually, because of this Don Quixote side of him he fell into a good many fantasies. He had this strange blend, you see, of extreme conservatism plus this sympathy with revolutionary causes, and the two things really didn't marry up. I don't think he had any idea of what his fellow human beings were at, but that was part of the oddity in him. But he wanted always to speak the truth, and he wanted to be completely straightforward. He had a loving heart, although he didn't find it easy to show it. But it was there.

Curiously, he thought he was repulsive. He was conscious of that. He felt he was physically unattractive, and I think it troubled him. And Sonia, you see, was like a dream person for him. He felt she represented this marvellous beautiful woman that he'd dreamed of but not actually had as a companion. And George realized, on his death bed, what he'd dreamed of. Sonia came to see us on the night that he died, and she wept copiously. I felt very sorry for her. I think she felt that somehow she might have given him more in their brief marriage than she had.

Orwell's niece Jane Morgan was one of those present at the funeral service.

It struck me as being rather an odd sort of funeral for Eric. It was all rather large and pompous and dark. Very formal, with lots of people there. I didn't think it was very Eric-like. It wasn't the sort of thing he would have arranged for himself.

In the funeral party that left the Albany Street church, David Astor travelled in the same car as Orwell's sister Avril.

I said to her, because I wanted to know, not just to make conversation, I said, 'Tell me, who did George admire most? What sort of person did he admire?' And she just turned to me and said quite easily and directly, 'The working-class mother of ten children.' At the time it took me by surprise, because I wasn't expecting that as an answer. But the more you think about it, the more true it was. And I think he meant the ordinary person's capacity to deal with lots of problems and to deal with them successfully, to manage. I think he revered ordinary people in a sensible way, and not in some sort of falsely romantic way. He was very close and simple and direct with everybody. I think a lot of nonsense has been written about his class. I think the reality was that he really quite transcended class. He adopted a position of equality towards everybody, including the privileged.

To me Orwell was a friend, and a very good friend. He was very capable of friendship. But he was something much more than that — two things, really. He was the writer I admired and envied more than any other. I think it's the most wonderful style to be able to write so strongly. But also he was a hero figure to me. He thought so courageously and so clearly, regardless of whether people would like it. He was the outstanding person of my day. I derived a great deal from the friendship.

In death Orwell had given his friends a problem to solve. He had asked in his will that he be buried in an English churchyard, a cemetery of the Church of England. Yet he was neither a practising Anglican nor a member of any congregation. Astor found a solution.

I have a house in the country, in a village called Sutton Courtenay, and I knew the vicar was an admirer of Orwell. He needed no explaining who Orwell was. He was a young man called Gordon Dunstan. I said, 'Is it possible to get him buried here although he didn't live in this village?'

The REVEREND GORDON DUNSTAN, who later became a professor of moral and social theology and a well-known figure in the Anglican church, remembers David Astor's request.

I was sitting in my study in the vicarage one winter evening and the telephone rang, and it was the voice of David Astor, my friend and parishioner here in Sutton Courtenay. And he asked if I could help him bury a friend. The friend was George Orwell, whose love of England and the English countryside was such that he wanted to lay his body to rest in an English churchyard, and not in some dreary municipal London cemetery. So I said of course I would gladly help.

But George was not a parishioner, and as you know, a village churchyard like this belongs to the village from generation to generation, and so there are laws about the burial of strangers. So I had first to consult the churchwardens, who are the lay keepers of the conscience, the perennial interest of the village. I went to see Mr Fred Towle, who was a retired company director living in the village, and Mr Cecil Allen, a farmer — his family have been farming here for generations. And I told them, I said, 'You don't know this man, but one day he'll be famous and people will come here to see his tomb.' And I gave farmer Allen a copy of *Animal Farm*, and I said, 'I want to bury the author of this book.' And they both said, 'Go ahead, Vicar, certainly.'

On the day of the funeral, January 26th, 1950, I was here and I met the coffin at the gate of the churchyard, properly, and walked before it into this beautiful medieval church, and I read the burial service from the Book of Common Prayer, straight. There was no music, no homily, no intrusive words. I read the pure service with whatever care I could as pertaining to a man who knew the truth attaching to words. We were a small company. There was the coffin and the bearers, and with him Sonia and David Astor and a gentleman whom by his demeanor and dress I guessed to be the family solicitor. And so we read the service here in church. And then I led them out into the churchyard.

His grave here has just an old English rose on it, which he asked for. He asked in fact that it might be left untrimmed, untended, but you know how roses grow, and they become straggly and a nuisance. Well, this is his grave. And it says, quite simply — again, I believe at his own request — 'Here lies Eric Arthur Blair, born June 25th, 1903, died January 21st, 1950.'

Acknowledgments

I must first thank the Canadian Broadcasting Corporation for allowing me to produce "George Orwell: A Radio Biography" and to record the interviews on which this book is based. In particular I greatly appreciate the support and encouragement of Eric Friesen and Bob Wagstaff for guiding my original proposal to a successful conclusion and generously giving me permission to use the interviews included here.

My colleague Edward Trapunski deserves my deepest thanks for his help in all stages of the production of "George Orwell: A Radio Biography." Without his tenacity in pressing me to do more interviews than I thought humanly possible, this book would be much thinner.

I must thank George Woodcock, not only for providing the introduction for this book, but for his uncanny and inspiring ability to make his friend George Orwell alive in my mind.

Professor Bernard Crick's generous and expert help in the planning of "George Orwell: A Radio Biography" was the only reason the radio program and therefore the book could come into existence.

I would also like to thank Peggy Riley in the London Bureau of the CBC who co-ordinated cheerfully and efficiently the research and field work in Europe.

The estate of the late Sonia Brownell Orwell and Martin Secker and Warburg Ltd. have kindly allowed me to quote from George Orwell's letters and poems. Livia Gollancz has generously given me permission to quote a letter written by her father Victor Gollancz.

I must thank every person quoted in this book for giving me as much time as was necessary to record fully their thoughts and memories of George Orwell/Eric Blair. I sincerely hope that in preparing their interviews for presentation in book form I have not distorted in any way the content or spirit of their remarks.

I am very grateful to David Kilgour, my editor at Penguin Canada, for his patience and painstaking professionalism.

Finally I would like to thank my wife Deborah, who has not only lived and breathed George Orwell with me for the past year without complaint, but has been an enthusiastic consultant whose reactions and suggestions were always unerring.

Selected Bibliography

Works by George Orwell

Down and Out in Paris and London. London: Gollancz, 1933.

Burmese Days. New York: Harper & Brothers, 1934.

A Clergyman's Daughter. London: Gollancz, 1935.

Keep the Aspidistra Flying. London: Gollancz, 1936.

The Road to Wigan Pier. London: Gollancz, 1937.

Homage to Catalonia. London: Secker & Warburg, 1938.

Coming Up for Air. London: Gollancz, 1939.

Inside the Whale. London: Gollancz, 1940.

The Lion and The Unicorn: Socialism and the English Genius. London: Secker & Warburg, 1941.

Animal Farm. London: Secker & Warburg, 1945.

Nineteen Eighty-Four. London: Secker & Warburg, 1949.

The Collected Essays, Journalism and Letters of George Orwell (four volumes). London: Secker & Warburg, 1968.

Other Works

BUDDICOM, Jacintha, *Eric and Us*. London: Leslie Frewin, 1974.

COMMON, Jack, *Orwell at Wallington*. Unpublished ms. in the Jack Common Collection, University of Newcastle Library.

CONNOLLY, Cyril, *Enemies of Promise*. London: Routledge & Kegan Paul, 1938.

CRICK, Bernard, *George Orwell; A Life*. London: Secker & Warburg, 1980.

DUNN, Avril, *My Brother, George Orwell*. London: *Twentieth Century,* March 1961.

FYVEL, Tosco, *George Orwell; A Personal Memoir*. London: Collier Macmillan, 1981.

GROSS, Miriam, *The World of George Orwell*. London: Weidenfeld & Nicolson, 1971.

JACKSON, Lydia, "George Orwell's First Wife." London: *Twentieth Century,* August 1960.

McNAIR, John, *George Orwell: the Man I Knew*. Unpublished ms. in the University of Newcastle Library.

POTTS, Paul, *Dante Called You Beatrice*. London: Eyre and Spottiswoode, 1960.

REES, Richard, *George Orwell; Fugitive from the Camp of Victory*. London: Secker & Warburg, 1961.

STANSKY, Peter and ABRAHAMS, William, *The Unknown Orwell*. London: Constable, 1972.

STANSKY, Peter and ABRAHAMS, William, *Orwell: The Transformation*. London: Constable, 1979.

WARBURG, Fredric, *All Authors Are Equal*. London: Hutchinson, 1973.

WEST, Anthony, *Principles and Persuasions*. London: Eyre & Spottiswoode, 1958.

WILLIAMS, Raymond, *George Orwell*. New York: The Viking Press, 1971.

WOODCOCK, George, *The Crystal Spirit: A Study of George Orwell*. London: Jonathan Cape, 1967.

Index of Contributors

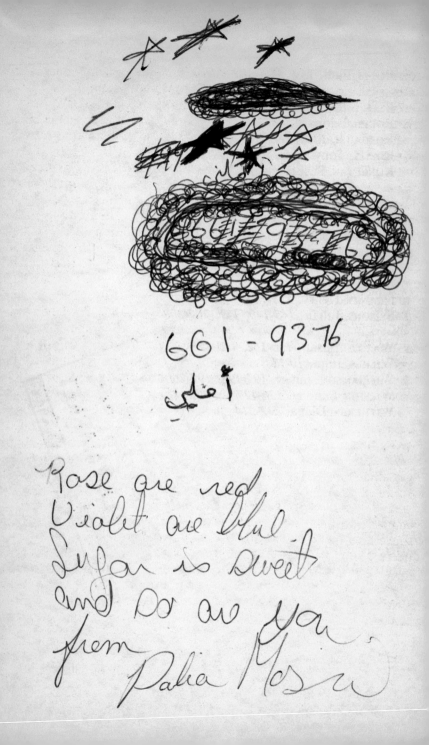

661 - 9376

أغلى

Rose are red
Violet are blue
Sugar is sweet
and so av you.
from Pama Mos